The Indexing Companion

Indexing is a crucial activity, but it is inconspicuous. Indexes are systematic guides that help people find information in a document, or documents in a collection. Although most people use them frequently, hardly anyone thinks of the creative activity that went into their making.

The Indexing Companion has something for all information professionals. It covers the basic principles of indexing, examines controversial areas and speculates on future directions. Based on publishing standards, textbooks, and the consensus of the indexing community, the book is packed with practical information. It describes the people involved in indexing; the processes, tools and software; and the special requirements of particular formats and subjects. It explores new challenges in indexing, such as working with indexes created by computers, and dips into emerging topics such as folksonomies and the semantic web.

Far from being dry, indexing is challenging and rewarding work. *The Indexing Companion* gives an overview of indexing for professional indexers, editors, authors, librarians, and anyone who may be called upon to write, contribute to, edit or commission an index.

Glenda Browne and **Jon Jermey** are freelance indexers with extensive experience in teaching and indexing.

D1190240

The Indexing Companion

GLENDA BROWNE

JON JERMEY

CAMBRIDGE
UNIVERSITY PRESS

CAMBRIDGE UNIVERSITY PRESS
Cambridge, New York, Melbourne, Madrid, Cape Town, Singapore, São Paulo

Cambridge University Press
477 Williamstown Road, Port Melbourne, VIC 3207, Australia

Published in the United States of America by Cambridge University Press, New York

www.cambridge.org
Information on this title: www.cambridge.org/9780521689885

© Glenda Browne, Jon Jermey 2007

First published 2007

Printed in Australia by Ligare

A catalogue record for this publication is available from the British Library.

National Library of Australia Cataloguing in Publication data
   Browne, Glenda.
   The Indexing Companion.
   Bibliography.
   Includes index.
   ISBN-13: 978-0-52168-988-5 paperback
   ISBN-10: 0-52168-988-0 paperback
   1. Indexing.   2. Information organization.   II. Title.
025.3

ISBN-13: 978-0-52168-988-5
ISBN-10: 0-52168-988-0

Reproduction and communication for educational purposes
The Australian *Copyright Act 1968* (the Act) allows a maximum of one chapter or 10% of the pages of this work, whichever is the greater, to be reproduced and/or communicated by any educational institution for its educational purposes provided that the educational institution (or the body that administers it) has given a remuneration notice to Copyright Agency Limited (CAL) under the Act.

For details of the CAL licence for educational institutions contact:

Copyright Agency Limited
Level 15, 233 Castlereagh Street
Sydney NSW 2000
Telephone: (02) 9394 7600
Facsimile: (02) 9394 7601
E-mail: info@copyright.com.au

Reproduction and communication for other purposes
Except as permitted under the Act (for example a fair dealing for the purposes of study, research, criticism or review) no part of this publication may be reproduced, stored in a retrieval system, communicated or transmitted in any form or by any means without prior written permission. All inquiries should be made to the publisher at the address above.

Cambridge University Press has no responsibility for the persistence or accuracy of URLs for external or third-party internet websites referred to in this publication and does not guarantee that any content on such websites is, or will remain, accurate or appropriate.

Cover images: (top) © Nicola Gavin/Shutterstock.com, (middle left) © Jaime Duplass/Shutterstock.com, (middle right) © Martin Garnham/Shutterstock.com, (bottom) © Sean Nel/Shutterstock.com, Platypus: © Lauren Statham, Alice Graphics.

Z
695.9
B76
2007

JUN 1 9 2007

Contents

Foreword

Information is useful. Accessible information is valuable. But easy access to pertinent information is crucial to success in modern life. Indexers provide this access, by identifying and ordering important aspects of the information we deal with.

In order to do our work properly, indexers must understand both the theory and practice of indexing. We are fortunate to have a number of publications worldwide that assist us in learning and applying indexing skills.

The Indexing Companion is the most recent addition, and the first Australian contribution, to the growing number of publications on indexing. In it, Glenda Browne and Jonathan Jermey contribute to the corpus of indexing in a number of significant ways: through their focus on interoperability, not only between the diverse strands of indexing but also among the various information professionals who create and use indexes; through their placement of 'traditional' indexing within the broader context of the information industry (including describing what other information professionals do and how indexing is incorporated into museum, library and archive activities); and through their treatment of the entire spectrum of indexing, from traditional back-of-book 'closed system' indexing to 'open system' journal cumulation, website and database indexing.

Browne and Jermey acknowledge that indexing is an international profession with much common ground but some regional differences, and explain the various standards and guides used in different countries and by different publishers. Their global perspective makes this text applicable to indexers in many countries, as well as being ideal for those working in Australia for either local or international clients.

The Indexing Companion draws its examples from every major indexing country, and it is a particular pleasure to see Australian indexing highlighted. Although Antipodean publishing is relatively small on the global scale, the Australian and New Zealand Society of Indexers is very active, due in no small part to members of the calibre of Glenda Browne and Jonathan Jermey. This, their latest collaboration, draws on their experience in indexing, librarianship, training and computing to present a work that will be a valuable resource for beginning and experienced indexers alike. I have no doubt it will improve the quality of indexing information available in Australia and elsewhere, and commend it to anyone with an interest in information organisation.

Lynn Farkas
President, Australian and New Zealand Society of Indexers, 2001–06

Preface

Indexing is a passion and a delight for those who are suited to it. For some people it is a full-time career; for others, including editors, writers and librarians, it is an occasional task. This book contains practical information about the process of indexing as well as specific techniques for a wide range of areas, and has something for all information professionals.

Those of us who index for a living are acutely aware of developments in the information industry. The authors have been indexing since 1988, and have observed significant changes in the work we do, the people we do it for, and the way we do it. Software developments have included tools that have aided us in our work (specialised indexing software, computers and the web); tools that may assist publishers but make indexers' lives more difficult (embedded indexing); and tools that threaten to take our work away (automatic indexing and search engines). This book is intended as a companion for indexers through times of change. We provide advice on working well, and we assess the future of indexing, identifying positives and negatives.

There has recently been an explosion in the use of indexing techniques in areas such as intranet and website search and navigation – often under different names, and done by different people. There is also significant and growing overlap in the work done by records managers, museum curators, librarians and indexers, although there is less communication between these groups than might be expected. Many of the tools and standards developed in one area have relevance in others, and software developments such as markup languages are having a wide impact. Along with convergence has come an understanding of the importance of interoperability (the ability of systems to exchange information), which is also a focus of this book.

The Indexing Companion covers the people involved in indexing, the processes and tools used in indexing, special formats and subjects that are indexed, the software used, and the future we can expect. The focus is primarily Australian, but the issues are international and the references and examples are relevant to indexers worldwide. The book contains enough information to get you started on an indexing project. Anyone with an urgent need to start indexing should begin with Chapters 3, 4 and 7, which cover the core of the process. However, indexing skills develop over a lifetime, and you will need to supplement this book with face-to-face training, online training, wide reading, and participation in online discussions. The bibliography provides a range of resources for further exploration, including many that are freely available on the web.

Many thanks to those who helped us develop our first book, *Website indexing*, which is where we gained the skills and confidence to take on this project, and to all at Cambridge University Press, who have been enthusiastic about this project. We are grateful to our three anonymous publisher's readers, who made useful suggestions about structure and content that we incorporated into the book.

Thanks to colleagues within ANZSI and the international indexing community who have generously shared work and ideas, indexing practitioners who make their writings freely available on the web, knowledgeable contributors to online mailing lists such as Index-L, friends who listen to us enthuse about indexing, and to libraries which have supplied us with books and interlibrary loans. Many of the quotations in this book were found at www.quotationspage.com.

This book is dedicated with love to our families, especially Bill and Jenny.

Glenda Browne and Jon Jermey

The Indexing Work Environment

The love of learning, the sequestered nooks,
And all the sweet serenity of books.
                    Henry Wadsworth Longfellow

INDEXING IS A CRUCIAL and widespread activity, but it is inconspicuous. Documents need indexes to help people find specific information within them, and collections need indexes to help people locate specific items they contain. Although most people use indexes regularly, hardly anyone thinks of the creative activity that went into their making. Despite inroads being made by computers, most indexes are still created by humans.

An index is a systematic guide that helps people find information in a document, such as a book, or documents in a collection, such as records in an archive. In addition to the terms that represent the topics of the document or collection item, an index also needs a syntax that allows expression of complex topics, such as a heading with subheadings; cross-references to lead from terms to other potentially useful terms; locators, such as page numbers, or links to lead users to information about the terms they select; and a way of filing the headings or making them searchable.

A glossary is not an index, because it does not link from its entries to other content. A concordance – an alphabetised list of words in a document – is not a true index because it simply lists words and phrases from the text, without analysis. Much the same is true of search engine 'indexes', which rely on the actual words in a document. A table of contents is not an index because it mimics the sequence of the material in the book, rather than providing an alternative view.

This chapter introduces the industry and the people who provide the context for the indexing process. Indexers need to know how to work with editors and authors, how to manage a business effectively, and how to create quality indexes quickly. Authors contribute the text – the clearer the writing and argument, the easier the job of indexing. Book authors usually have to provide indexes to their works, either by creating them or paying indexers to do so. Authors of periodical articles and intranet content may provide keywords for their writings (although these are often edited), while authors of articles in bibliographical databases have no role at all in indexing.

Book editors plan the indexing requirements; write briefs for indexers and occasionally index works themselves. Most other indexing projects have someone with the role of editor or project manager who coordinates the indexing and ensures the quality of the final product, especially when more than one person has contributed to the indexing.

All steps in the indexing process should take into account the needs of the end user. In some cases the typical user can be identified, but in others the indexing has to be appropriate for a wide range of users.

Indexers

> My biggest success to date has been convincing my mother-in-law that indexing is really, really cool. Seth Maislin, 2004

It is said that people study library science because they love books, but soon discover that they mainly deal with the covers of books. Indexers are more fortunate, in that we usually have to read the texts we are indexing. Indexers create indexes – A to Z lists of important topics – for virtually every type of document that exists. These indexes are a crucial key to detailed information.

Indexing is a very small profession. Most indexers train as librarians or editors, others as records managers or technical writers. A few learn the job from family and friends. It sounds like a paradox, but specialist indexers today are usually generalists. That is, they bring their indexing skills to bear on a wide variety of materials and subjects.

Book indexers tend to be employed by publishers or authors on a freelance basis rather than full time, although a few regular clients can keep an indexer in full-time work. Periodical indexers also tend to be freelancers, and may work throughout the year developing indexes that are published at the end of the year. Many collection indexing jobs are full time, although indexing may be only part of the person's job. Some indexers work with a wide range of formats, especially if they have learnt a variety of indexing types, but others specialise in either books or collections, and have only a vague idea of the requirements of the other types of indexing.

An indexer needs good general knowledge, the ability to grasp new concepts quickly, curiosity, attention to detail, interest in linguistic issues, and the ability to see things from somebody else's point of view. Although indexing jobs rarely have mandatory qualifications, most indexers have one or two degrees and at least forty years' life experience. Age is no bar to freelance indexing, but Kingsley Siebel once wrote to one of the authors (9 August 1996) that he was progressing well in a job application until he wrote his date of birth – 1917. No-one had known he was a near octogenarian, and this put them off.

Many writers have discussed the traits that make a good indexer, and a remarkable number find it a suitable task for prisoners. For example, 'a public-spirited contributor to *The Nation*' in 1883 suggested:

> Let all convicts who can read and write be set, under competent supervision, to indexing books . . . the kind of labor proposed is peculiarly suited to the reformatory idea, being incomparable for teaching order, patience, humility, and for thoroughly eradicating the last trace of the Old Adam in whoever pursues it.
>
> [Collins 2001]

Learning to index

The lyf so short, the craft so long to lerne.

Geoffrey Chaucer

The best ways to learn to index are:

- do a course run by one of the indexing societies or an online or video course (up-to-date details are available on society websites, including www.aussi.org)
- study indexing within another course; some editing and librarianship courses include a component on indexing
- learn on the job, in a library or a company
- take part in a mentoring program such as the one run by ANZSI (McMaster 2005)
- learn from an indexer who takes on 'apprentices' or offers training for payment
- read the resources: standard indexing textbooks, the international journal *The indexer*, content on the indexing society websites, websites of practising indexers, and the Index Students website (indexstudents.com)
- do practice indexes of well-indexed books (see the review excerpts in *The indexer*) and compare your results with theirs
- subscribe to mailing lists (see below)
- go to meetings of your local indexing society.

The April 2002 and October 2005 issues of *The indexer* feature articles on education for indexing and getting started in indexing. Dawney Spencer (1998–2004) has written many articles for beginning indexers.

Peer review by fellow indexers is a good form of feedback, especially for beginners. The Index Peer Reviewers discussion group (finance.groups.yahoo.com/group/IndexPeers) and colleagues in indexing societies may help, and some people pay for individual guidance. Some local indexing groups run peer review sessions in which you can get practical hints from other indexers. Martha Osgood (2004) writes that peer review can act both as a learning tool, through discussions of the application of indexing guidelines for different books, and as an editing tool, to bring an index up to professional standard prior to submitting to the publisher.

Societies of indexers

> To learn something about everything and everything about something.
>
> Thomas Henry Huxley

Many indexers work as freelancers. Some book indexers work in-house for large companies, especially legal publishers, or index as part of editing or technical writing jobs. Some database indexers work as librarians or for specialist companies, while others work from home on a contract basis. Most collection indexers work in museums, libraries, records offices and specialist companies.

Because indexing is such a small profession, networking with colleagues is an essential part of being a professional. There are now societies of indexers in eight countries or regions:

- Australia: Australian and New Zealand Society of Indexers, ANZSI, previously AusSI – www.aussi.org, soon to be www.anzsi.org
- Canada: Indexing Society of Canada/Société canadienne d'indexation, ISC/SCI – www.indexers.ca
- China: China Society of Indexers, CSI – www.cnindex.fudan.edu.cn (in Chinese)
- Germany: Deutsches Netzwerk der Indexer, DNI – www.d-indexer.org/welcome.html
- The Netherlands: Nederlands Indexers Netwerk, NIN – www.indexers.nl
- Southern Africa: Association of Southern African Indexers and Bibliographers, ASAIB – www.asaib.org.za
- United Kingdom and Ireland: Society of Indexers, SI – www.indexers.org.uk
- United States: American Society of Indexers, ASI – www.asindexing.org.

There was a society in Japan about ten years ago, but it no longer exists.

Most of the societies provide:

- communication between members, including meetings, newsletters, websites, e-mailed announcements and blogs
- advice to potential indexers and to clients
- training in indexing and related topics
- promotion of indexing; for instance DNI runs a stall and indexers' meeting at the Frankfurt Book Fair
- promotion of indexers' services through a database or register of indexers.

Experienced indexers also get a lot of their work through word of mouth, much of it through colleagues from their society.

John Simkin (2005) has summarised the history of the Australian Society of Indexers (AusSI, now ANZSI with the inclusion of New Zealand) and Hazel Bell (1997–2000) has written on the history of all of the indexing societies.

Indexers also join local societies of information scientists, secondary publishers, editors, technical writers, information architects, knowledge managers, and so on, depending on their specific interests.

Working for employers

Although freelance indexing is emphasised in indexing discussion groups, a number of book indexers work full-time for employers, often legal publishers. Editors of specialised publications such as cookbooks and technical writers of manuals and online help may also work in-house and spend some or all of their time indexing.

Database indexers may work for national, State and specialist libraries that have a responsibility for managing a bibliographic database. These jobs appear to have been falling in number in recent years. Intranet and website teams may hire indexers or information architects as full-time staff or consultants.

A few indexing companies, run by individuals, employ indexers for book and database indexing. They provide a collegial work environment and help to even out the individual's flow of work.

Full-time indexing jobs are advertised only occasionally, so they are easy to miss. Positions may be filled through internal promotion, word of mouth, or through employment agencies specialising in library and information work or technical writing.

Indexers who work on large projects for employers are likely to be in a team. Teams can consist of one indexer working with a variety of other staff, or a number of indexers working on similar aspects of the one project. Teamwork may involve various kinds of collaboration:

- with other professionals: for instance, information architects and programmers on an intranet search engine
- with non-professionals who are working as indexers: for instance, authors of intranet content who are expected to provide subject metadata for their contributions
- with other indexers on an open-ended project: for instance, as one of a number of indexers for a bibliographic journal database
- with other indexers on a large job: for instance, as one of a number of indexers for a multivolume encyclopedia.

Enid Zafran (in Perlman 2001: 67–70) has written about employing indexers as staff or subcontractors. See also *Consistency* in Chapter 8 and *Encyclopedias and other multivolume works* in Chapter 9.

Freelance indexing

To business that we love we rise betime
And go to't with delight.

William Shakespeare, *Antony and Cleopatra*

Freelance indexing suits people who like choice and variety and can live with some uncertainty. It usually entails working from home, and provides independence, freedom from office politics, and the chance to set your own working hours. It requires self-discipline to get the work done – particularly the less-favoured parts of the work – and it can be difficult to balance personal and work life. Freelance indexers often work one or two days a week in another job to ensure some security of income and human contact. In China a freelancer is called 'a person without a workgroup'.

When Caroline Colton (1996) spoke to the NSW Society of Editors about indexing, the society light-heartedly offered a prize to the person who could identify Caroline's star sign. Most picked her as a Virgo or Taurus, but Caroline replied:

> I am an Aries – reckless. This is an essential characteristic of an indexer. Anyone who tries to make a living out of full-time indexing would have to be reckless, because it is a very small industry. It's a bit like being a platypus; you can end up in a shrinking habitat. You have to be constantly conscious of marketing, of bringing work in, of having regular paying customers, of having a mixture of formats from books to journals to electronic publishing.

Small business management

> Talk of nothing but business, and dispatch that business quickly.
>
> Aldus Manutius (1449–1515)

To work effectively as a freelance indexer you have to develop small business skills as well as professional skills. You could do a small business course, read up on the topic, or consult an accountant. You will need to:

- build up a client base, and maintain a steady flow of interesting work
- quote realistically
- maintain adequate cash flow by pursuing prompt payment
- save for retirement
- manage your own computer maintenance and equipment
- maintain a safe workplace
- provide for training and professional development
- manage your time well, including slipped schedules and overlapping jobs (and know when to take time off)
- communicate with clients on the phone and online
- keep mandatory and useful records.

The Business Entry Point website (www.business.gov.au) provides excellent introductory material on starting a business, home-based businesses and occupational health and safety. Janet Perlman (2001) provides a wealth of advice on running an indexing business.

Records of the work you do are important for professional, business and legal reasons. Indexers have to record client details, including company style guides and special requirements. If you store templates in your indexing software according to each client's stylistic and output requirements, you will be able to deal with these automatically. If you keep records of the jobs you have done, the person you dealt with, the amount you were paid and the time taken, you will find it easier to select the clients that pay best and to quote more effectively in future.

Keep electronic copies of all the indexes you do in case you are asked to index later editions or similar works. When you deliver work ask the client to acknowledge receipt so you have a permanent record that the job was received. It may also be useful to ask for feedback on the job.

Keep financial records of invoices and payments so you can chase up late payment and fulfil your tax obligations. Business records have to be kept for seven years in Australia. A contact management program and dedicated billing application such as QuickBooks or MYOB may be useful. See also *Legal matters*, below.

Managing freelance work

Drive thy business or it will drive thee.

Benjamin Franklin (1706–1790)

Experienced indexers get most of their work from repeat clients, referrals from other indexers, and contacts through their listings on society websites. Many also do regular marketing to keep up a supply of new clients, who can fill gaps when clients disappear and provide an opportunity to say no to low-paying clients. Well-established indexers also start marketing again if they want to broaden their work to include other types of indexing, for instance, moving from book indexing to database or website indexing.

Experience is the most important factor in getting a job. You can build up work samples by doing voluntary projects such as newsletters, procedure manuals, minutes, books without indexes, genealogical materials, and websites. Some people work for another indexer as a subcontractor or mentee (see above) to get experience while building up a client base. To increase the chances of finding work, network with indexers, editors, writers, information architects and other people involved in the fields you would like to index in. It may take three years to build up enough regular clients to fill your schedule.

Marketing approaches should focus on any technical or subject skills you have. They can include:

- mailouts to publishers of a simple brochure about you and your indexing service, with details or samples of indexes you have created
- cold calls to editorial departments; first find out as much as you can about the person you should ask for, and the interests of the company
- combinations of mailouts and phone calls ('I'm phoning to see if you received my mailout') so your name is seen or heard several times within a short period
- a website with details of your training and experience, which may list the books and other works you have indexed, and link to sample indexes on the web (e.g., at Amazon.com) when they are available

- including your name in your indexing society's list of Indexers Available, and other directories as appropriate
- advertising in newsletters for authors and publishers, such as the Australian publication *Thorpe weekly newsletter* (the 'blue newsletter', www.thorpe.com. au/products/products_wbn.htm).

Authors occasionally write to indexing mailing lists seeking quotes for a job. As many people usually respond it is often not worth the effort to quote. Project managers tendering for a job may ask an indexer to quote for the indexing part of it. If they fail to get the job, the indexer misses out. Janet Perlman (2001: 57–65) describes the writing of proposals for large indexing jobs.

One of the hardest things about freelance indexing is estimating the fee to charge for a job. Indexing societies and colleagues can help by providing guidelines, but only experience can tell you how long a certain job is likely to take you. Given the economics of the publishing industry, there is often not enough money to pay the fee the indexer requests – in these cases a cheaper job can sometimes be negotiated. This can include leaving out certain items (e.g., names of cited authors) or doing a less detailed index overall.

A rule of thumb is that an in-house employee costs the company their salary plus 40%. So if you would expect to earn $40 per hour in an in-house job, you should be earning $56 per hour as a freelancer, as well as charging for expenses. You then have to add 10% Goods and Services Tax in Australia (and similar in some other countries).

The ANZSI recommended rate is $55 per hour. Technical indexing rates are often higher. Legal decisions in New South Wales aiming to reverse legally entrenched pay inequity based on the perceived breadwinner status of males have improved the pay of librarians, and may trickle on to indexers (Bonella 2003).

Per-job quotes are common in Australia. Nonetheless, it is handy to have a per-page rate as a rule of thumb – ours is the rather broad $2 to $12 per page, with most jobs costing between $3 and $8 per page. In the United Kingdom many indexers charge per hour. The Society of Indexers (UK) recommends a rate of at least £17.50 per hour, which works out at approximately £2.00 per page for a straightforward index. They are planning to replace this with a more detailed grid approach. If you charge by the hour you might be asked to quote an upper limit as well as an hourly rate.

The American Society of Indexers does not recommend a standard rate, but most indexers and publishers work with per-page rates, the average being about US$4.00. The ASI salary survey 2004 shows trends in indexing rates (www.asindexing.org/site/SalarySurvey.shtml).

When a per-page rate is automatically applied to all jobs, it does not take into account the complexity of the work or the number of words per page. The size of pages, the type size, the format (e.g., two-column), and the number of illustrations all affect the number of words. To better estimate the scope of jobs, some indexers count the number of words instead of pages. A rough guide is to charge one to two cents per word of text, so a 100,000-word book would cost $1000 to $2000 to index.

Other indexers quote per index entry or locator. To do this effectively it helps to have an idea of the number of locators to be included in the final index. Indexing policies can affect the cost – some people would index *25, 26, 27* as three locators, whereas others would compress it to *25–27* and earn one-third as much. It is also important to clearly define 'index entry': some people regard each page number as one entry, but to others everything connected to one main heading is an entry (see *Definitions* in Chapter 2). Charges per locator range from 50c to $2.00, depending on the complexity of the text.

An indexer's quote is usually for the creation of a subject index. If the indexer has to attend meetings or undertake extra jobs, such as keyword lists for CD-ROM search or author indexes, these should be quoted for separately. In addition, extra work caused by last-minute changes to the text or pagination requires extra payment. Many indexers do the first two hours of editing free but then charge an hourly rate for other changes.

Use of an index to a previous edition of the book may help with the selection of terms, but it usually makes little difference to the time taken to index a book. If there are only minor changes, it may be possible to edit the original index. This is best done by the original indexer, if they are available. If not, copyright and moral rights need to be considered.

For big projects that are likely to take many months, add about 10% of the estimated cost to allow for contingencies, and invoice monthly (on presentation of work to date) to maintain cash flow. Indexers often ask for more elapsed time than they need so they can accept other projects along the way while working part-time on the major project. Some indexers ask for partial payment in advance when working directly for authors.

Ongoing jobs such as journal or database indexing are more likely to be paid per hour or per piece (e.g., per article). Database indexers usually index between one and ten items per hour, depending on the number of fields that are required and the complexity of the subject matter.

When they have completed an index, indexers send an invoice for the job. Number your invoices, and show your own name and contact details, the client's name and contact details, a description of the work done, the payment formula (e.g., X pages at $Y per page) and payment requirements (e.g., within thirty days). In Australia you need to include your Australian Business Number, and the Goods and Services Tax if applicable.

Although most clients are reliable and pay reasonably promptly, problems with payment may arise (as Oscar Wilde said: Genius is born – not paid). Typical situations include:

- An author is unhappy with the index and refuses to pay.
- An invoice gets lost on the way to the pay section.

- A company goes bankrupt – in which case, as unsecured creditors, freelance indexers are not likely to get paid.
- A company is taken over by another company that does not fulfil earlier obligations.
- The pay system is inefficient; some companies do cheque runs only one day per month, so if you miss that run you have to wait another month.

Some approaches to speed payment are:

- Send a reminder with 'Overdue' in large letters.
- Send a letter of demand (you can view a sample at www.artslaw.com.au/ LegalInformation/DebtRecovery).
- Speak directly to staff in the pay section, reminding them about late fees.
- Claim copyright in the index and refuse to allow publication until you are paid.
- Take the case to a small claims court: the costs are relatively low and you do not need a lawyer.
- Use a mediation service, such as the one run by the Arts Law Centre of Australia (www.artslaw.com.au/LegalInformation/Mediation.asp).

A contract or written agreement with clearly stated terms can make this process more straightforward. A purchase order is beneficial as it means that the expenditure has already been approved.

Legal matters

Legal matters of importance to indexers include contracts, insurance, copyright and moral rights.

Some indexers use formal contracts for all jobs, but others rely on informal measures. Most make sure that they have a written (e-mailed) agreement covering:

- the agreed fee (plus GST) including charges for extra work
- timing and method for arrival of text, and sending of index
- expectations regarding the length, content, and style of the index
- any special expectations.

Other matters you may wish to cover include your rights to proofread the index, to receive a complimentary copy of the work, and to be acknowledged as indexer and as owner of copyright in the index. Examples of formal contracts for indexing can be found at www.wellchosenword.com/indxctrt.htm, pages.prodigy. net/jeanmidd/contract.html and members.aol.com/indexarts/samplecon.htm.

Employ a legal adviser to explain any clauses that are not clear to you, and do not assume that clauses will not be imposed, or accept any verbal guarantees that go against the wording of the contract. Do not accept a clause that says your work shall be 'satisfactory to the publisher' unless an independent forum for mediation of disputes is also proposed.

Clients may provide you with a contract to sign, especially for larger projects, which may include insurance requirements, confidentiality clauses and an agreement not to work for competitors.

Insurance requirements can be impossible to comply with or very expensive, and often stop indexers from taking on jobs. They include:

- **Workers' compensation insurance**: This is available only to registered companies.
- **Professional indemnity insurance**: This is expensive, and it has to be maintained long-term as it works on a claims-made basis – that is, you have to be insured at the time a claim is made, not just at the time the work was done.
- **Public liability insurance**: This is available through many home insurance policies, but does not always cover workplace-related injuries. Search www.artslaw.com.au for more information.

Some clients remove or adapt these requirements by doing a risk management assessment instead of having a blanket requirement for insurance.

There is a general consensus that indexes created by freelancers are protected by copyright law as 'compilations of information'. Claims of copyright in published but unpaid-for indexes have helped some indexers obtain payment, although for others this has not worked because of complex corporate takeovers or the use of packagers as an intermediate step in the production chain. (Packagers are independent companies that produce a book for a publisher).

The existence of moral rights in indexes is clear cut, at least in Australia (www.aussi.org/profissues/moralrights.htm) and Great Britain (www.indexers. org.uk/InAvail/useful/iaprac.htm). These countries have legislation that protects a creator's right of integrity (the right not to have one's work altered in a way that is prejudicial to their reputation), the right of attribution, and the right not to have authorship falsely attributed. The law in Australia could be used to support a claim against a publisher for distorting an index, or perhaps where a substantial part of an indexer's work is used in a later index without attribution or payment.

Publishers do have a defence for infringement, that of 'reasonableness'. This would depend on the nature of the work, the context in which it is used, and any relevant industry practice. This suggests that only inappropriate editing of an index would breach moral rights.

Working from home

To work from home you need to be self-disciplined and enjoy your own company. Some people cannot imagine this, but others love the freedom and the ability to get stuck into work without distractions.

And then there are those who work with children at home . . . Although freelance indexing can appear an ideal opportunity to work from home while being with young children, it can be very difficult to produce quality work with constant demands for attention. Whether it works for you depends on you, your children and your support networks. You can compromise by hiring a babysitter to care for children in your house while you are there, and using paid childcare when you are not.

For occupational health and safety issues, see *Health and safety* in Chapter 10.

Mailing lists for indexers

There are many international mailing lists about indexing and related topics – if you join only one of the ones listed here, it should be Index-L:

- aliaINDEXERS (Australia): alia.org.au/alianet/e-lists/subscribe.html
- cindexusers – groups.yahoo.com/group/cindexusers/join
- Faceted Classification Discussion (FCD): finance.groups.yahoo.com/group/facetedclassification
- Index Peer Reviewers: finance.groups.yahoo.com/group/IndexPeers
- Index Students: indexstudents.com
- Index-L: indexpup.com/index-list/faq.html
- Macrex: www.macrex.com/discuss.htm
- SIGCR-L for classification research: mail.asis.org/mailman/listinfo/sigcr-l
- SIGIA-L for information architecture: mail.asis.org/mailman/listinfo/sigia-l
- TaxoCoP for taxonomies: groups.yahoo.com/group/TaxoCoP
- SKY Index: groups.yahoo.com/group/skyindexusers
- Web Indexing SIG (ASI): groups.yahoo.com/group/web-indexing.

The announcement lists below send one or two messages per month to announce meetings:

- IA-Peers: send an e-mail to IA-Sydney-on@lists.ironclad.net.au to get on the Sydney IA-Peers mailing list for IA get-togethers (IAwiki.net/CocktailHours/Sydney). IA-Peers get-togethers are held in twenty-six cities, including Amsterdam, Boston, Canberra, Charlotte, NC, London, Sydney, and Tokyo
- NSW KM Forum monthly meetings: groups.yahoo.com/group/NSW-KM-Forum-Announce.

Other indexing-related mailing lists are listed at www.asindexing.org/site/discgrps.shtml.

Writers

> One writer, for instance, excels at a plan or a title-page, another works away [at] the body of the book, and a third is a dab at an index.
>
> Oliver Goldsmith – 'The Bee' n. 1, 6 October, 1759

The term writers here includes authors of books and articles, and technical writers who work on organisation-based projects including online help, manuals and intranets.

Authors can make the indexing process easier or harder by the way they write and organise documents. Normally the qualities that make for a good book also make for a good index. It is relatively easy to index a book in which the author has:

- structured the content logically
- provided meaningful chapter titles and section headings
- avoided unnecessary repetition of the same material
- defined terms, along with their synonyms, and used them consistently.

Authors sometimes comment, on seeing an index to their book, that it is interesting how the index brings together concepts that they had not explicitly considered, and shows an unfamiliar view of their work.

Multi-author works often raise the problem of synonyms: where one author uses the term *developing countries*, another *Third World*, and other *newly industrialised economies*, it may be difficult to know to what extent these terms are meant to be synonymous, and can thus be grouped together in the index.

The same applies to the indexing of collections, where work by multiple authors, written over a long period, is the norm. As consistency cannot be expected in the materials being indexed, it is usually imposed by use of a controlled vocabulary (see Chapter 6). Because of this, the specific words an author uses are less likely to be included in indexing terms than are the words used by a book author. Collections such as intranets can also be plagued by legacy data – old information transferred to the new medium – that has been structured and written for a different environment.

Payment for book indexes often comes out of authors' royalties. It is hard to see why this should be so; after all, the author does not pay the book designer or the cover artist, and a good index is just as much a marketing tool as a good cover. An author may:

- create the index themselves
- hire an indexer directly
- pay an indexer who is commissioned by the publisher
- create an index and hire a professional indexer for an overview and advice.

Authors can help indexers by providing assistance on synonyms and difficult terms. It is usually not helpful for the author to highlight the text or provide a list of keywords that should be indexed as these divide the indexer's attention between the indexing task and checking the lists.

Writers as indexers

My desire is . . . that mine adversary had written [an index].

Adapted from *Job* xxxi, 35.

Some authors choose to index their own books. Some do it very well, and several author-indexed books have won indexing prizes. Often, however, the author is too close to the text to be objective. Words and phrases that resonate with meaning for the author may convey little to the casual browser. There are author-created indexes in which section headings such as 'Seven routes to an alcohol-free life' are indexed under 'seven' but not 'alcohol'.

Many scholarly authors try to simplify the indexing process by using the 'concordance' feature of word processing software. This entails creating a list of words that should be indexed and asking the software to generate a list of page numbers on which those words occur. The 'indexes' that result are inadequate because they have many undifferentiated locators for many headings: there may be more than twenty page numbers after a word, not separated by any subheadings. In addition, they fail to pick up concepts that are not described using the words the author has listed; they fail to pick up complex concepts; and they do not show aspects of subjects using subdivisions. These indexes can be improved somewhat by looking up pages for the terms with the most entries and manually creating subdivisions to divide those sections, if not all of the index.

Authors who are creating their own indexes need assistance. Courses and textbooks can be helpful, and they should also have:

- a clear guide to house style requirements
- enough time (say, two weeks for 200 pages)
- careful editing of their indexes.

Technical writers often index the books they write, and develop skills in indexing technical material using embedded indexing, with last-minute changes to products and text as they work. See also *Handbooks and manuals* and *Online help* in Chapter 9.

Authors of journal articles may allocate keywords to their articles. These can be useful as a source of ideas for indexers, but are not usually adequate on their own. The reasons include lack of consistency with other indexing, and an inappropriate level of specificity. Article authors have been encouraged to index more appropriately using online templates with sections for research methodology and the geographical and historical period of inquiry, with the view to making the indexing shareable through use of Dublin Core and the OAI-PMH (Willinsky and Wolfson 2001). See *Standards* in Chapter 2.

Writers of intranet content are sometimes expected to provide their own indexing when distributed authoring systems are in place. Some problems with consistency and level of detail can be avoided by using a limited set of terms selected from a pick list, and having an editor check all the author-supplied indexing. The advantages of this approach are that there is no delay between the creation of content and its indexing (if the authors actually do get around to indexing), and the indexing is usually compatible with organisational language use.

Indexing is also a possible freelance occupation for authors.

Editors

> It is neither wealth nor splendour, but tranquillity and occupation which give you
> happiness. Thomas Jefferson

Book editors, as representatives of publishers, are pivotal to the indexing process. They usually decide whether or not an index is required. Nearly every non-fiction book is enhanced by an index, although some publications miss out. Evan Whitton (1997) comments on the Wood Royal Commission: 'An index would facilitate study of the data, but out of $64 million allocated he sadly failed to find a few thousand for an index.'

Editors also determine the characteristics of the index:

- the type of index(es) required, whether of subjects, cited authors, species, place names
- the parts of the book to be indexed: text only, or also appendixes, figures, tables
- the features to be identified separately, such as boxed text
- the types of content to be indexed (e.g., names and places)
- the amount of space available for the index, and the format (e.g., eight pages, two columns)
- the style: usually house style, but there may be specific decisions for special types of content.

In some cases the indexer may decide some of these matters, such as the type of content to be indexed, or an editor may have specific requests for a book for a special audience, such as children. Other decisions that editors make concerning the index include:

- who will index the book, if not the author(s)
- the budget (in conjunction with the author(s), if they are paying)
- the schedule for sending page proofs to the indexer, perhaps in batches, and returning the index to the editor
- the output format required; usually RTF is acceptable, but some require special coding or embedded entries.

Editors must then communicate the requirements to the author or professional indexer who will do the job, and check that the index that is delivered suits the needs of the book.

Editors of collection indexes are not a clearly defined group. A bibliographic database has a person with a supervisory and quality control role, as do large library cataloguing departments. Because union catalogues such as Libraries Australia can be edited by contributors, the whole library community plays a role in quality control. Intranets may have a writer or editor with overall responsibility for quality, as may online help projects.

Indexing briefs

A book indexer needs to know most or all of the information listed in the brief and style sheet below. The notes in square brackets would not be included in the brief.

> INDEXER'S BRIEF
> Title:
> Author:
> Readership: [general, school, academic, etc.]
> Number of pages, words and illustrations:
> Budget: [Include Goods and Services Tax and any other extras.]
> Space available for index/Comprehensiveness: [The editor may calculate the number of entry lines needed, or the indexer may work from a sample index page printout to calculate lines per page, width of entries and so on. Alternatively, a guideline such as 'medium level, x entries per page' can be given.]
> Date page proofs are to be received by indexer: [The indexer needs to know if this changes, as they will have scheduled time for the job.]
> Date completed index due to editor: [Indexing a book often takes about the same time as copyediting it. Try to allow at least a week for every 200 pages – if you are pressed for time an indexer may be able to do the job more quickly, especially if the requirements can be negotiated]
> Format for index: [Normally the index is e-mailed as a Microsoft Word or PDF document, but more complex formatting such as tagging is sometimes required]
> Special conventions or requirements: [For example, create an index to cited authors; do not index glossaries or appendixes]
> Indexer queries/Author liaison: [Let the indexer know you are available to respond to queries and to forward these to the author as needed.].

A collection indexer generally needs to know the following, although the items will vary depending on the needs and structure of the project:

- the scope, aims and typical users of the collection
- payment method (e.g., per piece or per hour)
- number of terms per item
- how they will access the items to be indexed
- parts of documents to be indexed (e.g., exclude editorials and advertisements)
- things to be indexed (e.g., authors, subjects, and an overall classification code)
- method of data entry or output of indexing terms.

Editing of indexes is discussed in *Evaluation* in Chapter 8.

Style sheets

Stylistic issues are often dealt with by providing the house style guide, or an instruction to follow a standard guide such as AS/NZS 999, *Style manual* (for Australian government work) or *The Chicago manual of style*. Most indexers have a preferred style, which they use unless otherwise instructed.

It is not useful for the editor to say 'Follow the style of the sample index provided' as this requires the indexer to trawl through the index to find the stylistic decisions that have been followed. This approach is especially frustrating when the sample index provided is of poor quality. It is much simpler if the editor makes the requirements explicit. Style sheets should cover the following:

- initial letters: upper or lower case?
- page numbers: how to separate from the index heading (comma or spaces before first page number)
- page ranges: whether to set these out in full (*10–12, 257–259*) or abbreviate (*10–2, 257–9*; or *10–12, 257–59*)
- illustrations: whether to index them and if so how
- tables: whether to index them and if so how
- filing order: word-by-word; letter-by-letter
- filing order: file as if or as is? (e.g., *Mc* as *Mac*, *St* as *Saint*, *2* as *two*)
- filing order: initial articles
- format of subheadings: indented, run-in, hybrid
- *see* and *see also* references: format and position
- alphabetical groups: should a letter of the alphabet appear at the head of each section, and should the sections be broken up by blank lines or paragraph spacing?

It would be save time and energy if these rules could be applied consistently by all publishers, but everyone has their own preferences. Some decisions can be made logically based on research into index use, and these should be applied where possible (see *Index users*, below). In other cases we advocate use of AS/NZS 999 (Australian and New Zealand Standard, see Chapter 2) unless there is a good reason to follow another style.

Collection indexers need to know

- whether there is a controlled vocabulary for selection of subject terms, and rules for its use
- rules for combination of terms
- whether there is an authority file for names.

See also *Evaluation: Book-style indexing* in Chapter 8.

Finding indexers

Indexers may be hired by an author directly, by an editor on behalf of the author, or by the editor on behalf of the publisher.

Professional indexers can be found through 'Indexers Available' listings on indexing society websites. In addition, specific groups of indexers such as the ASI Special Interest Groups also list indexers who are available for work.

ANZSI's list of Indexers Available can be accessed at www.aussi.org/indexersavailable/index.htm. The 'R' symbol next to a name indicates that an indexer is registered. This is done through an evaluation of their work by a committee appointed by ANZSI. Indexers Available can be searched by name, State, materials and formats, subject specialities, and additional services offered. The ASAIB directory of indexers (www.asaib.org.za/directory.html) has a list of interdisciplinary indexers to indicate those who index materials from a range of disciplines. This acknowledges the fact that most indexers consider themselves to be generalists, able to index a wide range of materials.

For information on fees, see *Indexers*, above.

Index users

The ultimate purpose of indexes is, of course, to provide a tool of value to the users of the index. Unfortunately, indexers rarely know the audience, or get any feedback from them. Indexers depend on editors and authors to tell them as much as possible about the expected readership, but also have to make commonsense decisions based on assumptions about the text. Most books have a wide range of users, so it is difficult to target specific approaches. Keep in mind the need to serve two types of users:

- Some are new to the book and may use a wide variety of terms to access a topic (no matter what it is called in the book).
- Some have already read the book and are familiar with the authors' terminology and argument. They might therefore consult the name of a case study subject, or an idiosyncratic term used by the author that would not be considered by someone who has not already read the book.

There is a subset of the first type of user – one who is not familiar with the book, but is browsing the index for interest rather than to fill a specific information need. Sometimes the unexpected index entries might appeal to them. In an index to a book on workers' compensation in the medical profession one of the authors noticed an index entry for *drowning*. It was the one entry she looked up, puzzled as to how a health professional could drown on the job. It turned out that the doctor was snorkelling during a medical conference!

In addition to showing a reader what is in a book, indexes also show that something is not covered, so the user can quickly try another source.

Keep the potential users of your index in mind as you analyse the content and select terms to use. Often the choice of term is clear cut, as it depends on the wording of the book. In many cases the audience cannot be clearly identified, and a variety of words and phrases will be potential terms. You would use *adipose tissue* for a technical book and *fat tissue* for laypeople, but a book with a varied audience may well need both. In some situations closer identification of user needs is possible. This includes multiple editions of textbooks, in which teachers using the books provide feedback to the publishers. Another is indexing for a narrow user group. When working on access to an intranet for an organisation you can study search logs and do studies on a sample of users to get a good idea of the needs and approaches users will take with the index.

There are also atypical index users, who might be quite important. For one periodical we indexed, the editors were major users; for many books the authors will also be regular users.

Although specific issues to do with users are discussed in this section, users are also the focus of most of the book.

Research into the use of indexes

> I find you want me to furnish you with argument and intellects too.
>
> Oliver Goldsmith – *The Vicar of Wakefield* Ch. 7 (1766)

To indexers, a well-formed index is a thing of beauty – a compact, efficient, elegant package of useful information. To users, indexes are often difficult to read and confusing to use. For this reason we need research to find out how users respond to indexes in practice. Research has shown that users often:

- do not understand indexes
- do not know the alphabet
- do not like cross-references
- want more alternative terms (yet do not like cross-references!)
- search more broadly than indexers index
- want a table-of-contents-style entry to lead them through the index
- perform better when subheadings do not start with 'little' words such as *in* and *of*
- perform better with indented (paragraph) subheadings than run-on subheadings
- do not read introductory notes
- need help to distinguish between main headings and subheadings
- appreciate alternative mechanisms to access information.

These findings come from research projects by Christine Ryan and Sandra Henselmeier (2000), Susan Olason (2000), Cecilia Wittmann (1990) and Corinne Jörgensen and Elizabeth Liddy (1996). Where research evidence exists in favour of certain approaches, it is discussed in the relevant sections below.

Informal approaches to research, such as asking people where they would look for topics in an alphabetical sequence, can also be useful. When a peer reviewer queried our indexing (in a book on management) of Captain Kirk and Albus Dumbledore in the inverted form, we asked friends and indexing students where they would look for these terms. Many people said they would file *Captain Kirk* under *C*, as his name flows as a whole, while they would file *Albus Dumbledore* under *D*, as he is often referred to by his surname. These responses do not always follow the 'rules', which would invert both names, so they suggest the need for double entry in many cases. Similarly, Pauline Sholtys' comments on *the* (see *Filing rules* in Chapter 7) show that basic assumptions about users may not be valid.

Talking to users can also bring unexpected results. When, as a new librarian, one of us surveyed users about their priorities in the development of the collections and services of the medical library, they wanted to have the walls painted and to get some armchairs. Presumably the collection had what they needed already. When we tested a corporate online help system with staff, their main requests were for larger type, and for a different font for main headings and subdivisions. Another surprise was their use of a linked glossary as a pseudo-index to lead them to useful content.

To make indexes easier to use, indexers can:

- involve users in index planning and evaluation
- add more internal guidance
- use font variation to guide users
- obsess less over minor issues and think more about the overall experience
- offer training in index use and search techniques
- integrate thesauruses to lead users to appropriate terms
- consider alternatives such as 'best bets' links to the most popular pages
- remember the 80:20 rule – 20% of the content gets 80% of the use.

Usability guidelines
Jakob Nielsen (1994) notes ten points for evaluation against recognised usability principles (heuristics):

- **Visibility of system status**: If you have an index, make sure it is easily found; if you have more than one index, make sure they are both easily found and the distinctions between them recognised.
- **Match between system and the real world**: Use the language of users, and respond to the perceived needs of users. The use of paragraph numbers as locators reflects the structure of a book more than page numbers do.
- **User control and freedom**: Offer a choice of index and other access tools (such as tables of contents, site maps and shelf order); let users move through the index following references.
- **Consistency and standards**: Index according to a nationally agreed standard; index all similar pages to a similar level of detail.
- **Error prevention**: Users sometimes get confused about the difference between *see* and *see also* references, so rewording one of these (for instance replacing *see* with *search using*) might help. Provide guidance within the index about rules that may be confusing, such as filing rules.
- **Recognition rather than recall**: Because indexes are browsable they allow users to recognise and select an entry, rather than choosing ('recalling') a term to search.

- **Flexibility and efficiency of use**: Large online indexes load more quickly if split into letter groups; smaller indexes are more efficient when kept in one file as this makes them readily browsable.
- **Aesthetic and minimalist design**: Use minimal capitalisation, so that when capitals must be used they stand out; avoid images and font variations that serve no purpose.
- **Help users recognise, diagnose and recover from errors**: Cross-references guide users from one location to another, possibly more useful, one; allow users to backtrack as needed.
- **Provide help and documentation**: Include an introduction explaining general index features and those specific to the individual index.

Lori Lathrop (1999) provides a useful checklist for evaluating indexes. For general research-based web design and usability guidelines including content, search and navigation see www.usability.gov/guidelines.

User-oriented, mission-oriented and document-oriented indexing

There are two main approaches to indexing – user-oriented and document-oriented. User-oriented indexing (also called request-oriented indexing) assumes that you can anticipate the potential needs and approaches of indexers, and target your choice of terms towards the topics they may seek and the search terms they may use. It is most likely to work within an organisation where needs are well-defined and there is a shared language; for instance some terms may have a special meaning within that organisation.

A subset of user-oriented indexing is mission-oriented indexing, in which you identify information within a document that pertains to a defined need. Your task may be to index all content in a range of documents that is about alternative therapies for endocrine diseases. Thus you ignore all other content, focused on the defined needs of the project.

Document-oriented indexing (also called entity-oriented indexing) assumes that the only thing you can know with certainty is the content of the document. Therefore you serve users best by indexing that content precisely, so that when they search the index they will find any content the document has that is relevant to their need. In the book *Inside indexing* (Smith and Kells 2005), Kari Kells describes her choice of terms according to her assumptions about potential users of the book (request-oriented indexing), while Sherry Smith based her decisions on the content of the book itself (document-oriented indexing). This provides an interesting comparison of the choices that can be made.

Indexing with a controlled vocabulary limits the extent to which you can create terms based on perceived user needs. Taxonomies and thesauruses can be user-centred (e.g., generated from terms in search logs) or document-centred (e.g., derived from documents as they are indexed). Some systems provide different views for different users, but these can be very frustrating when users need content that the system has not selected as being appropriate to their profile.

Raya Fidel (1994) has discussed user-centred indexing, including the use of automated indexing to tailor indexing to individual user needs. Hanne Albrechtsen (1993) has compared simplistic (keyword), content-oriented and requirements-oriented indexing, including domain analysis.

'Fiddling' or guidance for your users

Everything should be made as simple as possible but not one bit simpler.

attributed to Albert Einstein

Filing rules have typically advised indexers to put certain entries out of order, on the grounds that users do not always know the spelling of the words they are looking for. So the user who searched for 'McIntosh' in the correct alphabetical place would not find it, as it would have been filed at 'Macintosh'. The advent of computerised filing led to the revision of filing rules and the decision to file entries as they are written, rather than 'as if' they were spelt differently. We consider that the best approach is not to file entries out of alphabetical order, but to use guidance within the index (introductory notes or cross-references) to lead users to the correct alphabetical place.

As the old indexers' proverb says: 'Fiddle the filing rules and you have helped a user for today, but provide guidance in index use, and you have helped them for a lifetime'. See also *Notes in indexes* and *Filing rules*: *Filing Mt, St and Mc* in Chapter 7.

Synonym lists are used in intranet search engines to automatically expand searches to include alternative terms to help users find content they might have missed if they had not searched as widely. However, searches that retrieve hits that do not include the users' search terms may cause confusion. This type of assistance is often best provided by giving the user a choice: 'You searched for "ABC". Would you like to expand your search to include the terms "Australian Broadcasting Corporation" and "public broadcasting"?'

Views of users . . . as wild animals, berrypickers, stupid, and active

Ideas about how people might use indexes come from studies specific to indexing, and also from studies about how people approach tasks or categorise information. A sampling is discussed below.

Berrypicking, described by Marcia Bates (1989), is a model of information finding which goes beyond the traditional view of computer searching of databases to incorporate a range of information-seeking behaviours that operate in sequence, with the information need being redefined as the search progresses. She makes suggestions for the design of online search interfaces to enable a range of browsing activities including chasing footnotes, searching for citations, scanning a journal run, and searching for authors, as well as focused subject searching.

The paradox of the active user (Carroll and Rosson 1987) suggests that people have a 'production bias': they prefer to jump into activity with a system, rather than preparing carefully so that they get the most out of it. Thus people often do not read the manual (or they ask Index-L rather than reading a textbook), and they prefer to click through links rather than take time to explore an index. In a usability study searching for information in PDF documents, users preferred using full-text search, even when they got more accurate results using the electronic back-of-the-book index (Barnum 2004). The production bias is also apparent in approaches to indexing such as the 'ride a wild pony' approach, below.

People also have 'assimilation bias', in which they apply what they already know to interpret new situations. This is helpful when there are relevant parallels in the situations, but it can slow learning when there are significant differences. To aid users we should follow traditional patterns where possible, and make our new approaches explicit when we do not.

Information foraging (Pirolli and Card 1999) uses the analogy of wild animals gathering food to analyse how humans collect information online. Users estimate the likely success of a given hunt from the information scent, which provides clues to identify the prey (content) and show its value. The easier it is to find other sites with good information, the less time users will spend visiting any individual website. Websites should provide sample content on the homepage (to appear nutritious) and include links and category descriptions that explicitly describe what users will find at the destination.

The myth of the stupid user (Gaffney 2003) says that when usability problems are identified, creators should look for problems in the product, rather than blaming 'stupid users'. For example, even librarians misunderstand complicated Library of Congress Subject Headings, suggesting that the system needs simplifying.

See also *'Fiddling' or guidance for your users*, above.

Children as index users

> Keep me away from the wisdom that does not cry, the philosophy that does not laugh, and the greatness that does not bow before children.
>
> Kahlil Gibran (1883–1931)

Paula Matthews and KGB Bakewell (1997) researched indexes to children's information books. According to their findings:

- Children were aware of indexes and their role, but tended not to use subheadings and found cross-references difficult to understand. The use of double entries can avoid cross-references, but the unused term should be included in parentheses to make the connection clear, e.g., *farming (agriculture)*.
- Children had difficulty scanning pages to find the information the index had directed them to – the use of bold type to highlight key points on pages in the text might be useful here.
- Children were confused about page ranges. On encountering the locator *7–10*, they asked 'What does 7 minus 10 make?' This can be solved by the use of words in the ranges – *7 to 10*.

- Children may not know the alphabet, so it can be useful to print the entire alphabet on the same pages as the index, including letters in both upper and lower case as section headers.

One of the challenges in indexing for children is selectiveness. You may be able to use only one or two indexing entries per picture, so for a picture of crimson rosellas you have to decide whether to use *birds*, *native birds*, *parrots*, *rosellas*, or *crimson rosellas*. If there are other significant features in the picture you have to decide which of those are most important.

Children's textbooks are written with the curriculum in mind, and the index should conform to the language and directions of the curriculum guidelines. If there are questions for students at the end of each chapter, make sure that the words that children will search to find the answers to these can be found in the index. It is also worth remembering that the audience for early childhood books may be parents and teachers as well as children.

A number of websites organise content especially for children. These focus on topics of interest (such as space exploration) and select material at the level of children's understanding. KidsClick!: web search for kids by librarians (sunsite.berkeley.edu/KidsClick!/search.html) provides an advanced search capability that allows you to limit the search to certain fields, or by reading level or by inclusion of pictures. It also tells children how to truncate and use Boolean searching. (Boolean searching uses the operator *AND* to search for a document containing all of the search terms and the operator *OR* to search for any one or other of the listed terms.) KidsClick has a directory structure, and lets kids see the directory labelled with Dewey numbers ('What does this page look like through librarians' eyes', sunsite3.berkeley.edu/KidsClick!/dewey.html). This allows them to explore formal classifications while having an alternative to return to.

Hutchinson *et al.* (no date) discuss children's information processing ability and its implications for the design of information resources. They cover motivation, information processing skills, motor skills, searching and browsing, and book selection criteria. These ideas have been implemented in the International Children's Digital Library (www.icdlbooks.org).

The way people categorise things

The way people categorise and classify things has implications for indexing as it affects the terms people will search on and the places they will look for information.

Marcia Bates (1998) discusses linguistic and anthropological research on classification and approaches to information access. 'Folk classifications' – categories used for plants, animals, colours and so on – have been found to have consistent characteristics across different cultures. These taxonomies include from 250 to 800 terms; they focus on the generic level ('monkey', rather than 'howler monkey' or 'primate'); and they usually have a shallow hierarchy. Geraldine Triffitt (1999) has discussed folk taxonomies used in Aboriginal and Fijian cultures.

Other research has confirmed the importance of generic, or basic level, terms. Although it is not always easy to identify basic terms, Bates suggests that we would probably find people using these terms, rather than the broadest or narrowest terms, while searching. In a book on knowledge management, *librarians* might be a better term to use in the index than *corporate librarians*; in an immunisation handbook *Queensland* is more likely to be sought than *North Queensland*. To some extent this goes against the principle of specific entry, which says that every subject should be indexed using the most specific term available. In practice we often bend this rule by taking it to mean the most specific sensible term available.

Folk classification research also has implications for the number of categories and level of hierarchy that might be optimal for online information systems. Systems might aid users by providing a hierarchy from which they can select terms to start their search, or in which they can review search results. Display of a thesaurus allows users to move easily to the appropriate level of the hierarchy. This agrees with research by Susan Olason (2000) which found that users of book indexes liked to have a table-of-contents-style index entry at the main topic of the book, to give them ideas of the major topics included in the index and book. This has implications for the indexing of the metatopic (Chapter 4).

Steven Pinker (1999) has also written about the ways people categorise things, explaining that there are two approaches – classical (Aristotelian) and family resemblance. Classical categories include concepts such as odd numbers, which are clear cut and can have membership rules written for them. Family resemblance categories involve a range of topics from games to vegetables to reptiles, for which it can be very difficult to write clear definitions. Lizards have legs and snakes do not, but what about legless lizards? This issue applies equally to manual and automated categorisation, and in both cases the categories need to be tested by users. It also means that there might have to be different approaches to the automated categorisation of different types of content.

See also *Taxonomies: Automated categorisation and taxonomy generation* in Chapter 2 and *Websites: Collaborative tagging and folksonomies* in Chapter 9.

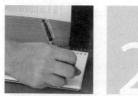

Definitions and Standards

THIS CHAPTER INCLUDES definitions of key indexing terms, and an overview of standards that are relevant to indexers.

Definitions

Here we define the key terms to do with indexing, especially some which are used in many ways. Specialist terms are defined in the sections they relate to, and are indexed under the topic.

Let us look at some typical index entries:

Daily Telegraph 20
    Vote-line 27–28
Islam 33–39 *see also* Muslims
    aggression condemned by 200–202
    in construction of 'Arab other' 33
    meeting hall *see* prayer centre
        application
    terrorists identified with 28–32, 206
'lost between cultures' *see* culture clash
swimming pool exclusive hire 156
Vote-line *see Daily Telegraph*: Vote-line

We can define these entries as follows:

- 'Islam' is a heading, also called a main heading or main entry – the term chosen to represent an item or concept.
- '*see also* Muslims' is a type of cross-reference, called a '*see also* reference'.
- 'aggression condemned by' is the first subheading under 'Islam'. The three lines below are also subheadings; also known as subdivisions and subentries.

According to the AS/NZS 999 standard (section 3.8), a subheading is a 'heading that is subsumed under a heading to indicate a subordinate or modifying relationship'. A subheading may have one or more subsubheadings.

- '200–202' is a locator – in this case a page number reference.
- 'lost between cultures' is a non-preferred term or entry point, that is, a term that is included in the index to lead you to another term.
- '*see* culture clash' is a type of cross-reference, called a '*see* reference'.
- '*see* prayer centre application' is a cross-reference (a *see* reference) from a subheading. It is not common to apply *see* references to subheadings.
- '*see Daily Telegraph*: Vote-line' is a way of directing readers to a subheading rather than a main heading. An alternative would be '*see under Daily Telegraph*'.
- 'application' is on a turnover line – a line which is too long to fit the page or column and therefore wraps to the next line.

Terms are words, phrases or symbols used to denote concepts, so all of the headings, subheadings and entry points for cross-references above are terms.

Multi-level headings are headings with subheadings. **Text headings** refer to headings of sections within the text (e.g., *Indexes* below).

Online sources of definitions include:

www.searchtools.com/info/classifiers.html,
www.willpower.demon.co.uk/glossary.htm,
www.dataharmony.com/taxonomy_glossary.htm and
www.webindexing.biz/Webbook2Ed/glossary.htm.

Indexes

According to AS/NZS 999 (section 4),

> the function of an index is to group together in a systematic and helpful order information on subjects scattered by the arrangement of the document or collection; to synthesize headings and subheadings into entries; and to direct users seeking information under terms not chosen for index headings to terms that have been chosen as index headings, by means of 'see' cross-references.

Alternatively according to James Anderson (1997), in NISO-TR02-1997, an index is

> a systematic guide designed to indicate topics or features of documents in order to facilitate retrieval of documents or parts of documents. Indexes include the following major components:
>
> (a) terms representing the topics or features of documentary units
> (b) a syntax for combining terms into headings (in displayed indexes) or search statements (in non-displayed indexes) in order to represent compound or complex topics, features, and/or queries

(c) cross-references or other linking devices among synonymous, equivalent, broader, narrower, and other related terms

(d) a procedure for linking headings (in displayed indexes) or search statements (in non-displayed indexes) with particular documentary units or document surrogates, and

(e) a systematic ordering of headings (in displayed indexes) or a search procedure (in non-displayed indexes).

When referring to web search engines, an index is an automatically generated list of all (or most) of the words (and some phrases) in full-text collections, arranged for quick access.

Keywords, entries and entry arrays

'When I use a word,' Humpty Dumpty said, in rather a scornful tone, 'it means just what I choose it to mean – neither more nor less.'

Lewis Carroll, *Alice's Adventures in Wonderland*

Keyword also means just what each user group chooses it to mean – neither more nor less! The common theme is that it always refers to an important word:

- When discussing search engines, keywords are the words that are used to search for a topic. Also called 'search terms'.
- When discussing metadata, keywords are subject metadata terms.
- When discussing displayed indexes, keywords are the meaningful part of a heading or subheading. An example is in the suggestion 'Invert "and" in the subheading "and school policies" to bring the keyword to the front.'
- In records management, keywords are the terms that are used to describe broad business functions. Each keyword is followed by an activity descriptor.
- In computer science, a keyword is an identifier that indicates a specific command, such as *end, goto, print*

Not to be confused with any of the above, the journal of the American Society of Indexers is *Key words*.

An index **entry** is 'a single record in an index, consisting of a header, a qualifier if required, subheadings if required, and locator(s) or cross-reference(s) or both' (AS/NZS 999 section 3.6). *The Chicago manual of style* words it as: 'An entry consists of a heading (or main heading), locators, and subentries and cross-references as needed.' Thus in the example on page 26, the block including 'Islam' and its four subheadings would be one entry. In common language when quoting 'per entry', however, each page reference or cross-reference is considered to be one entry. If you are getting paid per entry it is important to agree on the definition when you agree on a price. In the case of the 'Islam' block, it could be the difference between $1 and $7. For this reason a quote is better worded 'per locator' instead of 'per entry'.

James Anderson (1997), in NISO-TR02-1997, differs. He defines entry as 'the representation of a documentary unit in a displayed index'. It consists of at least a heading and a locator. More than one locator may follow a given heading in a displayed **entry array**, but each locator, in combination with its heading, represents a single entry. An entry may contain a multi-level heading and a document surrogate in addition to the required locator. This definition uses 'entry array' to define the block belonging to one main heading, which is called simply an entry above. NISO-TR02-1997 would call 'Islam, terrorists identified with 28–32' one entry, and the whole Islam block one entry array. This makes a useful distinction, which we have used in this book.

Depth of indexing, exhaustivity, specificity and granularity

Depth of indexing is the degree to which a topic is represented in an index, and depends on a combination of exhaustivity and specificity.

Exhaustivity refers to the number of terms representing a document in an index. A fully exhaustive index includes entries for all of the concepts that have been identified, while a less exhaustive index only covers the main topics.

Specificity refers to the exactness of match between the indexing term and the concept being indexed. If you index the concept of 'image indexing' using the term *multimedia indexing*, you do not have specificity, as the term is broader than the concept. If you use the terms *picture indexing* or *graphics indexing* for the concept 'image indexing', your specificity is closer. If you use the term *image indexing*, your specificity is perfect.

Specificity can be achieved by using specific terms, general terms with subdivisions, or a number of controlled vocabulary terms in combination. When using a thesaurus to index the topic 'children's computer games' you may have to use the terms *games for children* and *computer games* to achieve specificity.

Granularity is a measure of the depth of indexing, and refers specifically to the size of the indexable units. A book index is usually more granular than a periodical index, as it refers to small chunks of information the size of a paragraph or even a sentence. A periodical index, on the other hand, generally refers to a whole article or section.

Book-style, collection, and serials indexing

When indexing is used broadly to mean providing a pointer to information, it covers a wide range of activities in different formats producing quite different products.

This book divides indexing processes and tools according to whether they are book-style (closed-system) projects or collection (open-system) projects. Susan Klement (2002) has pointed out that there are significant differences in the approaches to these types of indexing, but that publications have rarely made the distinction clear when discussing them.

Book-style indexing is also called closed-system indexing, stand-alone indexing, information unit indexing, and publication-style indexing. It refers to one-off projects that result in a final product that remains unchanged after publication. In these projects the indexer needs to refer to the language of the book and the needs of users, but does not have to choose terminology based on past indexing, or in consideration of future possibilities (except, perhaps, to get ideas from similar books or earlier editions). Indexing of books is the typical form of closed-system indexing; other examples are e-books and web documents.

Collection indexing is also called open-system indexing, database indexing, bibliographic unit indexing, and continuing indexing. It refers to the indexing of collections to which new items are constantly being added. In these projects the indexer needs to follow rules of the project consistently. The indexer's decisions should reflect past decisions and be useful for future purposes. Most collection indexing projects are done by a team of indexers who refer to a controlled vocabulary such as a thesaurus to ensure the consistent use of index terms between indexers and across time. Bibliographical database indexing of periodical articles is the typical example of collection indexing; others are websites and collections in libraries, museums and archives.

Serials indexing has features of both book-style and collection indexing, depending on the nature of the serial and the type of index being created. We have grouped **periodical indexing** (journals, magazines and newspapers) with collection indexing, as these tend to be long-term, multi-indexer projects. We have grouped **book-type serials** (annual reports, directories) with book-style indexing, as they tend to be stand-alone, one-person jobs. The serial nature of their publication means that consistency with previous years' work can be achieved, and time can be saved by reusing some elements of the previous years' indexing.

Archives and digital libraries

The archives community uses the word **archives** to refer to inactive records that have been kept for their continuing value, and **Archive** (with a capital) as the place in which the archives are stored. On the other hand, the e-prints community uses **archives** as a 'synonym for a repository of scholarly papers' (www.openarchives.org/documents/FAQ.html).

Digital libraries are organised collections of electronic resources. They can include digitised portions of a library's collection, and resources paid for by subscription or licence fee that are available only to a library's clients.

Controlled vocabularies, thesauruses and taxonomies

Controlled vocabularies are lists of standardised terms used for indexing and searching. They include taxonomies and thesauruses.

Thesauruses are controlled vocabularies structured so that relationships among terms are displayed clearly. They contain preferred terms (subject headings), non-preferred terms (synonyms), broader and narrower (hierarchical) terms, and other related terms. They are used to ensure consistent application of index terms in many collection indexing projects.

Taxonomies are hierarchical controlled vocabularies used to organise and provide access to electronic content. They are often used to create the navigation structure for intranet or website browsing.

Standards

The nicest thing about standards is that there are so many of them to choose from.

Source: various

Indexers are affected by a number of official and unofficial standards, involving traditional indexing as well as the creation of metadata and taxonomies for digital resources. Different standards cover:

- the pieces of information (content) that should be recorded – AACR2 and Dublin Core metadata element set (see below)
- the way the information should be recorded – Dublin Core encoding schemes
- the way digital content should be marked up (structured) for transfer and display (See *Markup languages* in Chapter 8).

Standards for indexing

There is, unfortunately, no universal indexing standard. The **international standard – ISO 999:1996**, also known as AS/NZS 999:1999 and BS ISO 999:1996 – is the national standard in Britain, Australia and New Zealand, and as such has the broadest official coverage. On the other hand, many editors and indexers in the United States and Australia use *The Chicago manual of style* (*Indexes* 2003) as a de facto standard. The **NISO draft standard** (published as NISO-TR02-1997, Anderson 1997) attempted to broaden its coverage to include automated indexing, but a number of participants voted against it, so it has been published as a technical report rather than a standard.

Indexers can take various approaches. They may:

- follow the style provided by their editors
- follow AS/NZS 999 (ISO 999:1996) or *The Chicago manual of style*
- use a mixture of 'rules' from standards and textbooks
- follow their own instincts, often breaking standard rules such as those for filing entries, for the perceived benefit of their users.

Most indexers claim the right to adapt the rules as they see fit: Alan Walker (1995) has said 'A standard needn't be a straitjacket' and Fred Leise says 'There are no rules, only contexts.' Nonetheless, as Walker has pointed out, there is a body of theory about indexing and information access, and indexers should understand the principles behind the rules before they break them. Six basic principles he lists are:

- natural language (language of the text)
- direct order (non-inverted terms)
- specific entry (Chapters 2, 4 and 5)
- syndetic structure (Chapter 7)
- combination order: e.g., whether to use *Australia – history* or *history – Australia* (Foskett 1982: 80–82)

- coextensive entries: writing a multi-part heading that describes the whole topic of an article or book, e.g., *Organisms: Cells. Membranes. Osmosis –Reviews of research* (Foskett 1982, p. 267).

An indexing standard is not like an engineering standard, in which precise physical requirements can be established. Its creation requires compromises, and it cannot be expected to suit everyone perfectly. Nonetheless, the international standard (ISO 999:1996) generally reflects modern indexing practice. We have therefore used it as the basis for discussion of indexing rules in this book, while mentioning alternative approaches when they have something to offer.

Indexers often talk about indexing 'rules' that have no basis in agreed practice. These simply serve to confuse the issue, and would be better referred to as 'guidelines for use in certain circumstances'. These include the 'rules' *do not index under the metatopic* and *do not use chapter titles as index entries*.

Jeanette Smith (2004), a student of indexing, wrote: 'I bewail the dichotomy between the extreme detail-orientation required in indexing versus the ambiguity of the rules and subjectivity in the interpretation of the rules.' She describes the situation well. We have to be precise in applying the rules, but we can never get a firm hold on them, and as soon as we think there is a rule that is generally applicable someone will want to interpret it another way.

We will look at some of the official and unofficial standards.

AS/NZS 999:1999, *Information and Documentation – Guidelines for the Content, Organization and Presentation of Indexes* is the Australian and New Zealand standard for indexing. It is identical with ISO 999:1996, which is also the British standard (**BS ISO 999:1996**). The objective of this Standard is

> to provide the information industry with guidelines for the content, organization and presentation of indexes to a wide range of documents including books, periodicals, electronic documents, films, sound, images, maps and three-dimensional objects. It covers the choice, form and arrangement of headings and subheadings used in index entries once the subjects to be indexed have been determined.

ISO 5693:1985, *Documentation – Methods for examining documents, determining their subjects, and selecting indexing terms* (www.collectionscanada.ca/iso/tc46sc9/standard/5963e.htm) covers the selection of subjects (primarily for databases and other collection indexes).

There is no modern **US standard** for indexing as the committee was not able to agree on some issues, especially the recognition of computer-generated indexes as a valid type of index. The draft standard has been published as a technical report which can be downloaded free from the NISO site (Anderson 1997), as can their report on filing (Wellisch 1999).

The *Style manual* (2002) is the standard in Australia for government publications. It differs from AS/NZS 999 in a number of ways, including the filing of *Mc*.

The Chicago manual of style is a de facto standard in the US, and for many international publishers in Australia.

The **International Good Practice website** at www.aboutindexing.info is a fledgling wiki which offers a forum for discussion of indexing approaches.

Standards for controlled vocabularies

The United States standard, commonly used in Australia and New Zealand, is **ANSI/NISO Z39.19:2005**, *Guidelines for the construction, format, and management of monolingual controlled vocabularies*, which is equivalent to the international standard: **ISO 2788**. It is an update of the NISO thesaurus standard to make it more relevant to the online environment. It presents guidelines and conventions for the contents, display, construction, testing, maintenance, and management of monolingual controlled vocabularies. It includes lists, synonym rings (clusters of synonyms), taxonomies, and thesauruses (www.niso.org/standards/index.html).

The British standard *Structured vocabularies for information retrieval – guide* (BS 8723) is undergoing revision, and there is also an IFLA working group on multilingual thesauruses (www.ifla.org/VII/s29/wgmt-invitation.htm).

Standards for records and archives

The Australian standard is **AS ISO 15489:2002, Records management** (Sydney: Standards Australia 2002, based on **ISO 15489:2001**). It is the basis for the *Statement of knowledge for recordkeeping professionals* published by the ASA RMAA Joint Education Steering Committee (www.rmaa.com.au/docs/profdev/StatementKnowledge.cfm).

The **Open Archives Initiative Protocol for Metadata Harvesting (OAI-PMH)** provides a framework in which data providers create metadata, and service providers harvest the metadata (www.openarchives.org/OAI/openarchivesprotocol.htm). The main purpose of OAI-PMH is resource discovery; however, rights information to allow use (OAI-rights) is incorporated into the protocol. The protocol (www.openarchives.org/documents/FAQ.html) was developed to enhance access to scholarly communication held in e-print repositories (archives), but has since been used with other digital content resources as well.

ISAD(G): General International Standard Archival Description, the structural standard of the International Council of Archives, describes archival material using twenty-six data elements. It can be used with national standards as appropriate. ISAD includes some standards for administrative and physical control. Descriptions created in ISAD(G) can be stored in EAD (see *Markup languages* in Chapter 8).

ISAAR(CPF): International Standard Archival Authority Record for Corporate Bodies, Persons, and Families is used as a standard for names.

Standards for e-commerce

The book trade uses metadata throughout the supply chain to place orders, manage rights data and exchange conditions of sale. **ONIX** (**ON**line **I**nformation e**X**change) is an international standard for representing and communicating book industry product information in electronic format (www.editeur.org/onix.html).

ONIX is based on **Indecs** (**in**teroperability of **d**ata in **e**-commerce systems, www.indecs.org/action.htm), which is a metadata framework developed to assist the interoperability of e-commerce systems, especially in relation to intellectual property. Indecs is also used for DOIs (Digital Object Identifiers, see below).

ONIX has been mapped to UNIMARC and MARC21 for interoperability with libraries (www.editeur.org/onixmarc.html).

Dublin Core (see below) has a data element for rights which can be used to include a copyright statement.

Standards (schemas) for content and description

This section covers standards for the content that should be included and the way it should be written.

MARC and **AACR2** are discussed in the library collection section, while HURIDOCS is discussed in Chapter 4 and Library of Congress Name Authorities are discussed in Chapter 6.

The **Dublin Core Metadata Initiative** is an open forum of people from a wide range of backgrounds, including librarianship and information technology (dublincore.org). Its aim is the 'development of interoperable online metadata standards that support a broad range of purposes and business models'. Dublin Core has been kept as simple as possible to provide a basic framework for all users while allowing extensions for those who wish for more functionality.

The **Dublin Core element set** (dublincore.org/documents/dces) contains fifteen data elements that can be expressed in markup languages including XML and RDF (Chapter 8) and used for cross-domain information resource description. It has been endorsed as an ISO standard (ISO 15836:2003, www.niso.org/international/SC4/n515.pdf) and NISO standard (NISO Z39.85:2001, www.niso.org/standards/resources/Z39-85.pdf). The **Dublin Core encoding schemes** (dublincore.org/documents/dcmi-terms/#H4) note the way in which the selected elements are to be recorded.

Dublin Core can be refined (e.g., distinguishing between date created and date modified) and extended to allow for domain-specific applications. **AGLS (Australian Government Locator Service**, www.gov.au/recordkeeping/gov_online/agls/summary.html) and **NZGLS** (www.e.govt.nz/archive/standards/nzgls) have nineteen data elements, including availability, function, audience and mandate. The United Kingdom's **e-GMS** has twenty-five data elements. **Justice Sector Metadata Standard** is based on AGLS and has been designed for organisations providing legal information and services on the web (info.lawaccess.nsw.gov.au/lawaccess/lawaccess.nsf/print/jsms).

IEEE LOM (Learning Object Metadata) standard is used for the description of learning materials. These are digital and non-digital learning objects which can be used in e-learning, and include multimedia content, instructional content, and learning objectives. Pedagogical attributes such as teaching style, level and prerequisites can be included (IEEE Learning Technology Standards Committee, ieeeltsc.org/wg12LOM).

Categories for the Description of Works of Art (CDWA, www.getty.edu/research/conducting_research/standards/cdwa) is used for the description of art databases. The CDWA includes 381 categories and subcategories. CDWA Lite includes a small subset of categories for contribution to union catalogues and other repositories using the Open Archives Initiative Protocol for Metadata Harvesting (OAI-PMH, see above).

EdNA Metadata Standard (Education Network Australia, www.edna.edu.au/metadata) is a national framework for collaboration on the use of the web in education and training. It is based on Dublin Core and is consistent with AGLS. Metadata that conforms to the EdNA Metadata Standard or Dublin Core is electronically collected from trusted institutions using OAI-PMH (see above).

The multimedia sector, represented by the Moving Picture Experts Group (www.chiariglione.org/mpeg), has developed a number of standards for still and moving images. **MPEG-7** is an industry metadata standard for description and search of audiovisual content. MPEG-7 defines attributes of images such as format of the image file, resolution of the image, the application that originated the item and the date of creation and date of changes. **MPEG-21** is the Multimedia Framework that gives the big picture of how the data elements relate to one another. See also *Markup languages: SMIL* in Chapter 8, and *Video* in Chapter 9.

Standard application profiles (schemas developed for local applications) have been developed in specific fields (Heery and Patel 2000). *DTDs and schemas* are discussed under *Markup languages*: *XML* and *RDF* in Chapter 8, and MODS and METS schemas are discussed in *Digital libraries* in Chapter 9.

Standards for identification

Identifiers are 'names or strings adhering to certain conventions that, if properly employed, ensure uniqueness'. They are an important part of the 'political economics of information', in which the control of the technical means of accessing resources is as vital as control of the resources themselves. Giuseppe Vitiello (2004) examines features such as persistence and interoperability of identifiers, including ISBNs, ISSNs, and DOIs.

Digital Object Identifiers (DOIs, www.doi.org) are unique and persistent numbers that are assigned to 'chunks' of content (intellectual property) so that they can always be found, even if their location on the web changes. DOIs can be added to content at any level of granularity from paragraphs to entire books, and are interoperable with other international standards including ONIX, <indecs> and MPEG21 (see above). DOIs are important in e-commerce publishing models, as a component of rights management systems, and in the delivery of aggregated content in custom-published coursepacks. You can see DOIs for each article in *D-lib magazine* (e.g., 'doi:10.1045/march2006-crane') at www.dlib.org.

3

Planning Indexes

WE HAVE DIVIDED the steps in indexing into four groups:

- planning: scope, personnel and processes
- words, including concept analysis, term selection and controlled vocabularies
- structure, including subheadings, cross-references and filing rules
- evaluation, output and interoperability.

We consider each of these first from the point of view of all indexing, then specifically in relation to book-style indexing and collection indexing as appropriate.

The better you plan for an index, the higher its quality. Having decided that an index is needed, you need to consider the types of indexes (e.g., author and title), the size they will be, who will do them and when. The editor, and sometimes the author, has a major role in planning and editing book-style indexes, but the other parts are usually left up to the indexer. The project manager has a major role in planning and editing collection indexes, and will oversee all aspects of the process.

Book-style indexing

Most of the planning for book-style indexes is done by editors before they commission an indexer (See *Editors* in Chapter 1). In many cases it would be better if editors contacted indexers earlier in the process. Either way, an indexer has to confirm that the proposed brief is feasible with respect to index size, time and budget.

A book index is normally published with the content it refers to, but it may be separated: for example, a printed book may have an online index.

Selectivity of indexing

AS/NZS 999 (section 7.1.1) notes: 'Indexes should normally cover all matter in the documents.' In practice the level of coverage usually depends on the indexing budget and the structure of the book, and a book-style indexer is usually selective about the content (parts of the book) that is included. Some considerations are:

- **Preliminary matter**: Rarely indexed, although it may be if it contains substantive information not covered elsewhere.
- **Introduction**: Usually indexed at some level. Often it is read first to get an overview, but indexed last when the indexer knows how its content has been dealt with elsewhere.
- **Glossary entries**: Usually indexed under the term, with *defined* or *definition* as a subheading, so long as the definition has not already been indexed within the text. The whole glossary may also be indexed under the terms *glossary*, *definitions* or *terminology*. *Terminology* can be an important heading in legal indexes to gather glossary entries and definitions from throughout the document. A twist on this is the 'glindex', a combined glossary and index that is sometimes used as a way of grouping end matter and/or saving space. Glindex-style indexes have been used with pronunciation guides and chemical formula diagrams.
- **Appendixes**: Often indexed at a broad level only. For instance, a document reproduced in an appendix is indexed under its name or broad subject, but not by each specific subject term.
- **Bibliographies**: Not usually indexed. However, where there is an index of cited authors, the authors in the bibliography are indexed to the pages on which they were cited.
- **Footnotes**: Usually indexed if they provide significant information beyond that available in the text. They are not indexed if they provide only bibliographic citations, or if their content is easily accessible through index terms used for the main text.

A book-style index may also be selective about indexing features within chapters; for example, it may omit tables, figures, boxed text, study questions and case studies. Decisions depend on the space available, and the nature of the content. Boxed text that merely contains 'asides', with no substantive content, need not be indexed. Where figures are always placed on the pages on which they are discussed, they may not need indexing.

Where there are many tables, especially where they all relate to the same type of thing – for example, tables of exports by country – the use of table references may be beneficial in sending users directly to tabular information that they can then compare with other tables:

Cheese production 21, 33–37, 35t
Cotton production 55–61, 59t
Fruit production, 119–129, 120t

Table entries may also be useful when the sections are quite long:

Iron production, 228–264, 239t

Indexers are also selective about the types of topics chosen – this is discussed in Chapter 4.

Length of indexes

The optimum length of indexes is determined by the depth (comprehensiveness) of indexing. It is difficult to determine, and is influenced by the economics of the project, the content of the book and the perceived needs of the users. Unless there are obvious candidates for inclusion (such as 'index all names of films') it is hard to know until you start working on an index how much space you will need.

To calculate the space needed for an index, estimate the number of index terms per page. Then take into account the number of entries that will have more than one page number, which means each indexable topic you identify will take less than one line. Then estimate the number of long index entries that will have turnover lines, that is, will take more than one line each – often about 10%. Divide the number of index lines by the number of lines per page, and the number of columns, and you have an idea of the number of pages.

When an editor has told you the number of pages available, you can use a similar calculation, working backwards, to estimate how many index entries you can use. When indexing, keep in mind the average number of index entries you have allocated per page, so you index neither too deeply nor too shallowly as you progress. If there are strict space limits you can use a gradual indexing approach, starting with terms derived from section headings, and then adding more detail if space permits (see *Number of passes* below).

It is difficult to keep to a space limit in some books where there are lots of terms that are equally indexable. If you can have on average three terms per page in a book on pets, and one page lists cats, dogs, ponies, turtles and snakes, all with equal emphasis, you have no way of choosing between them. You have three choices: index none of them; index all of them, and use fewer entries for other pages; or devise broader groupings for them (such as *mammals* and *herptiles*).

It is usually best to index in more detail than you will need in the final product, as it is easier to remove headings and subheadings than to search through the text to find something you missed. However, do not add too many entries that you will not use, as that wastes time.

There are some rules of thumb about index length, but they are not always carried out in practice. One is that indexes to simple books should take up 2% of the book, while indexes to complex texts may require up to 15%. In practice, books average about 3.5% indexes, although they can go up to 58% (for instance, in dictionaries of quotations). Another rule of thumb says that the average number of entries per text page should be one to three for a light index, four to five for an average index, six to nine for a scholarly index, and ten to fifteen for an exhaustive index.

Although adequate space should be left for an index, this is not always done, and indexes are sometimes just squeezed into the last pages remaining in a signature. (A signature is a printed sheet that consists of a number of pages of a book, placed so that they will fold and bind together as a section. The sheet is folded into eight, twelve, sixteen or thirty-two pages.) Adding a whole section of eight pages when the index needs only one or two pages is expensive. On the other hand, indexing less deeply than the text warrants is not easy, and has been compared to fitting a size nine foot into a size five shoe.

When you have to artificially shorten an index you should first try structural approaches, including the use of smaller type, narrower margins, shorter indents, or a different number of columns. Some other strategies are: convert en-rules in page ranges to hyphens (115-16 instead of 115–16); squash the locators more (115–6 instead of 115–116); conflate page spans (115–8 instead of 115, 116, 117, 118); use run-in format instead of indented format; reduce the height of the drop (blank space) at the first page of the index; and reduce the space between letter groups (but do not remove it entirely).

One horror story tells of an editor shortening an index by simply removing every heading that had only one locator! Far better to look for:

- wordy entries that can be shortened
- 'boilerplate' text that has been repeated in the document
- subheadings that can be combined
- subheadings that can be deleted, with the locators moved to the main heading
- entries that can be replaced by a shorter cross-reference
- specific entries that are covered under a broader term; for instance, names of historic houses that are covered by the locators at the entry for *historic houses*
- less valuable *see* and *see also* references that can be deleted, especially when the alternative access points should be obvious; for instance, if you do not index 'Captain Kirk' under both *C* and *K*, you hope that someone who finds nothing at *C* will think to also look under *K*
- less important entries that can be deleted, including whole categories of terms such as places or names.

It is important for indexers to be involved in the shortening of indexes, as they know the structure of the index, and understand which entries will be affected when other entries change. If it is not the indexer's responsibility that the index has to be shortened, they should be paid for the time the revision takes.

It is rare to be asked to make an index longer, but it can happen when an editor does not want to leave blank pages at the end of a book, or wants to keep to the same number of pages for all books in a series. You can use double entry rather than *see* references, and also do the opposite of the instructions above for making an index shorter – retain wordiness, create subheadings, include less significant entries, and include more categories of terms.

Multiple indexes

Only one index should be provided for any individual document unless there is a good reason for having multiple indexes. This is because there is sometimes a need to refer between the indexes, and because users may miss the index that they do not see first. If there is more than one index, each should be clearly labelled, possibly with a footnote on each page letting users know about the other indexes. Multiple indexes are useful when:

- One category of entry would swamp the others, e.g., article authors in a scientific periodical.
- Some readers may be interested in only one part of the document, e.g., advertisements.
- Some readers may be interested only in specific items, e.g., legislation.
- It would be difficult to assimilate non-verbal headings into a verbal list, e.g., chemical formulas.

Instead of using multiple indexes you can use typographical devices to distinguish different types of entries within one index, being careful to avoid too much distraction.

Complete documents for indexing

AS/NZS 999 (section 6.4.2) notes that 'Indexers should have access to . . . complete documents . . . in their final form.' As deadlines get tighter, indexers are asked to index from documents that may lack images or tables, and may still be due for substantial revision. They are often sent a section at a time, out of page number order. It is also not unusual to receive manuscripts lacking pages, though these can usually be supplied by fax.

Dedicated indexing software has features that help with this type of project, for example, allowing the use of temporary page numbers that can be changed globally when final pagination is known. But this approach always adds to the time taken – it is an extra step as well as an extra worry, requiring more checking of receipt and indexing of each page.

If page numbers are changed after you have entered them, you will have to follow the procedure for repagination, below. Many projects that run on short deadlines send PDF documents via e-mail (see *Working with PDF documents*, below) or use embedded indexing (Chapter 8).

Ways of working

We describe here the general steps in book indexing, but many different approaches can be taken depending on the nature of the project and the experience and preferences of the indexer. Two books that focus on the indexers' personal approaches are Smith and Kells (2005) and Stauber (2004).

On receiving a brief, indexers familiarise themselves with the document to get an idea of the scope of the project, to make sure they understand the content, and to detect any potential problems. Familiarisation includes some or all of these tasks:

- Check that every page is present.
- Read the table of contents and some sample sections of the work. At this stage indexers who feel that they cannot index the work might return it to the client.
- Read the whole book. Few indexers have the time to do this, although Collison (1972: 26), who lived in more leisurely times, says 'the book should first be read through two or three times as a whole'!
- Mark up the page ranges for all sections: for instance note on the proofs that a section runs from pages 15 to 17.

Indexers may then go through the page proofs highlighting important words, and making notes of synonyms and other features of the terminology to be used. To decide whether to index a term or highlight a concept, they ask themselves 'If I looked up that term in the index, would I be pleased to find this information?' These steps are explained in Chapters 4 and 5, which cover various aspects of term selection and editing.

The next step is to enter the chosen terms into computer software, following the style that was provided or chosen. Most book indexers use specialised indexing packages such as SKY Index™, Macrex™ or CINDEX™, which automate much of the filing and formatting for the index. Chapter 10 discusses these and other software alternatives.

It is important to back up frequently as you work. One method is to use page numbers in the names of your backups. For example, in a book on reptiles you might use the filename *Reptiles206* when you have finished entering terms for page 206. Then when editing use a number for each pass through the index and a letter for the letter you are up to, for example, *Reptiles1p* for the first pass through, up to the letter 'p'. (Most indexers do more than one pass through the index when editing, although they may not always do it sequentially, so may need other codes for the stage they are at.)

Editing the index to ensure consistency of headings, to organise subheadings and to add and check cross-references can take 30% of total indexing time. A spell checker will identify some errors, while putting the index into page number order allows you to identify major problems including chunks that have not been indexed at all, and out of range locators (e.g., page 2111 in a 300-page book). See *Book-style indexes: Term editing* in Chapter 5 and *Evaluation: Book-style indexing* in Chapter 8.

You then need to convert the index from indexing software to word processing format and read through it again. After printing the final index it is helpful to have someone else check it. There are often still typographical errors and other inconsistencies at this stage. The index is then usually sent to the client as a word processor file by e-mail.

'Ride a wild pony' versus 'dressage'

Sonya Hartnett (2004), an author who now uses a structured method for developing a plot, says she used to use the 'ride a wild pony approach' in which she would throw all the bits of the story together when they came to mind. This nicely describes my (Glenda's) way of indexing. As a matter of some urgency, I like to get all my provisional content into my indexing software. Then I can relax and take my time to optimise the wording and structure. However, as I plod though my revision tasks I sometimes think it would have been better if I had thought a bit more about the structure as I went, so I didn't have to spend so much time editing. Harnett calls this her 'dressage' approach, in which everything is tightly controlled.

Sherry Smith (Smith and Kells 2005) describes how she delays decision-making about complex areas of the index until her final editing stage, by which time some issues have resolved automatically. She calls this process enlightened procrastination (which sounds a lot more professional than 'ride a wild pony'!).

To mark up, or not to mark up

Some indexers do not mark up (highlight) the text, but enter terms directly. They may or may not have read the book first, although they are almost certain to have examined the table of contents and other introductory material. Some indexers mark only page ranges (for chapters and sections) in advance. In effect, they perform the analysis, term selection and entry steps at the same time. The advantage of this approach is that it can be a lot quicker; the disadvantages are that concepts may be missed, and the significance of content early in the book may not be fully understood until the end of the book. For straightforward, highly structured books the method works particularly well.

Number of passes

Indexers also differ in the number of passes they make through a book. Occasionally indexers with abundant time read the book, then highlight important concepts, then enter the terms, then edit the index, but this is a luxury most indexers working to a deadline cannot afford.

Most indexers highlight terms in one pass through the book, and then enter terms in another pass. Others enter terms without marking up, as described above. Other indexers make a number of different passes through the book.

For structured computer books, Robert Saigh (2004) indexes chapter headings followed by text headings and any subheadings on his first pass. He then starts again and indexes any italicised, hyphenated or bold-face terms. If he has any space left, he selects terms from the text. He says: 'My process mimics Ford's automation in that I do discrete passes, which do not overlap.' If space is limited it can also be useful to index level by level as he describes. Linda Fetters (1996) describes a similar approach for indexing what she calls the forest and tree entries. She recommends writing the general (forest) entries for a chapter first to build the index structure, and then adding the specific (tree) entries.

Sherry Smith (Smith and Kells 2005) also makes at least two passes through the book. She often indexes scholarly books, and finds that the first pass allows her to determine the main structure of the index, while in the second pass she picks up points she has missed the first time, and refines the wording and structure. The first pass incorporates the highlighting step, and offers the advantage that some structure is being developed so she can start examining new terms in context.

Large team indexing projects can also benefit from a number of passes, allowing some issues to be resolved before the whole index is completed.

Working with PDF documents

> Working with PDFs and walking on water are easy if both are frozen.
>
> Source unknown.

PDF (Portable Document Format) is a universal file format that preserves the fonts, images, graphics and layout of any source document, regardless of the application and platform used to create it. PDF documents can be viewed and printed using free Adobe Reader software.

Publishers often e-mail PDFs to indexers instead of posting hard copy. This has transferred an extra cost to indexers, who have several choices:

- work from the electronic document, sometimes displaying it on a different monitor to the indexing software
- print hard copy and absorb the cost
- print hard copy and charge the publisher (about 10c per page).

Instead of e-mailing PDFs, some publishers provide the indexer with access to a website or FTP (file transfer protocol) site at which they, and all others working on the project, can access the PDF files. This adds to the work of the indexer, who has to seek out the documents. More importantly, these documents may be tinkered with after they have been loaded to the site, so the files the indexer accesses may differ from day to day. Ideally this should not happen: if it does, the editor has to inform the indexer, and the indexer may have to charge an additional fee for changes that have to be made.

PDFs can also cause problems with pagination. Some documents are initially sent unpaginated (e.g., for an encyclopedia), and in others the pagination displayed by the software and the pagination in the book do not always agree because the software includes pages which may be unnumbered, or numbered with roman numerals. This can be corrected by deleting preliminary pages that throw the correlation out, or adding mock pages where content such as illustrations is missing. Indexers who are sent multiple files often combine them into one, while others convert them into different formats (e.g., using *File > Save As Text*, or a program such as Able2Extract).

Access to PDFs can be beneficial as they are searchable, and can help you find topics you missed. But beware – this can lead to overindexing if you select every occurrence of a word without discrimination. PDFs can also be used to cut-and-paste terms into indexing software, reducing transcription errors.

Repagination and updating

Sometimes indexers have to change the page numbers in an index when the page numbers of the document have changed. This can happen to a few pages during the initial indexing of a book, for example, when a table has been moved within a chapter. It can also happen to entire books when the format changes, for example, from hardcover to softcover. Most indexers detest the work, but some who specialise in it and have developed efficient systems find it acceptable, and say it usually pays well. Editors who expect to publish in different formats should consider embedded indexing to avoid the need for repagination.

If you do have to repaginate, you should:

- Get the old book, the new book and the old index in page number order; either obtain an electronic copy, or scan it.
- Work systematically through the old index adding the new page numbers. If chunks of pages have moved exactly to new pages, you can simply increment the page numbers. Indexing software can do this automatically, but you should start at the bigger numbers or your new page numbers will be the same as some old page numbers.
- If it is not a simple movement of whole pages to new page numbers, you will have to mark the new page breaks on the old pages and change the page numbers one at a time.

Updating an index involves the addition or removal of index entries as well as repagination of existing entries. There are four main types (Wellisch 1996):

- **Mangled jobs**: Fixing these is almost impossible!
- **Yearbooks**: These retain most of their structure from year to year, and are often adapted throughout the year by editorial staff.
- **Revised editions**: Whether to redo an index or adapt an old one depends on the extent of changes, how easy they are to identify, and whether the old index is available electronically. It is usually quicker to reuse an original index if the additions, deletions, and rewrites total less than 10% of the book, especially if you indexed the previous edition. See also *Looseleaf services* in Chapter 9.
- **Unfinished work**: This may be needed if the original indexer is unable to complete a job, for example, due to sickness. It involves completing an index in the same style as it was started in. If not much work has been done, it may be better to start afresh. In this case you can use some of the work that was done on the existing index by importing it into software such as SKY Index and then deleting it. This leaves the existing entries available as prompts for 'typeahead', but does not impose them on the new indexer.

Non-English indexing

Indexing practices differ in different countries, and for different languages. Multilingualism is entrenched in constitutions such as those of the European

Union, Canada and South Africa, so attention to multilingual index access is important. South Africa has a small publishing industry, publishing mainly in English, and also in Afrikaans and the nine main Black languages.

French publishers interviewed by Bella Weinberg (2000b) believed that a minority of non-fiction books need indexes and that authors are the best people to create them. It appears that most of the indexes published in France are generated as simple keyword indexes using word processor concordance software. Although many books published in France do not have indexes, this does not apply to all books in French; French-speaking Canadians expect indexes. In Germany and other European countries, book index layout (e.g., of subheadings) and filing order of certain groups of letters (*Ll* in Spanish, and *Sch* and *St* in German) are different to those in English-speaking countries (Robertson 1995).

Non-roman scripts need special filing rules. Chinese indexes are filed either according to the number of strokes in the radical element of the characters, or according to the order the words would be in if transliterated into roman characters using the Pinyin system (Walker 2000b). Some African languages, such as those of the Khoi-San (Bushmen) and Xhosa, have clicks and other sounds that require the use of characters that may not be readily available in software, or easily searchable.

When a book is translated into another language, there are three options for the index: it can be machine translated, or professionally translated, or a new index can be created. Machine translation is sometimes used for technical books, but it does not work as well for books with less precise content or clear structure. Professional translation works better, but depends on the translator understanding the indexing terms out of context. Sharon Wright (now Sharon Bower, Index-L, 10 January 2005) gives the example of the indexing of the phrase *hurricane evacuation routes* as *hurricane bowel movement routes* in Spanish!

Translations often take more or less space than the original documents – if text has flowed to different pages or has been cut to fit the space available, the perils of repagination are added to the problems of translation. The ideal is to have the work re-indexed.

The 'Around the world' section of *The indexer* presents news from indexing societies which highlights differences in approaches to indexing around the world.

See also *Topical headings: Regionalisms* in Chapter 4.

Humorous indexes

Humorous indexes are a specialty that is not covered in detail here. Few indexers are commissioned to make such indexes, and those who are will develop their own style. In general, these indexes play with structure, delighting in inverted entries, little-used codes (such as *passim*) and long, descriptive entries that would rarely fit in a normal index. *The indexer* often features extracts of humorous or unusual indexes, and published an article on the creation of the name index to *The Atlantic monthly*, including entries such as *Rumsfeld, Donald, trademark swashbuckling panache as ultimate Achilles heel of* (Healy 2004).

Collection indexing

Collection indexing includes the indexing of bibliographic databases, periodicals, library catalogues, museum catalogues, records, archives, and multimedia databases, as well as the provision of subject metadata for intranets and websites. This is a wide range of indexing services and they obviously require very different approaches. They do, however, share many processes, including the use of controlled vocabularies.

The scope of a collection index is established when the project commences. Most indexers of these therefore use existing policies rather than select their own, although of course they have to change with developments in the information in their field. Medical databases, for example, have responded to the prominence of evidence-based medicine by making documents with this focus easily retrievable.

Since most of us will never plan the index of a library, museum or archive from scratch, this section focuses on bibliographic databases and periodicals. Other formats are covered in Chapter 9.

Planning bibliographic database indexes

Bibliographic databases are also known as abstracting and indexing (A&I) services or secondary publishing. They usually provide access to individual journal articles by subject, author and article title. They provide detailed bibliographic descriptions (citation details) of the items indexed, often including abstracts to provide a summary of the content. Book chapters, conference proceedings and other items may be included. Planning these projects includes decisions about:

- **Subject scope**: One database might be established to index all material about a specific place, or written by people from that place, while another might include all published materials on a certain topic.
- **Potential users and their needs**: For instance, engineers may be interested in hard facts and data rather than theory.
- **Documents to be included** (such as names of specific journals), other formats included, subject scope. For libraries and museums the aim is usually to index (catalogue) the whole collection, although priorities will be set with some categories being indexed first, or in more detail. For records and archives, legal obligations determine many of the priorities for indexing. For bibliographic databases, some organisations include web-based materials only if they are archived by Pandora (pandora.nla.gov.au; see *Digital libraries* in Chapter 9). Pandora works closely with indexing services and gives priority to materials that they suggest. Completeness may be dependent on the goodwill of document suppliers, as in the case of clearing houses that depend on donated journals.
- **Parts of documents to be included**, e.g., articles, editorials, book reviews. This is similar to the decisions made when indexing individual periodicals (see below). Articles and other substantial pieces are usually indexed, while

advertisements are often omitted, although in certain circumstances they can be important – for instance in the indexing of the *Australian women's weekly* for historical research in the social sciences.

- **Fields to be included**: These may include author, title, subjects, language, format. In database indexing, different types of entries are stored in different fields, allowing fielded search on one entry type only. Combined keyword searches usually allow search on a combination of different field types. Classification codes are also often provided to give a broad grouping for items. For a museum catalogue you also have to consider physical descriptions such as materials used and storage needs.
- **Types of subjects to be analysed**: For a multimedia database you might index colours and shapes, and perhaps also 'meaning'.
- **Depth of indexing**: This covers the number of entries per article and the use of major and minor indexing terms to cover major topics and peripheral topics.
- **Ways of entering terms**: Possibilities include typing into a template or selecting controlled terms from a pick list.
- **Structure of the database**, such as which fields will be searchable; and the search methods (e.g., displayed and non-displayed indexes; post-coordinate Boolean searching).
- **Structure of the indexing terms**: Whether to make the terms co-extensive with the document – that is, one complex term is used to describe the whole topic – or to create separate terms for each aspect of the topic, allowing searchers to combine them at the time of searching. Most modern databases do not aim for coextensivity.
- **Source of the indexing terms**, and rules for selecting them from controlled vocabularies (e.g., names from an authority file; subjects from a thesaurus; format types from a pick list). There may also be specific rules about combining terms (e.g., whether to use *lakes – Namibia* or *Namibia – lakes*) or using certain types of terms in certain circumstances. There are also standards for abbreviating journal titles.
- Approaches to increase **consistency** and prevent **bias**.
- Measures to ensure ongoing **funding** and support.

Planning periodical indexes

The planning of indexes for periodicals such as journals, magazines and newspapers is usually under the control of an editor, who either does the indexing or commissions an indexer. In many cases the editor's decisions merely follow past practice. Editors who have identified problems with the indexes they commission need to consider changes to the process, either writing a different brief or asking a different person to create the index.

Periodical indexes differ from book indexes as they are usually indexed in less depth (indexers may index mainly from title, abstract, introductions and section headings, rather than reading the whole text), and they are published after most of the content they refer to.

Technological developments are also changing the way indexes are done. For example, some legal publishers now tag legal cases within the text in XML format so that a Table of Cases (an index to named legal cases) can be automatically generated. In some ways this is moving the 'indexing' to an earlier part of the project.

Sometimes editors in new periodical indexing projects cannot simply follow or adapt past practice. For these, editors have to decide:

- The **types of index** to be provided. For instance, there may be separate author, title and subject indexes, or combinations (e.g., a combined author and title index and a separate subject index). Many indexes combine all types of entry, and use font variation to distinguish between them.
- The **sections** to be indexed. For instance editorials, if they contain substantial content; advertisements, sometimes in a separate index; news, selectively chosen; forthcoming events selectively chosen; product reviews; book reviews; articles (most important).
- The **size** of the index. This determines the average number of entries that can be generated per page.
- The **format** of the index.
- The **page ranges**. For instance, whether to give the page range of the whole article, or just the first page, or just the pages of the specific discussion.
- The **locator completeness**. If the indexes may later be cumulated, the locator must include the volume number as well as the issue and pages. Sometimes the article title is used as the subdivision.
- **Where** and when the index will be published. Some indexes are published with the last issue of the volume, others with the first issue of the next volume, others as a separate print document, and yet others as separate documents on the web.

A retrospective project – the indexing of a number of past issues that have never been indexed – may be undertaken by a large team. For these projects, editors also have to decide:

- The **purpose** of the index, and the potential **users**.
- How to set **guidelines** and train indexers.
- How to **record decisions** that have been made about terms to be used, e.g., in a thesaurus and list of instructions. This includes synonyms and terms that should be used for certain categories of headings. A company takeover may be indexed under the names of both companies involved, the heading *takeovers*, and a heading for the main industry or service involved.
- **Who** will do the indexing – sometimes volunteers or students are used for the bulk of the work
- Ongoing **funding**.
- **Promotion** and accessibility of the index once completed.

Cumulative projects combine separate past indexes into one large index. For these, editors also have to decide:

- how much they will change the existing indexing to ensure consistency
- whether they will change all terms to modern language, or use cross-references between variants
- whether they will go back to the original documents to ensure accuracy.

If you know that an annual index you work on will be cumulated in future, you need to ensure consistency with previous indexing and to anticipate future requirements. If you are sure your index will be published only as an individual yearly index, you can afford more variability in terms, although you should still aim to provide predictability for users.

Continuous cumulative indexing is easier when the indexes are available electronically. See *Microsoft Access* in Chapter 10.

Multiple authors in periodical indexing

Multi-article, multi-author journals can be difficult to index. Many of the authors will be connected with a number of different papers, and many co-authors are not named on the text pages and can be identified only by consulting the list of references. For this reason, author indexes typically have one entry for the main author of a paper, with references to that entry from co-authors, resulting in unwieldy entries in which co-authors have lost their connection to topics of papers.

> Breyer, Benjamin; Jiang, Wei; Cheng, Hongwei; Haydon, Rex; Zhou, Lan; Feng, Tao; Ishikawa, Akira; He, Tong-Chuan; Development and use of viral vectors for gene transfer 45–63

> Cheng, Hongwei *see* Breyer, Benjamin *et al.*

Max McMaster and later Tordis Flath led discussions on this topic at two AusSI/ANZSI conferences (Flath 2005), which came up with a consensus decision. The preferred approach is to keep the cohesion of the full citation under the name of the first author, but to also give title or subject and first author details under the names of the co-authors in place of a reference:

> Breyer, Benjamin; Jiang, Wei; Cheng, Hongwei; Haydon, Rex; Zhou, Lan; Feng, Tao; Ishikawa, Akira; He, Tong-Chuan; Development and use of viral vectors for gene transfer 45–63

> Cheng, Hongwei, (Breyer, Benjamin *et al.*) Development and use of viral vectors . . . 45–63

Ways of working – collection indexing

Before indexing anything, the collection indexer has to familiarise themselves with the overall policies and procedures of the database or periodical as described above.

Database work practices are often documented in procedure manuals, and they depend on the requirements of the system and the traditions that have developed. Freelancers do some database indexing, but much of it is done in-house.

To familiarise yourself with individual items, skim titles, abstracts, topic sentences and bold-face terms. The title of the journal that an article is from can help place the article in context. It is more difficult to familiarise yourself with non-print items. For audiovisual materials you may have to work from textual material or watch or listen to some of the content.

There is probably less variation in working methods with database indexing than with book indexing, as these are long-term projects with highly structured content. A controlled vocabulary such as a thesaurus is usually created for collection indexing projects and determines the terms that can be used for indexing, although some databases allow the use of free-text terms as well.

Database indexing is often done by a team. Either many people do the same type of work, or different team members do different parts of the job. For example, some may procure the articles to be indexed, others add descriptive details of authors and titles, and others add subject terms. See also *Encyclopedias and other multivolume works* in Chapter 9.

Because collection indexing projects are usually ongoing, more time can be spent analysing user needs and evaluating the appropriateness of the service. This is particularly so with respect to intranets and websites, for which usability is a major focus.

Library cataloguing is nearly always a specialist job done by librarians. Copy cataloguing (adapting cataloguing done by someone else) is also done by library technicians or para-professionals.

Many small collection indexing projects are done by professionals other than indexers, particularly those who are expert in the subject area or format. For example, artists might index visual media, and web managers may index websites.

See also *Collection indexes: Free-text searching and machine-aided indexing* (Chapter 5) and *'Automated indexing' applications* (Chapter 10).

Ways of working – periodical indexing

Periodical indexers normally receive issues throughout the year, and submit an index in December. This gives some control over the workload, although you can end up with a very busy December. Try to select journals with different schedules to spread the load, for example, one with four issues per year and one with six per year. There are a few disadvantages in periodical indexing – you may start work in January but not get paid until December; you have lots more paperwork to store throughout the year; and it can be more time-consuming to index in a piecemeal way. One alternative is to index all but the last issue in one hit, and then quickly enter the last issue when it arrives.

Non-English indexing

Non-English collection indexing is affected by the linguistic issues discussed under *Book-style indexing*, above. In addition, databases and thesauruses may have to be multilingual (see *Interoperability: Mappings between thesauruses* in Chapter 8), and the development of the services can be affected by the cultural, political and financial circumstances of the countries involved.

Marlene Burger (1999) describes the indexing of a collection of traditional African musical instruments. This involved popular English-language terms, such as *drums*; international terminology, such as *membranophones*; and vernacular terms in many languages, such as '*ingqongqo* (Xhosa); *moropa* (Pedi); and *ongoma* (Herero).

The development of modern bibliographic databases in China started in 1956 with the translation of abstracting and indexing services from Russia. The Cultural Revolution destroyed much of the work that had been done, and made it difficult to restart as there were few experienced professionals available, documents from outside China had not been purchased, and existing services were in disarray. From 1977 the situation improved, with indexing of Chinese documents in addition to translation of documents published overseas (Zeng 1990). China now ranks fifth in the world in the number of published papers, and Elsevier has launched a collection of Chinese journals on ScienceDirect (info.sciencedirect.com/content/journals/china). The China Society of Indexers is also thriving.

Masoumeh Bagheri (2005) spoke at an ANZSI conference on the need for Persian-language thesauruses because translations of thesauruses from other languages had proved inadequate. After the Islamic revolution in 1979 the need for Persian thesauruses intensified, especially in the fields of history and government, while the Iran–Iraq war increased the need for access to information in scientific and technical fields. Indexing education in Iran has developed to fill the needs of the indexing services being provided (Mansoureh Bagheri 2005). In Iranian libraries books are catalogued in the language they are written in, so users might have to search Iranian, English and French sequences to find all the books they need.

Ajibola Maxwell Oyinloye (2000) wrote of the difficulties faced by Nigerian information workers when trying to establish indexing databases for Nigerian periodicals. They encountered economic and staffing problems, and also found that publication of Nigerian periodicals was erratic. Indexers in Australia are fortunate that, although some bibliographic databases have closed (Chapter 11), a wide range of databases is still produced.

4

Concepts, Topics and Names

THIS CHAPTER COVERS the analysis of concepts and the selection of terms. Determining the concept (topic) and deciding how to word it are two distinct steps, especially in collection indexing where the terms may have to be selected from a controlled vocabulary. Term selection processes are discussed at the end of this chapter and in Chapter 5, and controlled vocabularies are discussed in Chapter 6.

Concept analysis

Concept analysis involves reading a text (viewing images, etc.), understanding the content, and identifying topics that should be indexed. In many cases this involves marking up the text – that is, highlighting words that describe concepts of interest, sometimes also adding marginal notes about possible wording and references.

Concepts can be analysed primarily from the point of view of the item (document-centred indexing), or of the audience (user-centred indexing). In-house indexing in particular aims to bring out concepts that are potentially relevant to members of the organisation. Bibliographic database indexing for a general audience relies more on the text alone, although the scope of the database influences the indexing of individual items. Intranet indexing is very user-focused, and the indexers have the advantage of being able to talk with users and determine their interests. See also *Ways of working* (there are sections on books, periodicals and collections) in Chapter 3.

For books, concept analysis usually involves reading the whole book, and identifying indexable topics for both large and small chunks. The indexer might allocate a term for a whole chapter, a range of pages, a paragraph, or even one significant sentence. For periodicals, concept analysis relies mainly on the title, abstract and introduction; the indexer may only skim the whole text. Usually it is between book and collection indexing in its level of detail. In periodical and collection indexing terms usually refer to the topic of the whole document, but may occasionally apply to individual sections within the document. The indexing of specific subjects, genres and formats is covered in Chapter 9.

Aboutness and meaning

'Aboutness' (extensional aboutness, topicality) describes the inherent topic, or subject, of a document, while 'meaning' (intentional aboutness, informativeness) expresses the meaning that a document may have for a person. A document can have more than one 'meaning', depending on who wants it, why, and what for. The purpose of information retrieval systems is to retrieve documents whose 'about-nesses' (topics) suggest that a user might find them 'meaningful' (Beghtol 1986). Document-centred indexing emphasises aboutness, while user-centred indexing emphasises meaning.

Identifying the 'aboutness' of imaginative texts and multimedia items is usually more difficult than for factual text. *Animal Farm* by George Orwell is 'about' management of a farm by animals, but as a political satire it has a wider connotation. See also *Users* in Chapter and *Fiction* and *Multimedia (audiovisual) materials* in Chapter 9.

Types of analysis

Arlene Taylor (1999) has named four approaches to analysis:

- **Purposive method**: You try to identify the author's purpose.
- **Figure-ground method**: You try to determine a central figure that stands out.
- **Objective method**: You count references to various items to see which are mentioned most often (computers do this well).
- **Unity, or rules of selection and rejection**: You try to find out what holds the work together, and what has been said or not said.

These approaches relate most to collection indexing, as they are methods of determining the overall purpose and content of a document. They can, however, also be applied to smaller chunks of content, such as finding a central figure in a paragraph. The unity method assumes prior knowledge of the field, so that the indexer can determine the emphasis the writer has given.

Sources and categories of concepts for analysis

The major concepts are usually derived from the document title, chapter headings and subheadings throughout the text. Abstracts can be useful when indexing articles, and artefact descriptions when indexing museum items. Bold-face words and topic sentences provide clues to the author's intended meaning. For a detailed index the text provides the remaining topics, and context for wording of subhead-ings to fully describe them.

You need to take into account the expected exhaustivity (detail) of indexing when analysing the text. If you will be entering just a few terms per page or docu-ment, you need to look for the overall theme. If you will be indexing exhaustively, and picking up every topic that is covered, you look at both the broad level and the detailed level. For exhaustive indexing you are also more likely to select individual names in addition to general topics.

Once you have decided to index certain topics, you must select all substantial references to those topics. This is Do Mi's First Rule (Stauber 2004), and can easily be forgotten or misdone. If you choose to use a general heading such as *lifestyle diseases*, which is not named in the text, you have to know which of the diseases mentioned fit in this category, and you have to be alert to them when they occur. These groupings can sometimes make interesting sections of an index. One school chemistry textbook mentioned a number of scientific discoveries that depended on accidents (such as leaking equipment), so we grouped these in the index as a point of interest.

Indexers sometimes use checklists to make sure they have considered all categories of topic. Types of terms include: actions, objects, agents, instruments, locations, time periods and viewpoints. Although these may remind you to consider all types of entry, they do not help you to select instances of those topics to be indexed. In some disciplines (subject domains) you may also have to consider different priorities for indexing, for example, a greater emphasis on theoretical approaches in the social sciences and humanities.

Bias in indexing

> It is only about things that do not interest one that one can give really unbiased opinions.
>
> Oscar Wilde (1854–1900)

Most indexers assume that they should not show bias, and deplore its use to hide certain viewpoints. Michael Mallory and Gordon Moran (1994) have observed that 'when academic controversies are involved, problems in indexing have arisen in disciplines as diverse as art history and medicine'. They presented examples of a perceived lack of objectivity in the abstracting of articles about the Guido Riccio controversy in art history.

Susan L Gerhart (2004) examined the ease of finding information about controversial issues using web search engines, and concluded that web searches tend to present the 'sunny side' of controversial topics. This bias reflects authors' links and searchers' choices. The National Library of Medicine Classification tries to avoid bias in its classification of non-traditional approaches to health; for example, it uses the term '*Quacks. Quackery*' only for 'works the subject of which the author considers quackery'.

Some writers have challenged the need for total objectivity, suggesting that value judgements in the selection and indexing of documents could be useful. Albrechtsen (1993) suggests that user-oriented indexing involves 'subjectivity and responsibility in choosing among the qualities of documents'. Dagobert Soergel (1985) also suggests the use of more qualitative judgements in user-oriented indexing, including the use of terms such as 'read immediately' and 'danger to our business' to emphasise the importance of certain documents.

In practical situations, 80% of problems are caused by 20% of situations. These 20% should therefore receive the most detailed indexing. When creating metadata for an intranet, we provided numerous access points for the instructions on how to get a password reset, as this was something we had found we needed.

Indexing non-inclusion

Occasionally you may wish to index a part of a text that mentions that a topic is *not* discussed. This can be useful as it may save the user wasting time searching under alternative terms. It does, however, go against the grain as it does not lead users to useful information on a topic. If used, the wording of the index entry should be clear so that the user is not disappointed when they look up the page.

Negative results (such as 'this research found no adverse effects from taking drug X for six months) should be indexed, but there is no need to include discussions of possible work (such as 'this research will be followed by an investigation into . . .') or work that was not covered in the report.

Elizabeth Wood-Ellem made an entry in the index to her biography of Queen Salote of Tonga which read: *Coward, Noel, not mentioned*. This indicated that she was aware of his quip about Salote, but had not deigned to mention it (Cauchi 2000). (Queen Salote visited London in 1953 as an official guest at the coronation of Queen Elizabeth. When asked who the man sitting next to her was, Coward is said to have replied 'Her lunch'.)

Although occasional negative references can be useful in print indexes, in non-displayed online indexes they are likely to be misleading as subheadings cannot be used to clarify the reason for the entry. This also applies to abstracts, in which a sentence 'Cost issues are not discussed' will be retrieved by a search for 'cost'. Some people use this to draw traffic to sales on sites such as eBay, for example, by saying 'Not a genuine Dior outfit'.

Passing mentions

In general, do not index passing mentions of a topic, in which a person, place or subject is mentioned, but no substantial information about them is provided. This applies particularly to examples ('Many marsupials, including possums and bilbies, are nocturnal'), lists ('among those present were Harry Hall, Bill Brewer, Peter Davy, Peter Gurney and Uncle Tom Cobley') and asides ('she wasn't a Margaret Thatcher').

On the other hand, in a book on movie stars we created three entries for the subheading *look-alikes* under *Monroe, Marilyn*. They were passing mentions in that they told us nothing about Monroe herself, but they did emphasise her lasting mystique, which in itself says something about her.

Absences may be indexable. 'Kerry Bruce didn't turn up for the first meeting' probably would not merit an index entry, but 'surprisingly, the Minister for Roads was absent from the high-level discussion' could.

Some indexers, especially of biographies, correspondence and family histories, index discussions that others would consider passing mentions, on the grounds that each mention tells us something, and that the accumulation of brief mentions can be significant in itself. This approach often results in the accumulation of long strings of undifferentiated locators (see also *Locators* in Chapter 7).

It is especially important to avoid indexing passing mentions in children's books, as children often take a long time to identify relevant content on the page they are directed to, and waste time and get frustrated if there is little of substance there.

Wording of topics and names

> Zounds! I was never so bethumped with words
> Since I first called my brother's father dad.
> > William Shakespeare, *King John*

Term selection (also known as translation, wording, phrasing, typing up) is central to the indexing process. Term selection in book-style indexing depends mainly on the words used in the item being indexed, along with possible alternative entry points that the indexer thinks of; in collection indexing, terms are usually selected from a controlled vocabulary. Rules for structuring index terms for book indexes and for controlled vocabularies are similar, for example, emphasising the use of natural language and direct order.

Along with term selection goes data entry – recording the decisions that have been made about wording of terms and adding the page numbers or other locators that those entries refer to. Most professional indexers use one of the three major indexing software packages discussed in Chapter 10. They type entries and locators into the software. As they watch the index grow they make wording decisions based on entries that already exist in the index. With SKY Index you can work on the index in the bottom panel and see the structured alphabetical index in the top panel. Macrex and CINDEX offer similar options.

General approaches to term selection that apply to all types of indexing are discussed here, along with the issues of missing information, dealing with the metatopic (main topic) and classification in indexes. Chapter 6 covers the development of controlled vocabularies, Chapter 7 covers subheadings and cross-references, and Chapter 9 discusses specific issues in term selection for various subjects, genres and formats.

Sylvia Coates (2001) has described the principles of term selection using 'Humpty Dumpty' as the document. Before you look at her article, try creating an index of up to ten entries for the nursery rhyme (en.wikipedia.org/wiki/Humpty_dumpty), then compare results.

Topical headings

> Think like a wise man but communicate in the language of the people.
> > William Butler Yeats

The word topics is used here to mean subjects that are not names, places or time periods. Deciding on the wording of topics is not difficult when they are explicitly mentioned in a document, although there are always decisions to be made about the precise term to use: for example, *bush foods* or *bush tucker*. It is a lot more difficult to name complex topics that have not been named in the text, and to name concepts in non-text items.

Sometimes the word you need may be used only in part of the book, or you may discover it through wider reading. Until you learn that the tips of shoelaces are called *aglets* (www.fieggen.com/shoelace/shoelacetips.htm), you can index them only under *tips* and *shoelaces*.

Write terms as they are written in the text, following its spelling and use of inverted commas and italics, unless this would cause clutter or confusion in the index. Inverted commas may be significant to the meaning of a term, such as the use of *'half-bloods'* in a book about Indigenous people. If the meaning of a term is unclear out of context, you may wish to add inverted commas in the index: for example, *'staircase construction'* in a book on film.

Abbreviations and acronyms can be used as index entries if they are used in the text. Sometimes the acronym is more important than the full term, which may no longer be used (*OCLC*, *UNESCO*). Make references or double entries at alternative versions that may be consulted.

Entries should be clear and succinct, and as full as necessary to make sure that the person who comes to that term has a good idea what it will lead them to if they follow the link. This has been called the 'principle of safe arrival'.

Indexing principles should be used when wording topics unless there is a good reason to follow another method. Some of these principles are derived from library science, and most apply equally to book-style and collection indexing, although in collection indexing they may be applied at the time of thesaurus construction (Chapter 6) rather than at the time of indexing. These include:

- Use the **language of the text**. Thus, if the book consistently uses the term 'sodium chloride', this should be the main term in the index, though the indexer may want to include cross-references from *salt*, *common salt* or *cooking salt*.
- Use **direct order**. For instance, prefer *hospital libraries* to *libraries, hospital*.
- Use **indirect order** (**inversion**) in double entries or *see* references if you think the second word in the term will be consulted. This is likely with noun phrases in which the inverted term provides a useful grouping point: *libraries, hospital* as well as *hospital libraries*. It should not be done when the phrase as a whole is essential for meaning (*Freudian slips*, *data processing*), or in most legal terms. It is rare to use indirect order without also using direct order; you might choose it when the uninverted term is so specific that it is unlikely to be consulted, although the specificity might be relevant when the user finds the term. You could use *lettuce, cos* and *lettuce, mignonette* in an index to the *Healthy canteens handbook*. Use inversions as sparingly as possible: thus 'breeding of red roses in Picardy' becomes *Picardy, breeding of red roses in*

not *Picardy, roses, red, breeding in*. (It would also be indexed under *roses* and *breeding*.) See also *Filing rules: Initial articles* and *Subheadings: Filing of function words* in Chapter 7, and *Inverting names* and *Geographic names*, below.

- Use **nouns and noun phrases**. Occasionally, useful phrases for indexing start with adjectives or adverbs. Examples are *very high frequency, newly industrialised economies (NIEs), most-favoured-nation principle*, and *as low as reasonably achievable (ALARA)*.

- Enter terms under their **specific name**. If the subject is Siamese cats, use the index entry *Siamese cats*, not *cats*, or *pets*. Entries that turn out to be too specific are easier to change later if necessary than those that turn out not to be specific enough. In collection indexing use the most specific term available in the thesaurus. You may have to combine more than one term to create full specificity; for instance the topic forensic neuropsychology can be covered by the terms *forensic medicine* and *neuropsychology*.

- Do not **capitalise** initial letters in index or thesaurus entries unless they are normally capitalised. Thus proper names and acronyms can be easily distinguished from other entries in the index. In some cases the same word with or without a capital letter may have different meanings, e.g., *Archives* as the building and *archives* as the documents. Some people use initial capitals on main headings to distinguish them from subheadings, but this can usually be better achieved by using bold-face for main headings. Some thesauruses capitalise every word in a heading, but because we primarily scan the tops of words as we read this can make the headings harder to scan.

- Use the **plural form** for all items that are countable; this allows the use of the singular for other meanings. All of the following pairs have different meanings: *trust* and *trusts, interest* (in banking) and *interests* (hobbies and activities), *storm cover* (insurance against storms) and *storm covers* (covers to protect boats during storms). The choice will sometimes differ for different users; e.g., construction indexes might use the term *cements* to indicate the different types of cement available. Sometimes when there is only one instance of an item the singular might make more sense (e.g., *code of conduct* in an organisational manual). ANSI/NISO Z39.19:2005 agrees with the recommendation above. Some museum thesauruses use the singular form because the institution only holds one instance of most artefacts. Nonetheless, Leonard Will (1992) recommends the use of the plural even in those cases, because it indicates the class the item is in, rather than the number held. German and French-language indexes, on the other hand, often use the singular form.

- Use **positive words**, unless the negative is essential to convey the required meaning. You may have to use the terms *non-response bias* and *non-haem iron*. A cross-reference from the base term is often useful, e.g., 'combatants, *see also* non-combatants'.

See also *Legal publications* and *Scientific and medical publications* in Chapter 9.

Disambiguation

Where the same entry refers to two different entities, distinguishing information should be added in parentheses after the name. These glosses are known as parenthetical qualifiers, and are considered to be part of the heading. This process is called disambiguation, and it applies to topical, place and name homographic terms:

golf clubs (equipment)
golf clubs (institutions)
Rose Bay (bay)
Rose Bay (suburb)
Walker, Alan (activist and theologian)
Walker, Alan (indexer and librarian)

Disambiguation works well for displayed (browsable) indexes, but not so well for searchable indexes, in which searchers are likely to use unqualified terms and retrieve irrelevant information. This was apparent in the sponsored links provided by Amazon after a search for *indexing*. The first two hits were for 'the Bible of Index Funds' and 'Vanguard Investments' – both retrieved because they are about economic indexes.

Clustering of results so that similar items are grouped can provide a rough form of automatic disambiguation. This can be seen on the web at clusty.com and vivisimo.com. One of the strengths of Wikipedia (en.wikipedia.org) is that it explicitly disambiguates search terms. Try all of these using the search term 'indexes'.

Regionalisms

In response to the question on Index-L 'What is Canadian style and spelling?', Martin L. White replied: 'Every subheading ends with "eh"?'   5 January 2006.

An index reflects usage in the documents being indexed; however, indexers must also be aware of alternative usages. This may require simple translation of terms used in different countries (*flats* and *apartments*) or noting usage which is potentially confusing (*public schools* in the United Kingdom are equivalent to *private schools* in Australia).

Usage may vary within a country. The first year of school in different States of Australia is called *kindergarten*, *preparatory*, *reception*, *transition* or *first class*. To confuse matters more, *kindergarten* is also a synonym of *preschool*. Other regional variations include *tuck shop* and *canteen*, and *slippery dip* and *slide*. These issues are discussed in Australian Word Map (ABC and Macquarie Dictionary, www.abc.net.au/wordmap/default.htm).

Lisa Rasmussen (1992) has studied the problems inherent in indexing within a Canadian context. These include the mixture of British and American English

(Australia is in a similar situation), words of Canadian origin, and divergence of Canadian French from French French.

See also *Non-English indexing* in the book-style and collection indexing sections of Chapter 3.

Name headings

Index personal names (people's names) and corporate names (organisations' names) when they are:

- subjects of documents (in all types of indexing)
- authors of documents (in collection indexing)
- authors who have been cited in the text (in book indexes).

Cited authors

To create an author index you include all citations, sometimes limiting entries to the first author or the first three authors. For scientific works authors are often put in a separate author index, as they could swamp the subjects. See also *Collection indexing*: *Multiple authors in periodical indexing* in Chapter 3.

In the humanities some names might be indexed as both subjects and cited authors, so it is useful to combine the two indexes. Having them in the same index also makes it easier to create cross-references from subjects to names, for example, 'zone of proximal development *see also* Vygotsky, Lev'.

If you are not asked for a separate author index you may choose to include cited authors who are mentioned prominently or whose works are discussed in detail, for example, *Mead, Margaret* in an anthropology book. Some indexers include cited authors if they are named in the text, for example, 'Eybers (1995) said X causes . . .' but not if they are merely mentioned in parentheses, for example, 'X causes . . . (Eybers 1995)'. Sometimes this difference is significant, but often it is simply a result of the choice of expression.

The authors of a book or book chapters are not normally indexed in a list of cited authors in that book, as they are noted on the title page or table of contents. They should, however, be indexed when they are subjects of the book. When authors who have written a chapter of a book are cited in other chapters of that book, some indexers include all chapter authors because otherwise a one-line citation would be indexed but a whole chapter by the same author would not.

If a separate author index is being created, author entries can be typed into the same computer file as subject entries with a code before them so they can be extracted later, or into a second window open on the screen. They can also be entered in a preliminary pass through the document – this can be a good way to get a feel for the content of the book before starting the subject indexing. In bibliographic databases authors are always indexed, and can be searched in a separate field. Their names are often controlled through the use of a *Name authority file* (Chapter 6).

Names as subjects

People as subjects are usually included in the general subject index, although some works, such as local histories, may use a separate name index. When there is a substantial discussion of a person or corporate body in a document, the names should be included in the index. In family histories, biographies and collected correspondence most names, no matter how brief the mention, are indexed. See also *Biographies*, *Correspondence and diaries* and *Genealogical and local history materials* in Chapter 9 and *Passing mentions* above.

Indexees sometimes notice their own entries in indexes. Michael Thorn (1993) wrote:

> The Times Index for 1992 contains two separate listings for my name: Michael Thorn, biographer of Tennyson, and Michael Thorn, deputy head of a primary school. The entries clearly apply, in the minds of the Index editors, to two separate people. I'm amused that my double life should be so formally acknowledged.

Resources for name indexing

There are complex rules for indexing names. Book indexers use the form of name that is used in the book; however, they still have to decide what entry point to use. Most indexers follow the rules of *AACR2* (1988), either directly or because these rules are reproduced in indexing textbooks. Biographical dictionaries and library catalogues show the form of name that other people have used. *HURIDOCS* (2001), which is based on *AACR2*, the *IFLA manual* and *The Chicago manual of style* is available on the web. It provides:

- general guidelines on matters such as surnames, compound surnames, no family name identifiable, titles, articles
- guidelines for determining entry form in certain languages and language groups, including African, Afrikaans, Arabic, Asian, Burmese and Karen.

Noeline Bridge (2003) has written on web sources for verifying personal names. National library catalogues can be useful for identifying national preferences – you can find these listed at 'Cybrary: National Library Catalogues Worldwide' (University of Queensland, www.library.uq.edu.au/ssah/jeast). The AIATSIS library catalogue (mura.aiatsis.gov.au) is a useful source of ideas for indexing Australian Aboriginal names. A number of websites link to sites with information about surnames from different countries (cyndislist.com/surn-gen.htm#general, digiserve.com/heraldry/surnames.htm). The October 2006 issue of *The Indexer* has a pull-out Centrepiece feature – to be posted on *The Indexer* website – on the indexing of personal names, including the 'Hundred Chinese Family Names', and French, Italian and Dutch names.

Formats for indexing names

Issues to be considered when indexing names include:

- choosing which form of a name to use: *Mao Zedong* or *Mao Tse-tung*
- dealing with name changes: single and married names
- dealing with identical names – add parenthetical qualifiers (glosses) to distinguish them, such as *Joan (d.1891)* and *Joan (shopkeeper)*
- entry point for names.

In the 'Internet Movie Database' (www.imdb.com/title/tt0108052), personal names are gathered in one format, but information about each film shows the name used in billing for that film. For *Schindler's List* (1993), two of the fifteen top billed were credited with different names to those stored in the database, that is:

Jonathan Sagall. . . . Poldek Pfefferberg (as Jonathan Sagalle)
Shmuel Levy. . . . Wilek Chilowicz (as Shmulik Levy)

Sometimes the name used for a particular individual varies throughout the book, or the name used in the book is not one that ordinary readers are familiar with. When the same person, place or thing is known by several names, your options are to use:

- both (or all) names for the period in which they were current
- the name that was current at the period the book is about, and refer from other names
- the best-known name.

Titles, thank goodness, are not of major importance in Australia. They can be used to distinguish between two people with the same name, and may be expected in military books. Usually the title of the highest position reached is used. Titles that are quite different to the person's name are useful entry points, for example, 'Home, 14th Earl of *see* Douglas-Home, Sir Alec' and 'Beaconsfield, Lord *see* Disraeli, Benjamin'.

Inverting names

Normally in English-language indexes personal names are inverted so that the surname appears first, for example, *Jones, David*. Foreign names are entered according to the rules in the country of origin of the person; for instance, the Dutch use *Gogh, Vincent van*. Names that have been anglicised are entered under the first part of the name (*de la Mare, Walter*). Foreign names in common use in Australia are usually entered under the first part of the name (*van Gogh, Vincent*) in addition to, or instead of, the foreign entry point.

Some Aboriginal names are inverted (*Yunupingu, Mandawuy* and *Yunupingu, Galawarry*) and others not (*Oodgeroo Noonuccal*) so it is best to consult an authority (see *Resources for name indexing*, above, and *Name authority files* in Chapter 6).

Fictional characters with authentic-sounding names are inverted (*Hornblower, Horatio*, and *Finn, Huckleberry*), but obviously made-up names are usually entered in direct order (e.g., *Bugs Bunny* and *Wile E. Coyote*). There are, however, exceptions. In the Last words of fictional characters website (www.geocities.com/Athens/Acropolis/6537/fict-a.htm), Little Boy Blue from the poem by Eugene Field is indexed as *Blue, Little Boy* (tongue-in-cheek, perhaps?).

A message to Index-L headed 'a quick inversion question' brought nineteen replies, showing that there can never be a quick inversion question. Discussions on whether or not to invert Malcolm X and Iggy Pop brought no consensus. The basic rule in library cataloguing is that the name is inverted if the second part is acting as a surname. The fact that Malcolm X's wife also took the name 'X' suggests that X was acting as a surname, but many people still felt that the name was better entered directly. Double entry is therefore the best option.

When checking indexes, you need to look under titles such as Captain and Queen to find any entries inadvertently entered there. When indexing for children (and even adults) it can be useful to have double entries – *Cook, Captain* and *Captain Cook*; *Elizabeth, Queen* and *Queen Elizabeth* – or at least references from the title to the specific entries containing the title.

Corporate names (names of organisations) are entered in direct order, possibly also with a reference from another part of the name, for example, 'Dior *see* Christian Dior'. Corporate names starting with 'The', 'A' and 'An' should be indexed under the second word in the name and, preferably, doubled under *The, A* and *An* (Abrahams 2006).

Geographic names

It can be difficult to decide whether to index places or not. The decision depends on the relevance of places in the text, the potential uses of the book, the number of places, and the space available for the index. If you choose to index some places you have to index all places of the same importance, so it is an important decision to make early.

Place names are usually qualified with the name of the area they are in, especially if there could be ambiguity, for example, *Auburn, South Australia* and *Auburn, New South Wales*. In the past indexers often inverted geographic names (*Geneva, Lake* or *Fuji, Mount*), to bring the unique part of the name to the front. There were always exceptions to the rule, such as *Cape of Good Hope* and *Isle of Man*. Many indexers now prefer direct order, in line with modern practice for other heading types.

Place names starting with 'The' are indexed under *The*, including *The Northern Road* (in street directories) and *Los Angeles*, although not *The Netherlands*. *The Chicago manual of style* indexes *Den Haag* under *Den*, but its English version under *Hague, The*.

The Getty Information Institute Thesaurus of Geographic Names Online (www.getty.edu/research/conducting research/vocabularies/tgn) and Geoscience

Australia Place Name Search (www.ga.gov.au/map/names) provide useful information about place names. See also *Geographic materials* in Chapter 9.

Titles of books, articles and shows

Titles should be indexed as they are written in the text, with italics or inverted commas where they are used in the text. Subtitles can be omitted unless needed to differentiate between two different works. See also *Filing rules: Initial articles* in Chapter 7.

Errors and missing information

AS/NZS 999 (section 6.4.2) recommends that indexers notify publishers of possible errors or inconsistencies in documents. Most jobs have just a few errors, but for some it simply takes too much time and is beyond the indexer's brief. Some of the errors that an indexer finds are detected through concurrent proof-reading, although you never know which of the ones you notice will be missed.

If inconsistencies in the text affect the index, indexers have to query them. If the same name is spelt in different ways, you have to choose one for the index. An indexer's note to the editor might read: 'p. 556 has adrenocorticotrophic; p. 976 has adrenocorticotropic. I've used -tropic.' In this case they are alternative spellings.

Many indexers feel that index entries should be complete, even if the text is not, and will research a reference to 'Ms Moody' to find out what given name to enter. In our opinion this is not the indexer's responsibility, except in the case where there is more than one person with the same name and the index has to distinguish between them. In this case the indexer should work out the differences if they can, and consult with the editor if they cannot. In a work on medieval English history, where the author has not distinguished the names of monarchs by numbers, the indexer may have to determine whether any given 'Edward' means 'Edward I', 'Edward II', 'Edward III' or 'Edward IV'.

The malignant, mighty or maligned metatopic

Many indexers believe that you should index under the metatopic (main topic) of the book only when absolutely necessary, to avoid the problem of having most of the book indexed there. Other indexers, just as strongly, feel that the metatopic is a useful gathering point.

You can avoid the metatopic in two ways – by converting subheadings to main headings, and by removing the metatopic as an adjective as the first part of a term. When the metatopic is a main heading with subheadings, you could have an entry:

    wattles (*Acacia*)
        allergies caused by
        as national symbol
        birds and
        weed potential

Alternatively, you could use the entries *allergies*, *national symbols*, *birds*, and *weeds* as headings in their own right. When the metatopic is the first part of a complex term, you can avoid it by simply removing the metatopic word and using the remainder of the term. Thus in a book on pharmacology, as the whole book is about drugs you could use the term *information* rather than *drug information*.

Indexing at or avoiding the metatopic

As with many indexing controversies, this one is not new. Kingsley Siebel wrote to the indexer of *The indexer* in 1991 pointing out that that indexer had not fully followed his 'self-imposed stricture' that 'the term "indexing or its cognates" is not used except as a title entry', as he had included an entry for *indexing programs*. Siebel's suggestion was to loosen the stricture and include even more under the metatopic, but Geoffrey Dixon's response (1991) was to remove the offending entry in the next volume's index, commenting: 'once the term is used as a subject heading there is no drawing back'.

Following a middle course, Wilfred Lancaster (2003) notes in the introduction to his index: 'Because the entire volume is about indexing and abstracting, the use of these terms as entry points has been minimised in the index.' The entries that remain are appropriate for inclusion at the metatopic:

> Abstracting and indexing, comparison of, 6–7
> Abstracting exercises, 379–387
> Abstractors as indexers, 123
> Indexing: as classification, 20–22; defined, 6–7; exercises in, 365–378; practice of, 24–49 . . .

Yet other indexers use the metatopic positively. Research by Susan Olason (2000) showed that users find the metatopic useful as a table-of-contents-style entry or gathering point that can lead them to places within the index that they might not otherwise have considered. Many biography indexers use the metatopic as a structured entry point into the index, rather than expecting users to search throughout the index for key points in the person's life. Experience in libraries also suggests that users like to start with a broad category into which their specific questions fit, from which they can then narrow the search.

Problems with avoiding the metatopic

There are problems with avoiding the metatopic. Firstly, you cannot always assume that because a book is about a topic that all the information referred to in the book is on that topic. For instance, a book on drugs may have content on patient information and disease information as well as drug information, so the use of the term *information* alone to describe drug information is misleading. Similarly, in a book on indexing you cannot use the term *software* to refer to indexing software, as you will also have entries for other types of software such as word processing, accounting and speech recognition. And sometimes the wording just does not work without the metatopic word. In a book about the bladder, how can you avoid the metatopic when referring to the 'bladder neck'?

There is a further problem: even if, for instance, drug information is the only information being indexed, you may avoid the metatopic but your users may not, nor may the indexers who follow you. In *LISA (Library and information science abstracts)* the preferred term for an article on agriculture libraries was *Agriculture*, as every topic in the database was related to libraries. But because indexers often followed their instincts instead of the controlled vocabulary, the term *Agriculture libraries* was used in error. The inconsistencies were dealt with in the second edition by the addition of a scope note: 'AGRICULTURE: (Occasionally and incorrectly as: AGRICULTURE LIBRARIES)' (Browne 1992).

In addition, while you can avoid the metatopic in entries that you structure, you cannot avoid it in titles and names that you are copying verbatim. So an index to *The indexer* will still have a lot of entries starting with 'index', but they will not be those selected as being most relevant, merely those that were worded that way in the text. For example, there may be entries for journal sections such as '*Index makers of today*', book reviews of *Indexing from A to Z* and so on.

When indexes are used to guide purchasing decisions, the lack of entries at the metatopic could mislead customers, who will be unable to readily identify the focus of the book. It also makes it difficult for them to identify the distinguishing features of a new edition.

Finally, with the trend towards the deconstruction and reconstruction of texts (see *Custom-built publications* in Chapter 9) it is useful if index terms can be reused in contexts different to the ones for which they were first written. So the entry 'drug information' is more useful than 'information' for a chunk of text that might be moved to a new document collection with a different subject focus.

Classification in indexes

In a classified index, topics are entered as narrower terms of the class they are in, or a thing they are part of. For example, schools and universities could be grouped under the heading *education*, and heroin and cocaine under *illicit drugs*.

Classification in book indexes is generally avoided; the specific entry is preferred so that topics can always be found by searching for them under their own name. Nonetheless, many indexers use some classificatory structure, either as a gathering point or because it takes less space than referring to specific terms. Legal indexes have traditionally been classified, and many still are. Good cross-referencing is needed if classified indexes are to work: otherwise a user does not know that rods and cones are indexed under *eyes*. Also, classifications change over time. Borko and Bernier (1978: 14) provide the example of *computers* being classified under the broader term *calculating machines*!

Classification is important in free-text searching of unindexed text, where it is relatively easy to search for specific narrow topics, but harder to get an overview of an area. Wilfrid Lancaster (2003: 270–271) has suggested the creation of hybrid search systems that use human-created broad subject codes and geographic area codes, supplemented with full-text keywords and phrases from titles or texts. This system would help avoid false drops caused by different meanings of the same word in different contexts. Classification is also important in web gateways, providing a way of browsing the content. See also *Taxonomies: Automated categorisation and taxonomy generation* in Chapter 6 and *Digital libraries*: *Subject gateways* in Chapter 9.

5

Selecting Terms

ONE OF THE biggest differences between book-style and collection indexing is the term selection process. This is because book-style indexes are stand-alone items, and the indexer can usually choose any wording and combination of headings and subheadings within the bounds of proper indexing practice. In collection indexing, on the other hand, indexers are usually constrained by the need to maintain consistency with past indexing, or with other indexers working at the same time, and may have to select terms from a controlled vocabulary (Chapter 6).

Book-style indexes

Index entries for book-style indexes are created using the language of the book, informed by the guidelines discussed above, as well as the rules for using subheadings and cross-references discussed in Chapter 7.

There are more individual choices in book-style indexing than in collection indexing, as all terms and subdivisions are coined specifically for the content being indexed at that time. Editing for clarity and conciseness therefore plays a big role in creating terms in book-style indexing.

Term editing as you index

> It is easy enough to make an index, as it is to make a broom of odds and ends, as rough as oat straw; but to make an index tied up tight, and that will sweep well into corners, isn't so easy.
>
> John Ruskin

Editing is the process by which the raw index entries are written and grouped to make them as useful as possible. Editing is necessary because there are many ways to write the same concept, and because subheadings need to be worded to fit with the main term they relate to, and with any other subheadings that are needed. Some indexers do most of their editing as they go, changing wording of pre-existing entries when adding new ones. Others do nearly all of their editing at the end.

A compromise including at least some work during entry is probably ideal, as this allows the index structure to develop, but not get too firm. If no editing is done during the typing-in stage, it is possible to get to the end of data entry and realise that the terms *patents*, *pharmacological patents* and *intellectual property* have been used almost as synonyms, because most of the patents being discussed in the document are pharmacological. It is then necessary to combine the entries, but if you are not sure they are all on exactly the same subject, you have to go back to examine each one. Some checking on the way would have saved time.

But you cannot do all the editing as you go, as it is only when the whole text has been indexed that final decisions about what to include and how to group entries can be made. For example, terms from the last chapter may create the need for subheadings for a whole section of the index. The different mindsets when adding entries are discussed in *'Ride a wild pony' versus 'dressage'* in Chapter 3.

Often about one-third of the time taken to create an index is spent in editing. For complex projects (such as embedded indexes) and team projects, this figure can be much higher. People who edit as they go report less time spent, but it has been spread out throughout the indexing process, rather than being gathered as one task at the end. Experienced indexers spend less time editing because they are better at making the right choice from the beginning.

Some index terms are straightforward, and the wording and relationships offer no problems – 'Australian Broadcasting Corporation *see* ABC'. For others, terms may have a number of synonyms and a range of terms related in various ways. When this happens it is often helpful to draw a simple concept map showing all the terms that are related, and using arrows and circles to show the relationships between them. For example, the term *hydration* relates to *hypohydration* (*dehydration*), which is improved by *fluid replacement*, and the fluid may be *water*, or may contain *electrolytes*, and needs *drinking*, and so on. A map of all these terms suggests the cross-references that should be made in the index.

Most professional indexing software programs allow you to group index entries according to certain characteristics. Many indexers use this to edit major areas of their index. For example, you could group all entries containing the words or fragments *cardiac*, *cardio* and *heart* to ensure appropriate treatment of this area throughout the index.

To edit an index, you need to arrange it in alphabetical order and go through it from start to finish ensuring that it reads as a coherent whole, and that the editor's brief has been followed. Indexers need to check all the things that editors check (*Evaluation: Book-style indexing* in Chapter 8). They should make sure that subheadings are listed under the main headings, indented and arranged alphabetically:

macropods
    gestation, 44–68, 341–2
    habitat, 24
    X chromosomes, 66

They should also make sure that closely related terms are grouped together. Take for instance this sequence:

Australia, seagoing vessels 432
Australian boats at sea 55
Australian camaraderie 34
Australian mateship 45
Australian ships 21

It would be better as:

Australia
    mateship in 34, 45
    seagoing vessels 21, 55, 432

Other points to check in editing the index are:

- There are no chunks without index entries. Perhaps a whole chapter has somehow been forgotten – this can happen with urgent projects in which the text is sent to the indexer in batches.
- If a category of indexable concepts has not been included, explain this in the introductory note (e.g., 'Names of set textbooks have not been indexed')
- All entries in the index are important and useful to the reader; all trivial or misleading entries have been removed.
- Headings and subheadings are worded clearly and concisely, as appropriate for the user group (*heart attack* versus *myocardial infarction*), with the most important keywords to the front (e.g., *musical instruments, purchase of* not *getting a musical instrument*)
- Equivalent entries in different locations should have the same locators. Thus *editing, cross-references* must have the same locators as *cross-references, editing*.
- Cross-references are given between synonymous or related terms; for instance, 'tiger cats *see* quolls'; 'Rottnest Island, 35 *see also* quokkas'. Check that *see* and *see also* references all lead to appropriate topics, and make *see* references into double entries if appropriate. See also *Cross-references and double entry* in Chapter 7.
- All notes and queries have been dealt with.

Indexing software can be used to check for errors, including identifying cross-references with no target entries.

Collection indexes

Term selection for collection indexes involves selecting subject headings from a controlled vocabulary, and possibly selecting names from an authority file and classification codes from a list (Chapter 6). In automatic indexing the terms may be extracted (derived) from the text rather than being assigned. The subject headings used in intranet and website tagging are called subject metadata (see *Metadata* below).

Translation of a concept into a controlled vocabulary requires an understanding of the text and familiarity with the language and policies of the controlled vocabulary. The closer the vocabulary is in scope and specificity to the item in hand, the better the fit of the term that is selected.

Items should always be indexed under the most specific term that covers the topic. If one term does not cover it, a combination of terms may be used, for example, *appendix* and *surgery* for the topic *appendectomy*. If an item covers a number of topics that are all narrower terms of a broader topic, apply each of the narrower terms – *grevilleas*, *banksias* and *correas* instead of *native plants*. When searching some databases you can automatically search for all narrower terms of a term in a process called explosion. An 'exploded' search for *native plants* will retrieve items indexed with the terms *grevilleas*, *banksias* and *correas*.

The thesaurus deals with synonyms by providing references from terms that are not used to the term that is used. These are normally phrased as 'X use Y'. In online systems a search can be automatically performed on a term and all of its identified synonyms. This should improve recall as the search is broadened to include all useful terms.

The number of terms that are allocated will depend on the policy of the project, and normally ranges from three to fifteen subject terms per item. Exhaustive indexing means coverage of all of the topics in the item; selective indexing includes only terms for the main subjects. Some databases divide terms into major and minor subjects; in MEDLINE, for instance, traditionally the major subjects were the only ones printed, but both were available for searching online. Others allow inclusion of controlled vocabulary and free-text terms.

Index terms are often entered into templates, with separate fields for information about subject, audience (e.g., age group), format of material (e.g., book chapter, article) and so on. MEDLINE has specific check tags for age groups, pregnancy, research about animals, and so on. Indexers can normally search the database while they index to see what terms have been used for similar items in the past. This ensures better term selection and greater consistency between indexers.

In the past methods of enhancing indexing, such as term weighting and role indicators, have been used to increase the precision of search results. The use of major and minor terms in MEDLINE indexing is an example of simple weighting. Most of these have been stopped because they were too difficult or time-consuming to apply, and too difficult for users. Subheadings can increase the precision of results by reducing false associations, but their use also results in loss of recall when indexing usage does not match search usage.

Free-text searching and machine-aided indexing

Human indexing, especially of bibliographic databases, is being challenged by the use of free-text searching and of machine-aided indexing. With free-text searching, term selection is the listing of every word in the document (the full text) with the exception of common words such as *and* and *but* which have been designated as stop words. With machine-aided indexing, term selection (translation of the concept to the controlled vocabulary term) is performed by the computer.

Studies in the 1960s and 70s suggested that free-text searching could provide results that were equal to or better than searches using human indexing based on a controlled vocabulary. Later studies using larger databases with realistic search queries have challenged these findings. Free-text and controlled vocabulary searches usually each provide unique hits (that is, each search type finds some relevant items that the other does not find) and are therefore complementary. They also each work better for different types of searches.

Free-text searching is needed to find names of individuals (if these are not indexed by the database), while controlled vocabulary searches are particularly useful for broad concept searches where the topic of interest is not explicitly mentioned in the text (Lancaster 2003). Indexing is also useful as it allows for a displayed index from which users can select terms of interest, rather than having to think of search terms.

TREC (Text Retrieval Conferences, trec.nist.gov) has provided the opportunity for systematic controlled tests of retrieval from large full-text files. They have confirmed that statistical approaches to information retrieval do function, as although individual words are ambiguous, word combinations are less so, and false drops can be reduced.

But not all automatic methods have exactly the same aims. When Larry Page of Google was invited to submit the Google search engine to a standard evaluation of performance using measurements of recall and precision, Page replied that he considered those metrics irrelevant – his measure of performance was simply 'the time it takes our user to find what he is looking for' (Diakoff 2004). This is a reminder that although Google performs extremely well for some searches, it is not the way to find everything important that has been written on a topic.

Deerwester *et al.* (1990) have written on latent semantic indexing. This approach has been used by MiTAP (mitap.sdsc.edu/about.html) for monitoring global events; capturing, transcribing and translating documents; extracting 'named entities' such as people, places and diseases; and summarising texts.

When databases do employ indexing, the trend is towards machine-aided indexing (MAI), although in most cases these projects still use human editing. The Center for Aerospace Information at NASA uses machine-aided indexing with human review to map text to NASA thesaurus terms (Lancaster 2003: 309), apparently with comparable recall and better precision than human indexing.

Anecdotal evidence from indexers suggests that MAI systems require a lot of editing, and that while they are good at picking out concrete nouns, they are not as good at identifying more complex topics such as behaviours. For an article titled 'Behavioral and auditory evoked potential audiograms of a false killer whale (*Pseudorca crassidens*)', the MAI descriptors were: *auditory evoked potentials*; *hearing*; *rubber*; *electrodes* and *gold*. The last three terms were extracted from the phrase 'responses were received through gold disc electrodes in rubber suction cups'. The more complex concepts in the abstract were not identified. The manual descriptors were: *auditory evoked potentials*; *sound spectrography*; *auditory thresholds*; *bioacoustics*; and *go/no-go discrimination learning*.

MAI techniques also do not work well when language is used creatively. For an article on endothelins (vasoconstrictive compounds) entitled 'ET: Phone home', the MAI suggested *Emergency Department* and a range of telecommunications terms (Greenhouse, Shelley, pers. comm. 12 May 2006).

For overviews of automatic indexing see Marjorie Hlava (2002), Karen Sparck Jones (2004) and James Anderson and J Perez-Carballo (2005, Ch. 8). See also *Taxonomies: Automated categorisation and taxonomy generation* in Chapter 6.

Computers are challenging the role of human indexers in term selection for bibliographic databases, but human indexing skills are still needed:

- to establish and maintain policies and procedures for indexes
- to set up rules for machine-aided indexing systems
- to edit the output of machine-aided indexing systems
- to index the most important documents
- to evaluate the quality and appropriateness of content for certain users
- for databases with inadequate MAI systems (anecdotal evidence suggests these are in the majority, so published results might be biased towards successful experiments)
- to provide broad classifications for documents.

John Farrow (1995) has said: 'If academic [bibliographic database] indexing is to have any purpose . . . it is to identify the principal topics of the document, at a level of exhaustivity somewhere between the title and the abstract.'

To remain viable, human indexing must be:

- high quality
- up-to-date
- targeted to user needs
- affordable.

Elizabeth Swan (2003), a professional searcher and manager of a specialised bibliographic database, spoke at the AusSI conference in Sydney about the value (or not) of indexing. As a searcher she appreciates the selection of quality material, the use of codes and weighting, and the ability to limit searches by the date a document was published or amended. Her database, EDGE, which indexes material about packaging, uses relatively simple, quick indexing, and has managed to stay economically viable when other services have closed.

Re-indexing when thesaurus terms change

When a thesaurus changes either its terms or its policies, database managers have to decide whether to re-index old records in the database or to note the date of the change in the thesaurus and rely on searchers to adjust their searches. Libraries have to make similar decisions when there are changes to the classification scheme – these are more onerous as they require re-shelving as well as re-cataloguing.

Prue Deacon (2003) has written about changes to the *Health and Ageing Thesaurus* which resulted in the narrowing of the scope of the term *prevention and control*, the addition of three new terms (*living with disease, primary prevention* and *prophylaxis*) and widening of the scope of the term *disease management*. These changes affected 20% of the records in the HealthInsite database (www.healthinsite.gov.au).

The team decided to re-index the records, and the changes took a number of months. One interesting finding was that for many records they deleted the term *prevention and control*, rather than replacing it with one of the new terms. It appears it had been too easy to add this term by checking it on a list of *MeSH (Medical Subject Headings)* subheading terms, even when it was not a major feature of the article. They regretted that they had not made this change years earlier when they became aware of problems with the use of the term; one of the reasons was that they had been trying to remain compatible with *MeSH*. There is often a pull between the desire to serve your users as you see fit, and the desire to comply with an international 'standard'. You cannot always have it both ways.

See also *Thesauruses: Term selection* in Chapter 6.

Abstracts

Abstracts are often included in bibliographic databases to provide summary information about items. These summaries may provide all the information a user needs, or at least enough information to enable them to decide whether they need to obtain the whole article. A good abstract is concise, accurate, clear, and avoids redundancy.

Marcia Bates (1998) has written on research by Resnikoff and Dolby into the way people respond to information in steps of about one in thirty – it is useful to have a text, then an abstract about one-thirtieth of the length of the text, then indexing terms which provide an even more compact summary.

A very brief abstract is called an annotation, as in an annotated bibliography; however, in video indexing, annotation is used to mean indexing. There are three main types of abstracts:

- Indicative (descriptive) abstracts describe the content.
- Informative abstracts summarise the content and provide substance from the item, including results.
- Critical abstracts, like book reviews, evaluate the content.

In online systems there is now overlap between the purpose of abstracts and indexing terms, as both may be used to learn about the content of the item, and both offer searchable access points. An abstract is a good place to use natural language terms or names that are not authorised by the controlled vocabulary.

Some journals now require very structured author abstracts, including categories such as aims and methods. In websites and intranets the description (abstract) field is often presented to users in the list of hits. If there is no description, the first few lines from the page, or sentence excerpts containing the search text, are used.

Periodical indexes

Term selection for indexes to individual periodicals is similar to book-style indexing to the extent that the indexer is free to choose terms. It is similar to collection indexing to the extent that the indexer is constrained by past use, by index policies, or by a controlled vocabulary of some type. Periodical indexes that cover a number of years have to deal with new topics, changes in terminology, and changes of names, for example, 'AusSI *see* ANZSI'.

Periodical indexes may include both general and specific entries for the same topic. An article on healthy policies for school canteens could be indexed under *school canteens* as well as *fat content*.

Because locators in periodical indexes can be long and complex when they include full citation details, sometimes only one entry has the full details and all other terms refer to that entry. For an article on the pig farming interests of an ex-prime minister of Australia, *Guidelines – a subject guide for Australia libraries* used the reference 'Keating, Paul *see* Pigs' (Column 8, 1994).

Metadata

Metadata is structured data about data, and resembles the information in library catalogue records. As Jessica Milstead and Susan Feldman (1999) point out: 'Like the man who had been writing prose all his life without knowing it, librarians and indexers have been producing and standardizing metadata for centuries.'

Subject (keyword) metadata, titles and descriptions (abstracts) are the most relevant metadata fields for indexers. Others include date, rights management information and information to aid workflow and record management. Metadata is often structured according to the Dublin Core standard (see *Standards* in Chapter 2).

Subject metadata is usually taken from a controlled vocabulary. It has been used to enhance retrieval of websites by search engines. However, because of the use of inappropriate metadata to improve ranking (spamming), most search engines now pay little or no attention to hidden metadata (but see *Web as a whole: Metadata and paid search* in Chapter 9). Title and description metadata remain important, however.

Metadata is of much more use on intranets (see *Intranets and CMSs* in Chapter 9), which often suffer from information overload and access problems, and are less susceptible to spamming. Synonym rings (clusters of synonyms) can be important for broadening searches to include all synonyms of the term the user entered. For example, using a synonym ring, a search for any of the terms *fees*, *charges*, *costs* and *payments* would retrieve all documents containing any of those words.

Government departments are not all convinced of the value of metadata. A US survey found that many supported the hypothesis that: 'For the majority of government information, exposing it to indexing with commercial search technology is sufficient to meet the information categorization, dissemination, and sharing needs of the public and as required by law and policy' (GSA 2005).

Metadata can be used to dynamically generate browsable lists of search terms (indexes), for example, at the Montague Institute Review site (www.montaguelab.com/Public/indexes.htm). It can also be used as the basis for a website's navigational structure (Lider and Mosoiu 2003). Tony Gill *et al.* (no date) have written on the use of metadata and crosswalks (mappings between fields in different databases). See also *Thesauruses* and *Taxonomies* in Chapter 6 and *Websites: Collaborative tagging and folksonomies* in Chapter 9.

Metadata for intranets is sometimes created by content authors rather than specialist indexers. The simplest approach is to ask authors to tag content using natural language, and to have an indexer or editor check the terms and translate them into controlled vocabulary terms as appropriate. A number of organisations retain the natural language terms as well as creating controlled vocabulary terms. If authors are expected to use controlled vocabulary terms, processes have to be developed to make the controlled vocabulary easy to navigate. This can include providing:

- a drop-down list of terms that can be used (works well with short lists, such as a list of formats)
- a navigable classification scheme or hierarchically displayed thesaurus
- a search facility for the controlled vocabulary.

Provision of pick lists, a browsable thesaurus and a search facility also aid user searching of the intranet (Haynes 2004: 165).

Faceted metadata

Faceted metadata is the application of metadata terms from structured categories. These include categories relevant to a certain topic, and those that are generally applicable, such as *format, user appropriateness, type of material* (e.g., *overview*), *genre, time* and *place*. A recipe index could have the facets *ingredients, cooking method, cooking time* and so on, as well as generally applicable facets such as *for children*. Use of faceted metadata is considered to be a good way of combining the best of browsing and searching. Marti Hearst (2006) has compared information exploration using clustering and faceted categories.

A faceted classification is based on a controlled vocabulary, and implementation requires indexing of documents with metadata from the controlled vocabulary. FacetMap (facetmap.com/index.jsp) is a software package that allows you to create and test your own faceted classification scheme on the web (facetmap.com/demosetup/index.jsp). Flamenco code for faceted metadata is now available as open source code, stored at sourceforge (flamenco.berkeley.edu).

Facets have been important in library classifications since at least the time of Ranganathan, whose PMEST facets have been well studied. PMEST refers to personality (the main topic), material, energy (that is, activity, operation, process), space and time (Steckel 2002). A faceted approach has been implemented at NCSU – see *Library collections* in Chapter 9 for details.

Controlled Vocabularies for Selecting Terms

WHEREAS MOST BOOK-STYLE indexing is a stand-alone process requiring only the item in hand, collection indexing is a long-term process dependent on the use of controlled vocabularies for maintaining consistency between indexers. In traditional bibliographic database and library indexing, this is done through authority files for names and thesauruses for subject terms. On intranets and websites the same basic tools may apply, although name authority control is less likely, and the controlled vocabulary may be a taxonomy used for navigation as well as for term selection. Ontologies and topic maps are important for more automated approaches to information access on the web. For an introduction see Warner (2002).

Name authority files

In library catalogues and other collection indexes, decisions about the form of names are recorded in authority files that list the preferred forms of names and alternative names from which references can be made. The alternative names may be earlier or later names, pseudonyms, or fuller forms of the name, and often include birth and death dates to distinguish different people with the same name. Authority files either provide cross-references or work behind the scenes enabling automatic searches for different forms of names.

Authority files may also include the source of information about the name. For example, *Library of Congress Authorities* (authorities.loc.gov) has a record for my great-great aunt, Alice M Browne, with a reference to *Ryce, John*, her pseudonym, quoting a book by RL Wolfe on nineteenth-century fiction that states: 'John Ryce is the nom de plume of Alice M. Browne'.

Denise Bennett and Priscilla Williams (2006) have explored cost-effective options for name authority generation, including the use of computers to assist disambiguation.

See also *Name headings* in Chapter 4.

Thesauruses

Thy firmness makes my circle just, and makes me start where I began.

John Donne

An information retrieval thesaurus is a structured list of subject headings (preferred terms) to be used as index terms. Thesauruses are used to ensure the consistent application of index terms, and to improve information retrieval by controlling synonyms and homographs, and by providing information about relationships between terms. They may also be used as an aid to searchers, enabling them to choose the best search terms and to broaden or narrow their searches.

The thesauruses discussed here are different to Roget-style thesauruses in purpose and structure, and it is unfortunate that the same name (meaning *storehouse* or *treasury* in ancient Greek) is used for both tools. The plural of *thesaurus* can be *thesauruses* or *thesauri*, as the word was originally Greek not Latin (Peters 2004).

Thesauruses show three types of relationships – equivalence, hierarchical and associative – and these are all reciprocal. Equivalence refers to synonymous terms (or terms treated like synonyms, such as abbreviations and opposites) and is indicated by 'USE' and 'Used For' or 'UF'. In the example below, *eggplant* is the preferred (authorised) term and *aubergine* is the non-preferred term. 'USE' usually translates to '*see*' when the reference is written for index users.

> aubergine USE eggplant
> eggplant UF aubergine

Hierarchical relationships comprise broader (parent) terms and narrower (child) terms. These are also reciprocal, and are indicated using 'BT' and 'NT':

cetaceans
NT whales

sperm whales
BT whales

whales
BT cetaceans
NT sperm whales

Hierarchical relationships can also be displayed in tree structures:

cetaceans
... **whales**
...... **sperm whales**.

The broadest term in a hierarchy is called the top term.

Associative relationships are provided between terms that are related, but not synonymously or hierarchically. The types of terms paired in associative relationships are listed in *Cross-references and double entry* in Chapter 7. The example below is from *Thesaurus for graphic materials I: subject terms* (*TGM 1*):

Bloody shirt
RT Prejudice
RT Sectionalism (United States)

Prejudice
RT Bloody shirt

Sectionalism (United States)
RT Bloody shirt

Scope notes define terms and describe their scope in a specific thesaurus. They should be used when the meaning or scope of a term might not be clear and when the same term has different meanings in different contexts. *TGM1* has a public note (scope note) for *Bloody shirt* saying: 'Means employed to stir up or revive party or sectional animosity'.

Categories can be used to divide a thesaurus into topic groups. A motoring organisation that provides travel services might use the categories *motoring*, *travel*, and *membership information*.

ANSI/NISO Z39.19:2005 (Chapter 2) provides guidance on the use of thesauruses in the online environment. Other useful publications include the book *Thesaurus construction and use* by Jean Aitchison *et al.* (2000), an introductory tutorial by Tim Craven (1997, updated 2002), and lists of links maintained by Mike Middleton (2006), Mary Sue Stephenson (2005) and the Government of Canada Core Subject Thesaurus (en.thesaurus.gc.ca/bib_e.html).

Planning

Creating a thesaurus is a major undertaking, and maintaining one can be a difficult task. Initial plans should keep the thesaurus as simple as possible for the needs of the job. It is possible to purchase ready-made thesauruses, but these do not always suit specific projects.

To create a thesaurus can take anything from one month to three years, depending on its size and complexity, and updating each edition can take up to six months. Alternatively, updating can be continuous.

The first step is to determine who the users will be, then how many terms are needed, how specific they should be, what categories of terms should be included and how they should be worded (for example, in scientific or natural language).

Concept analysis

There are two main approaches to selecting concepts to include in a thesaurus: bottom-up and top-down. In bottom-up (stalagmitic) construction, indexers gather concepts that exist in documents used within the organisation or subject area the thesaurus will serve. In top-down (stalactitic) indexing, indexers identify all the potential subjects that could ever be covered in the field and create headings for them, whether or not they will be needed immediately. Most projects use a mixture of these, considering it important to cover terms that are used (called literary warrant, user warrant, and organisational warrant) and to put these in a logical structure that will expand as the collection expands.

Specifically, concepts can be identified in:

- literature from the organisation or user group, including manuals, glossaries and mini-dictionaries created as groups define terminology within their specific area
- general literature on the subject, including dictionaries and encyclopedias
- sample user questions and search log entries
- existing thesauruses and indexes on related topics, which are particularly useful for identifying relationships.

In some systems, such as intranets, thesaurus terms are searched in conjunction with free-text terms from the documents. In these cases it may be possible to rely on the thesaurus for controlled indexing of broad categories of information, and to use free-text searching for specific details.

Term selection

> There is no greater impediment to the advancement of knowledge than the ambiguity of words.   Thomas Reid (1710–1796)

The concepts identified and grouped in the previous steps have to be given their final wording, following the principles discussed in *Topical headings* in Chapter 4, including the use of natural language and direct order. In a thesaurus for a specific subject area, the language used in that field is the 'natural' language for that user group.

Complex compound terms should be avoided, as computer systems allow for post-coordination of terms – that is, combination of terms at the time of searching, previously called post-correlative indexing. It is simpler to manage the terms *child rearing* and *single parents* than the compound term *child rearing by single parents*. Compound terms are used when the component words would not make sense as individual words, or when the phrase is commonly used as a phrase, for example, *stonewalling tactics* and *Key Performance Indicators*.

For each group of synonyms, one term is chosen as the preferred term and the others are included as non-preferred terms. These may be used to generate references to the preferred term or, preferably, to automatically generate a search for the synonyms along with the preferred terms. Some websites and intranets do not create full thesauruses but rely on simple synonym rings (clusters of synonyms) to generate searches for all of the terms in each group when any of the terms is searched for.

Thesauruses such as *MeSH (Medical Subject Headings)* maintain lists of topical subheadings and formats. These are applied to main headings to narrow their meaning or to provide information about the type of content. *MeSH* topical subheadings include *rehabilitation* and *drug therapy*, and formats include *examination questions* and *handbooks*.

Frequently a general term is used to mean a specific one. For example, *vehicles*, *motor vehicles*, and *cars* are often used synonymously. Indexers need to make early decisions about the specificity of term to use. In most cases it is best to use the most specific term because otherwise you may find a later addition to the thesaurus clashes. For instance, if you decide to use *batteries* for *car batteries*, you might later find that you are also indexing *mobile phone batteries*, and need to revise the first entry. The more general term should be added as a broader term.

After the initial concepts for inclusion in the thesaurus have been identified, they are grouped to provide the structure of the thesaurus. Synonyms and broader and narrower terms should be identified first, and categories tested by users. One method is to ask users to sort cards with topics written on them into categories; another is to ask them to allocate the topics to categories you have already created. It can be a shock to see how different user approaches are from the draft structure.

Thesaurus construction software (Chapter 10) allows output of thesauruses in alphabetical and hierarchical order, and in XML format for use in online search engines. The standard XML output may not, however, be appropriate for the specific search engine being used, and extra programming may be required.

Thesauruses need continual maintenance, as language, knowledge and needs change. Maintenance tasks include:

- Add new terms after checking that they represent new topics. If they are synonyms of existing terms they should be added as non-preferred terms.
- Delete unused and unnecessary terms.
- Amend terms by changing either their wording or their place in the hierarchy. Terms that are heavily used may be divided into narrower terms.

Indexers who use a thesaurus should be able to propose 'candidate' terms. These are evaluated by the coordinator, who adds them to the thesaurus if appropriate. See also *Collection indexes*: *Re-indexing when thesaurus terms change* in Chapter 5. For a discussion of interoperability between thesauruses and systems see Chapter 8.

Taxonomies

There is a serious lack of vocabulary control in the literature on controlled vocabulary.   Bella Hass Weinberg (quoted in Klement 2002, p. 23 n.1)

> Each taxonomy assigns a set meaning to a word (the group noted that it was ironic that the word taxonomy itself is so hard to define).
>
> *Records Management Society Bulletin* i.120, June 2004 p. 5

> It is a rich irony that the word 'ontology', which has to do with making clear and explicit statements about entities in a particular domain, has so many conflicting definitions.
> Clay Shirky 2005

ANSI/NISO Z39.19:2005 depicts taxonomies as hierarchically displayed controlled vocabularies without associative relationships. They are normally used in the creation of the navigational structure of websites and intranets, while thesauruses are used as sources of indexing terms.

Yahoo's directory structure (on the left-hand side at dir.yahoo.com) is an example of a displayed taxonomy. Taxonomies are often used for browsing, and are therefore more likely than thesauruses to use compound terms, as there is no possibility of combining terms in searches when browsing a site. An article on Builder.com (2003) discusses the application of taxonomies in information architecture and their relation to thesauruses. See also *Information architecture* in Chapter 9.

Automated categorisation and taxonomy generation

Automated categorisation software is available with a number of content management systems (see *Intranets and CMSs* in Chapter 9). The software can create taxonomies from content on a site, and can make links from terms in the taxonomy to relevant content. Most systems now allow for human checking and editing of the results.

Some proposed uses of automated categorisation are: to generate the navigation structure of intranets (or multiple navigation approaches for different users), to categorise the results of searches on the web, and to organise news feeds.

See also *Index users: The way people categorise things* in Chapter 1 and *Taxonomy management software* in Chapter 10.

Ontologies

An ontology (www.cmswiki.com/tiki-index.php?page=Ontology) is a controlled vocabulary that describes objects and the relations between them in a formal way, and has a grammar for using the terms in the vocabulary to express something meaningful. In its broadest sense, ontology is used to include a range of controlled vocabularies including glossaries, taxonomies and thesauruses. In the narrower sense, a formal ontology is a vocabulary that can be can be expressed in an ontology representation language and used for automated reasoning support (that is, can be used by a computer to make logical inferences).

For example, if a man claims health insurance for obstetric consultations, an ontology which 'knows' that men do not get pregnant can infer that the claim is not valid. Deborah McGuinness (2001) has described the mandatory and typical requirements of ontologies, and Michael Wilson and Brian Matthews (2002) have pointed out that if existing thesauruses are to be used on the semantic web they will have to be converted into ontologies with more precisely-defined relationships.

Topic maps

Topic maps and RDF format (Chapter 8) are both used to represent data on the web. RDF is used to annotate resources directly, while topic maps 'float above' the resources they provide access to, and are therefore reusable over a number of resources in the same way that a thesaurus is. Topic maps are linked (e.g., by URL) to the resources they are describing. Links are created manually in many cases, but can be automated for structured information.

Topic maps are based on principles used in traditional indexes and thesauruses, with inspiration from semantic networks. They are based on topics, associations (the relationships between topics) and occurrences (resources that discuss the topics).

Topic maps can be useful for structuring information repositories and navigating through them. Application areas include web portals, intranets, and content management systems. The topic map data model allows automated merging of information from diverse sources including databases, thesauruses, automatic tagging tools, and metadata from RDF Dublin Core documents (Tramullas and Garrido 2006). This feature allows the integration of information from many sources within an organisation into a coherent whole.

Topic maps have been used by the IRS Tax Map (www.missouribusiness.net/irs/taxmap/tmhome.htm) to provide central access to all the content Tax Map has about a subject, linking to the topic pages of related topics, as well as to relevant forms, instructions, and publications. Nikita Ogievetsky and Roger Sperberg (2003) have suggested that topic maps could be used for selection and indexing of content in custom publishing.

Data dictionaries

Data dictionaries define all the types of information stored in a database. Data dictionaries have similar aims to controlled vocabularies, but they are more structured and they work at a more granular level, dealing with specific bits of data rather than overall concepts. A data dictionary can ensure the use of a consistent format for fields such as dates and telephone numbers, as well as ensuring consistent use of language for organisational concepts. A data dictionary could clarify the relationship between the terms *total salary*, *total remuneration*, *remuneration*, *salary*, *bonuses*, and *superannuation*. Taxonomies, thesauruses and data dictionaries used within one organisation should be compatible with each other.

Many data dictionaries can be found on the web, including the Australian National Health Data Dictionary, Version 10 2001 (www.aihw.gov.au/publications/hwi/nhdd10) and the Canadian Heritage Information Network Data Dictionaries: User Guide (www.chin.gc.ca/English/Collections_Management/ Humanities_Dictionary/user_guide.html).

7

Structuring Indexes

Book-style indexes are usually printed or otherwise displayed in alphabetical or other order (see *Filing rules*, below), and are readily accessible for browsing. Collection indexes may be displayed, but are often accessible only through searching. Thus the onus is on the user to type in the ideal search term, whereas browsing lets them select the best terms from a list. The ideal approach is to allow both searching and browsing.

Indexes are more than just lists of terms that describe subjects within documents – they also have a structure that provides additional information and guidance to users. All indexes, displayed and searchable, may include:

- introductory notes and footnotes to provide guidance on approaches used
- subheadings to provide additional subject information
- locators (page numbers, links etc.) to show users where to find the information
- cross-references to lead users to alternative headings.

In addition, displayed indexes have:

- a filing order to arrange headings in the order in which they are most likely to be found
- a layout to make the index easy to access.

Searchable (non-displayed) indexes have search protocols instead of page layout to enhance access.

Non-displayed index search design

For non-displayed indexes that rely on search, indexers have to consider the best approaches for users. These include:

- placement of search buttons on webpages and throughout websites
- default search commands: the default may be to provide webpages that contain all of the words typed (Boolean AND), or to provide webpages that contain any of the words typed (Boolean OR)
- provision of fielded searching, e.g., limiting searches to author or subject fields
- provision of automatic search expansion, e.g., through the use of synonym rings that automatically search for all synonyms of the term that was entered
- provision of spellcheckers and suggestions for search expansion, e.g., 'You typed *categorisation*, would you like to search for *categorization*?'
- relevance ranking
- the amount and types of information to be provided in search results, e.g., page titles and descriptions
- advice to be presented on the main search page and when searches fail.

Indexers may also have a role in writing search manuals and training staff in search procedures.

Notes in indexes

Introductory notes are often not noticed, but nonetheless they are an important potential contact with users, and give indexers the chance to explain the decisions they have made. Footnotes are sometimes used in addition to, or instead of, introductory notes, to provide information on every page to make it more likely to be found. Here are the main topics dealt with in notes and some examples:

- multiple indexes: 'See also Index of First Lines.'
- style: 'Page numbers in **bold** refer to major sections of the text.' 'References to figures and tables are indicated by an *f* or *t* after the page number.'
- filing rules: 'This index is in letter-by-letter order, so hyphens, en-rules and spaces within index headings are ignored in filing.'
- abbreviations used in the index: 'JBW = John B Watson', 'FDM = Frequency Division Multiplexing'.
- where an index refers to a multi-volume work, the pages in each volume: 'Vol. 1: 1–604; Vol. 2: 605–1300'.
- possible search approaches: 'For drugs, consult the disease you want to treat rather than the drug name.'
- special approaches, such as avoidance of indexing under the metatopic: 'Since the major subject of this title is public health, entries have been kept to a minimum under this keyword and readers are advised to seek more specific references. Entries under specific countries have been limited to major topics. Additional statistics may be found within the text.'

Less common notes request information or apologise for the index. The Que 'Special Edition' manuals ask: 'How can we make this index more useful? E-mail us at indexes@quepublishing.com' while one of the *Therapeutic guidelines* says:

'Manual indexes have limitations: use our *intelligent electronic index* in our electronic product (mentor, www.emispdp.com) for exploring and explaining *combinations* of signs, symptoms and test results.'

Searchable indexes are less likely to have notes embedded in the index, but should have a manual that provides general information.

Indexers rarely write notes within indexes apart from standard cross-references. Notes should be used more, we feel, to alert users to the types of decisions that indexers make, and to allow space-saving approaches to be taken. Useful notes include:

- The: 'For titles starting with *The* search under the second word of the title.'
- Saint 'For Saint, *see also* headings beginning with St.'

When alphabetical order has been used throughout a book it can be supplemented by indexing, without the index having to duplicate all of the entries. In *Growing grevilleas* (Don Burke, Kangaroo Press 1983), one entry says: 'Grevillea – since the grevillea varieties are listed on pages 46–79 in alphabetical order, they are not included in the index. The following list consists of alternative or incorrect names only.'

Borko and Bernier (1978: 33) recommend the use of interfiled notes that provide information about headings and their arrangement. They give the example 'Finland (including periods under Sweden & the Russian Empire)'.

Subheadings

> The subsubhead's a subhead of
> The subhead that's above it
> And that in turn's a subhead of
> A heading – gotta love it!
> But just as headings spawn subheads
> And subsubheadings under 'em
> We have subsubsubheadings
> And so, ad infinitum!
> > Based on a rhyme by Augustus de Morgan that was based on a rhyme by
> > Jonathan Swift . . . and so, *ad infinitum*. JJ&GB

Index headings are created for names, places, topics and concepts that have been discussed. Subheadings are applied to headings for two main reasons:

- To show aspects of the topic: The entry *peanut allergy* is less useful for deciding whether to follow a lead than *peanut allergy, teachers' knowledge of*.
- To break up long strings of locators (page numbers): Normally a heading or subheading should have no more than five to seven undifferentiated locators.

Consider the entry:

open access journals 15–17, 19, 21–25, 116, 119, 252–253, 277, 279–280

This has too many locators to be easily consulted. If space permits it should be restructured to something like:

> open access journals
> >   author-pays publishing models 15–17, 19, 277
> >   list of major players 21–25, 116
> >   self-archiving 119, 252–253
> >   timeline since 2000: 279–280

Subheadings should be worded concisely, so they are easy to scan and, if possible, do not spill over onto the following line. (This is called a turnover.) Subheadings should be worded consistently. This applies both within each heading (under the heading *pets*, use *feeding* and *washing*, not *food* and *washing*) and within the index (*Australia, crime rates* should be matched with *New Zealand, crime rates*, not *New Zealand, levels of crime*). This is known as parallel construction.

Subheadings in book-style indexes are usually coined to suit the specific situation, while subheadings in collection indexing come from a controlled vocabulary and are added in a set combination order. Subdivisions cover aspects of the subject, place, time and format:

> Ice skating – Competitions – History – 20th century
> School accidents – Tonga – Prevention – Handbooks, manuals, etc.
> School administrators – Bahrain – Biography

The Macmillan study (Ryan and Henselmeier 2000) and research by Corinne Jörgensen and Elizabeth Liddy (1996) found that users are helped if main headings and subheadings are visually distinguished, for example, by use of bold type for main headings. This applies to online help as well as to books – some of the major feedback we had in user tests of an online help index was that people wished that the type was bigger and the subheadings were easier to distinguish from the main headings.

Over-analysis in subheadings

One of the main areas of disagreement between indexers and authors is the degree to which multiple subheadings for a page range should be included at a heading. Authors often like a list of subheadings following the structure of the text, as in this example from a book on SARS:

> SARS Coronavirus genetic structure 126–127
> >   man-made origins theory 127
> >   coronavirus family 127
> >   animal origins 127–129
> >   extra terrestrial origins theory 127

Most indexers would call this over-analysed. Over-analysis is not necessarily a fault, but it usually reflects uneven indexing and takes space from more useful entries. In this example there are five lines referring to two pages (126 and 127) within one entry array, but there are no headings for any of the topics named in the subheadings in their own right (e.g., *animal origins* as a main heading) and there is no entry for *genetic structure*.

Function words (prepositions) in subheadings

Articles, conjunctions and prepositions – *a*, *and*, *in*, *on* – are function words. They have no meaning alone, but they indicate the function of other words and thus enhance their meaning. They are therefore important in indexes. Indexers disagree about

- the extent to which function words should be used in subheadings
- the position of function words within subheadings
- whether function words should be considered in filing.

AS/NZS 999 (section 7.2.2.5) states: 'Prepositions should as far as possible be used only if their absence might cause ambiguity.' Indexers of technical works tend to omit prepositions, while indexers in the humanities are more likely to keep them, perhaps to make their subheadings more expressive. Function words are likely to be needed when the subheading precedes the heading grammatically (as in the first example below), although this does not always apply. Most indexers would agree that the function words are needed in:

> people of culturally and linguistically diverse backgrounds
> > teaching by
> > teaching of

In contrast, many would not consider them necessary in:

> teaching
> > of geography
> > of science

And is often used to indicate unspecified connections between headings and subheadings. It can be a quick and easy way of creating subheadings that can be used for a number of locators, but is easily overused. *Community life: design of public places and 15–17, 118–126* is shorter and simpler than *community life: design of public places to enhance interaction in 15–17* and *community life: design of public places as a reflection of 118–126*.

When function words are used, some indexers invert them – *cauliflowers, green olives with* – while others keep them at the front of the subheading – *cauliflowers, with green olives*.

Filing of function words in subheadings

George Levick (1993) wrote an article for the *AusSI newsletter* on inverted headings and subheadings, which he revised into a commentary when he discovered that Kingsley Siebel (1993) had just written an article on the same topic. He wrote: 'I found that Siebel and I diverged on almost every salient point' – which is not an uncommon occurrence in discussions about indexing.

Siebel believed that people got used to reading subheadings that may be awkward for those not familiar with the field:

Reserve Bank,
    Treasury bills, issue of, by

Levick, on the other hand, felt that users were prepared to experiment and reformulate wording to arrive at satisfying main headings, and that having done so, they 'relaxed' and browsed through the subheadings, reading them consecutively. This makes it less important to have firm conventions for subheadings than to have good style. He considered this to involve the use of prepositions with restrained liberty, placed where a reader would expect to find them, and filed as written.

AS/NZS 999 (section 8.6) does not provide a firm instruction, merely saying: 'a decision may be made to ignore the prepositions or conjunctions for filing purposes. Such a decision should . . . be recorded in an introductory note.'

Our preference is to avoid prepositions in subheadings where possible, as in the example below:

storage
    bathrooms
    bedrooms
    disks and tapes
    home offices
    kitchens
    living areas
    small areas
    under stairs
    walls
    wine
    wood for fires

We also advise that prepositions should be considered in filing. This can give useful groupings of similar subheadings:

storage
    in bathrooms
    in bedrooms
    in home offices
    in kitchens
    in living areas
    in small areas
    of disks and tapes
    of wine
    of wood for fires
    on walls
    under stairs

Alternatively, some indexers include prepositions but ignore them in filing:

storage
   in bathrooms
   in bedrooms
   of disks and tapes
   in home offices
   in kitchens
   in living areas
   in small areas
   under stairs
   on walls
   of wine
   of wood for fires

Research into function words

Research suggests that it is best to omit function words in subheadings when possible, and that they should be inverted to the end of the subheading if they are used. Cecelia Wittmann (1990) found that subheadings in award-winning indexes had these characteristics:

- They started with a significant word, either a noun or a verb; they especially avoided beginnings such as 'and' and 'in'.
- They were not related syntactically to their main headings. For instance, *statistical material: units of measure in* is syntactically related, whereas *statistical material: units of measure* is not.
- They did not exactly match words from the text.

Susan Olason's research (2000) also suggested that 'prefix words' (that is, function words) should be avoided in indexes.

Research by INSPEC on the use of indexes to *Science Abstracts* found that 30% of users scanned subheadings alphabetically, 24% scanned all initial words; and 63% scanned all subheadings under a main heading from beginning to end. The latter point 'may be explained by the user's realisation that a relevant document may be indicated by a phrase containing terms which he would not have thought of in advance' (Gould 1974: 282, in Wellisch 1993; some respondents used more than one method so percentages exceed 100%.) This suggests that lists of subheadings should not be so long that they are difficult to scan.

Non-alphabetical sequencing in subheadings

Subheadings may be filed in chronological, evolutionary, classified and canonical (scriptural) order if appropriate. It is rare, however, to find a compelling reason for not using alphabetical order consistently throughout an index. In Australian government publications the States were often listed in descending population order, as follows:

> wheat production
>> NSW 34–55
>> Vic 62–70
>> Qld 74–80
>> SA 82–6
>> WA 88–91
>> Tas 94–5

The correct order for populations changed in the 1980s, when Western Australia overtook South Australia. The order has not always been changed to reflect this, which illustrates one of the problems with this approach. See, for example, the order of States in various sections of the ABS website (www.abs.gov.au).

Subheading style

Subheadings can be displayed with indents or run on. The indented style is also called set out; line-by-line; entry-a-line; stacked. The run-on style is also called run-in or paragraph-style. Although run-on format is popular for humanities books, it is harder to read and should be used only when there is a shortage of space. The examples in this book are in indented format. The content from the first prepositions example above would appear thus in run-on format.

> storage: bathrooms 15; bedrooms 14, 23–25; disks and tapes 99–101, 103, 105; home offices 199, 203; kitchens 15, 203–205; living areas 77; small areas 204, 206; under stairs 155; walls 168; wine 110–112; wood for fires 79–80

Susan Olason (2000) found that indented indexes were ranked as user-friendly 90% of the time, while run-on indexes were never ranked as such. 'Comments about run-on indexes included frustration about being forced to read rather than scan, confusion about sorting and confusion about which page references went with which sub-entry.'

The indexes to the second edition of *Indexing books* (2005) and the fifteenth edition of *The Chicago manual of style* (2003) both use a hybrid style, with indented subheadings and run-on subsubheadings, to make the whole entry array easily scannable (Baker 2005).

If a heading has only one subheading it is known as an orphan subheading. In this case, the subheading should be run on after the main heading, unless the structure of the index is for all entries to be subheadings indented under a main heading (as in some legal indexes). Use a colon instead of a comma to distinguish the entry from an inverted heading:

> Thailand: cultural values in

Indention

Subheadings, subsubheadings and so on are progressively indented one em. An em is the width of the letter M in the font being used:

Abydos
☐ royal necropolis
☐☐ excavation of
☐ temple of Sety I

AS/NZS 999 (section 9.1.2.4) says that in all cases that run on to another line (known as turnover lines, wraparound lines or line wraps), the line should be indented more deeply than the deepest subheading indention employed in the index:

Catholic Schools Commission Decision
☐☐☐ of January 2005
☐ implications of for staff and
☐☐☐ students 145–6
☐ events leading up to
☐☐ in Australia 128
☐☐ in New Zealand 66–9

A simpler, tidier alternative is to indent turnover lines for each level more than the first line for an entry at the next level down:

Catholic Schools Commission Decision
☐☐ of January 2005
☐ implications of for staff and
☐☐☐ students 145–6
☐ events leading up to
☐☐ in Australia 128
☐☐ in New Zealand 66–9

Some indexes use bold type for main headings and have a space after each entry array. This means they do not have to indent the first subheading, thus saving space and reducing turnover lines:

leadership
by example 136
challenges for 113, 119–125
no substitute for 123

learning organisations 123–125, 137

legal issues 55, 289

Bold-face main headings can also be used with indented subheadings without the extra space between entry arrays. In both cases the bold face makes it easier for users to ignore subheadings until they find the right main heading.

Cross-references and double entry

> Ruth Pincoe was born to be an indexer. Her family was so organised that the milk jug in the fridge had a note that said 'See also back shed.'

Cross-references are used in most indexes to lead to synonyms (and sometimes antonyms) and other related terms. In book-style indexes cross-references are created according to the needs of the item in hand, while for most collection indexes they are generated from a thesaurus (Chapter 6).

See references direct users from entry terms that have no locators (non-preferred terms) to preferred terms that do have locators. In the reference 'shiraz *see* syrah', *shiraz* is an entry term and *syrah* is the preferred term. You can have more than one *see* reference from an entry term, for example, 'monotremes *see* echidnas; platypuses'.

See also references are used in index entries that have locators; they suggest additional places to look. For example, 'drawing 99 *see also* charcoal; pencils'. The entry 'meningitis 15–17 *see also Haemophilus influenzae*' leads the user from the disease to an organism that causes it. *See also* references are usually reciprocal, and you would expect to find a reference such as '*Haemophilus influenzae* 77–91 *see also* meningitis'.

General *see also* references can be made if it would take too much space to list all the terms being referred to. This works best for small knowable lists ('Australia *see also names of States and territories*') rather than long, unspecifiable lists ('emotions *see also names of specific emotions*') – who can predict which emotions have been included in the index?

See also references are normally made from broader terms to narrower terms, although arguments have been made for the value of upward references from narrower to broader to help orient users within the index and guide them to broader terms at which they might find additional information. The broader terms are not always obvious, as their choice depends on the context in which the concepts are being indexed. When thesauruses are displayed on websites and intranets, users are guided to both broader and narrower terms.

See under references are used occasionally to refer users to a subheading rather than a main heading. They can be worded: 'transmission *see under* AIDS' or 'transmission *see* AIDS: transmission' or, if brevity is paramount, 'transmission *see* AIDS'.

AS/NZS 999 (section 7.5.2.2) summarises the circumstances under which *see also* cross-references should be used:

- from general to specific
- from a discipline to its constituent studies
- from a class to its individual members
- from an entity to its parts or kinds
- from a discipline to the object studied
- from a theoretical study to its application

- from an activity to its agent
- from an activity to the thing acted upon
- from an activity to its product
- between similar topics differentiated in the index but not in common parlance
- between related topics separated by common usage – e.g., *mouth* and *oral hygiene*.

Cross-references can also be used to tease – until 1996 the United Kingdom *Yellow Pages* contained the reference 'Boring *see* Civil engineers'. It was finally removed after lobbying by the Institution of Civil Engineers.

Double entry

If space permits book indexers can create double entries instead of *see* references. That is, they put the locators at both entries rather than making the user look in a different place in the index. The first pair of terms below takes up as much space as the second pair, and also takes more of the user's time:

> shiraz *see* syrah
> syrah 15, 25–26
>
> shiraz 15, 25–26
> syrah 15, 25–26

If either term is not used on the pages being referred to, they should be included in parentheses to clarify the connection, for example, *syrah (shiraz)* and *shiraz (syrah)*.

Virgil Diodato (1994) found that double entry was used less often in science indexes than it would have been if indexers followed the rule above. It may be that indexers wanted to provide access through 'incorrect' terms, but not to validate them by including them as preferred terms in the index. They may prefer to include the reference: 'energy of motion *see* kinetic energy' than to double the locators at 'energy of motion'. This also applies to references from terminology that may be considered offensive or old-fashioned, such as *Third World* and *crippled*.

See references in collection indexes can be applied in two ways: the system may automatically link from a non-preferred term to the content indexed using the preferred term without the user knowing this has happened. This is like having a double entry. Alternatively, the system may provide a *see* reference so the user can search using the appropriate term.

Some intranets use synonym rings (clusters of synonyms) that automatically broaden searches to include all of the synonyms in the list, no matter which one was searched for. Others display parts of a thesaurus so users can see ways to broaden or narrow their searches, and get ideas for alternative terms they may not have considered using.

Cross-reference placement and style

Cross-references in book-style indexes can be placed either before or after the page numbers, or on the same line as the main heading, or as the first or last subheading. There may be a full stop (period), comma or simply a space before them, and the first 's' may be upper or lower case. An upper-case 'S' when the reference comes after the last subheading is said to make the reference more noticeable. Here are examples of these alternatives:

> trolley buses *see also* trams, 34, 57
> trolley buses (*see also* trams) 34, 57
>
> trolley buses 34, 57 *see also* trams
>
> trolley buses 34, 57
>   *see also* trams
>   consumer attitudes to 15, 17
>   route planning for 32–33
>
> trolley buses 34, 57
>   consumer attitudes to 15, 17
>   route planning for 32–33
>   *See also* trams

When one or both index terms in a reference are in roman (non-italic) type, *see* or *see also* are written in italics. When both index terms in a reference are in italic, *see* and *see also* are written in roman: '*And Then There Were None* see *Ten Little Indians*'.

It is important to check that all cross-references lead to useful content. Dedicated indexing software can check that there are entries by the name of the target of the cross-reference; that is, if you write 'canines *see* dogs' it will confirm that there is an entry *dogs*. You may also have to manually check *see also* references to confirm that there are additional locators at the target term. If you have 'pets 15' and 'dogs 15' you would not make a reference 'pets 15 *see also* dogs'.

Library catalogues have traditionally kept 'tracing' records to show which terms have been used. When the last book on a subject is removed from the collection, any cross-references to that term are also removed. Nowadays this process is likely to be automated.

Research into cross-reference use

Research into index use shows that users sometimes find cross-references confusing and frustrating. The Macmillan study (Ryan and Henselmeier 2000) found that '*see* references were not a problem . . . *See also* references, on the other hand, were confusing to some. For example, if they saw "Webpages. *See also* Web sites," some expected to see "*Webpages*" as a subheading under "*Web sites*."' That is, they were reading *See also* as *See under*.

We worked on an online help project that used the words *Search using* rather than *See* because of anecdotal evidence that users were confused by the *See* reference. When we asked on Index-L for other people's experiences, one librarian replied that she had seen a cartoon that had a frustrated librarian asking 'Just what is it about "See" that you do not understand?' She shared the frustration.

Obviously the meaning is clearer to librarians and indexers than it is to some users. Jörgensen and Liddy (1996) found that common errors in using cross-references included

> reading the see/see also as part of a main heading, part of a subheading, running separate references together, or reading a heading and subheading as part of a see also. Across all uses of the Basic Index, many users did not understand the structure or the function of see also references, and many exhibited an openly hostile reaction to them, saying, for example: 'This thing is so trivial. [Why?] Because it keeps going back and forth and it does not ever give you a page for what you're looking for.'

Robert Collison (1981), president of the Society of Indexers (UK), also found cross-references annoying, complaining that they 'sent us scuttling halfway around that very handsome architectural masterpiece', the Reading Room in the British Museum. He persuaded Clio Press to eliminate *see* and *see also* references in the indexes of a series of bibliographies. It is easy to replace a *see* reference with a double entry, but he does not explain how he satisfactorily compensated for the lack of *see also* references.

Locators

A locator is an 'indicator of that part of a document, or that item in a collection, to which the heading or subheading refers' (AS/NZS 999 section 3.9). Locators are sometimes also called references or reference locators. In book-style indexes locators are usually page numbers, but paragraph or section numbers are more logical units (Anderson and Perez-Carballo 2005). The use of paragraph numbers enables indexing to start before the pagination is finalised. It can also reduce the need for embedded indexing, as paragraph numbers do not change when page format changes.

Indexes to serials such as annual reports have the same type of locators as book-style indexes, while those for multivolume works include volume numbers as well as page numbers. Periodical indexes require more complex locators, including journal volume, issue number and page numbers. Author and title details are sometimes used as the subheading. A journal index locator might be '17(5): 16–17' or it might be a full citation such as:

> Lee, P 2002. 'History of vegetable farming in South Australia' J. horticulture vol. 12 iss. 4, pp. 16–19.

When bibliographic database indexes are displayed (printed or otherwise available for browsing), they may use locators similar to the full periodical citation format above. When they are merely searchable, selecting an index term retrieves a subset of content from the full information available for that item. This is different for each database, but usually includes the full citation. Links may be provided that allow the user to select more information, including abstracts and index terms. This progressive display of information allows users to explore more deeply the portions of the database that are of interest to them.

The *PsycInfo* database includes the following fields: accession number, title, year of publication, language, author, e-mail address, correspondence address, institution, source (citation), formats available, ISSN, document type, abstract, digital object identifier (Chapter 2), subject headings (index terms), classification code, population group, methodology, tests and measures, conference information and cited references. You can view samples at www.apa.org/psycinfo/about/sample.html.

In some databases users can follow a link to the full text of the content they are interested in, while in others they have to note the citation details and obtain the actual articles. In other online indexes the 'locator' may simply be a link to the relevant content. In book-style indexes for websites, for example, each heading or subheading may link to a webpage. In library collections the 'locators' are classification numbers or shelf numbers that indicate the physical location of the items. The locators might include a general area (e.g., AV or BIG), a classification number indicating the subject of the item (e.g., 025.4) and a running number to show the specific location on the shelf.

For non-print collections indexers may have to create locators, for example, by numbering items sequentially.

Locators after a main heading

When an index heading has at least one subheading, some indexers insist that all locators should be at subheadings, with none at the main heading. This is because locators left at the main heading usually indicate one of two extremes: the major discussion of the topic in the book, which often covers many different aspects of the topic, or very minor discussions that do not warrant subheadings of their own.

Creating subheadings for all locators is not always practical, as most indexes have space and time constraints. Some solutions that have been suggested include:

- Use bold type to indicate major discussions.
- Create a subheading for major discussions called *about, overview, introduction* or similar. *About* has the advantage of filing near the top of any list; some indexers file subheadings such as *introduction* out of order at the top of the list to make them more prominent.
- Create a subheading for all minor discussions that do not warrant a subheading of their own; this subheading may be labelled *mentioned, alluded to* or similar. While this would solve the problem, it seems unlikely that the average user would understand its purpose.

It may be that users just have to live with the uncertainty – unfortunately, we cannot always communicate every subtlety we would like to in a compact index.

Locators for special purposes

Illustrations such as photographs and diagrams may be indicated by the use of *italic* or **bold** locators, or the addition of various letters after the number. As italic numbers can be hard to distinguish from roman numbers, and bold-face is often used to indicate major discussions, letters are usually the best choice. Common ones are *f* for figures, *t* for tables, and *ill.* for illustrations. Subheadings can also be worded to indicate graphic material

> Sydney Opera House
> photographs of 15

One useful code we have seen is the use of (R) and (L) to indicate that images being referred to were for right- or left-handed clinicians.

For some large documents, locators give an indication of the position of the content on the page. Encyclopedias may divide a page into four quarters, and use the letters *a*, *b*, *c* and *d* to indicate which part of the page the content is on. Similarly, newspaper indexes may indicate the appropriate column. Exhaustive indexes can use indicators as precise as line numbers.

Locators for footnotes usually include the page number followed by *n*, for example, *125n*, while endnotes require the note number and the page number, for example, *212n.5*.

Locators for major discussions

> A thousand names are toss'd into the crowd;
> Some whisper'd softly, and some twang'd aloud.
> *William Cowper*

Major discussions of a topic may be identified by the use of **bold** locators, and occasionally by the use of colour. This is especially useful when there are long lists of locators, or where some information is particularly important. For example, a book on first aid can emphasise the locators that lead to practical information by printing them in red. Occasionally locators for general information such as introductions are emphasised by being filed at the top of a list of subheadings.

On websites, tag clouds (also called weighted lists) are groups of terms in which the more often the term has been used, the larger it is. This means users can search for items by popularity or use as well as by alphabetical position (www.tagcloud.com; en.wikipedia.org/wiki/Tag_cloud).

Collection indexes sometimes identify subject headings that indicate the major focus of an article. *MEDLINE* uses asterisks beside subject headings for major discussions. This system originated because only major terms were included in the printed version of the index, but it remains as a useful way of focusing searches. You can see this at PubMed (www.ncbi.nlm.nih.gov/entrez) if you do a search, select a hit that says 'PubMed – indexed for MEDLINE' then select 'MEDLINE' from the dropdown list at 'Display'. Scroll down to the subject headings, which have the code 'MH'.

Punctuation before locators

Commas are used between page numbers. A comma and a space, a double space or other unambiguous punctuation mark is used between headings and subheadings and the first page number after them (AS/NZS 999 section 7.4.5). If the entry ends with a number some indexers add a colon to visually separate the entry from the page numbers:

> construction timetables, 15, 19 [comma and space]
> sporting venues   22–24, 29 [two spaces]
> Sydney Olympics 2000:   201, 203 [colon after number, then two spaces]

Page ranges

When a topic is discussed over a range of pages, the range of page numbers is shown, normally with an en-rule (a dash a bit longer than a hyphen) between them, thus: 105–106. Page ranges are sometimes referred to as inclusive numbers or continuing numbers. Occasionally only the first page in the range is given, and users have to keep reading until the topic runs out. Page ranges should not be split onto separate lines as below:

> bicameral parliaments 55–56, 101–
>   108

Page ranges can be typed in full, or they can be contracted (compressed; elided) in one of two ways: by transcribing only the last two digits, or transcribing only the digits that have changed. Sometimes fuller forms are used for numbers in the tens, and the more abbreviated version for other numbers, as this reflects the way we speak (e.g., we write '115–16' because we say 'one hundred and fifteen to sixteen'). AS/NZS 999 (section 7.4.3.1) recommends use of the full form, as does Nancy Mulvany (2005), 'when possible', although it is not used in the index to her book.

- full page ranges: 22–23, 85–87, 111–115, 228–231, 1153–1178
- final two digits only: 22–23, 85–87, 111–15, 228–31, 1153–78
- changed digits only: 22–3, 85–7, 111–5, 228–31, 1153–78
- changed digits only, except for the teens: 22–3, 85–7, 111–15, 228–31, 1153–78
- *The Chicago manual of style*: 22–23, 85–87, 111–15, 228–31, 1153–78

The authors prefer the full form as it is easier to immediately comprehend, although we make exceptions for numbers in the thousands where the full range becomes unwieldy, and for indexes that have to be shortened. Dedicated indexing software (Chapter 10) can output page numbers in the standard formats.

Noncontinuous discussions

Where several consecutive pages mention a topic but do not discuss it continuously, many indexers use individual page numbers (e.g. '3–5, 7, 8, 9–10') to indicate that there are separate discussions in the text. Others feel that these should be combined, as the distinction provides no useful information. Indexers are divided into three groups:

- Those who think locators tell you a lot about the value of an index entry, such as how much information is available at that place. They like to keep the locators undifferentiated ('3–5, 7, 8, 9–10'). To save space they may combine the locators and use the word *passim*, meaning 'here and there', after the page range to indicate that the topic is dealt with intermittently throughout that range ('3–10 *passim*'). Some would say '3–5, 7–10 *passim*'.
- Those who think locators should not or cannot carry much meaning. They tend to combine the locators into ranges including all pages on which the topic is discussed, but no more ('3–5, 7–10'), knowing that this will tell the users 'There is something about this topic on each of the pages from 3 to 5 and from 7 to 10.'
- Those who value conciseness and ease of reading over precision. They would combine the numbers into page ranges including the pages within the range that do not cover the topic (3–10) (e.g., *Style manual* 2002: 282).

The authors usually take the middle course, including only the page numbers that actually discuss the topic but doing so in the most concise way possible. This both saves space in the index and makes it easier for users to move from the index to the text. We are not convinced that five separate references to a topic in five consecutive pages can be considered discontinuous. Our only exceptions (barring editors' requests) are for directory-style documents in which each occurrence of a topic is distinct from all others.

When there are many diagrams or tables that are indexed separately, long strings can become especially unwieldy. Compare these two entries:

adolescent smoking rates 15, 16, *16*, 17, 18, *18*, 19, 20, 21, 22
adolescent smoking rates 15–22, *16*, *18*

Undifferentiated locators

An undifferentiated locator is a locator at the main heading or subheading that is not distinguished through the use of subheadings or subsubheadings. Ideally, most entries should not have more than five undifferentiated locators. One of the rules of indexing is to 'save the time of the user', and if the user has to go to fifteen different places to look for the information they need, we have not saved their time. Solutions to undifferentiated locators include:

- Combine individual consecutive page numbers, as in the *adolescent smoking rates* example above.
- Differentiate the locators using subheadings to indicate the aspects of the main heading that they cover.
- Delete unnecessary locators.
- Use bold type to emphasise the most important locators, so users can start at the most likely place.

Some biography indexers consider that long strings of undifferentiated locators are necessary for minor mentions of people in a book. (See *Concept analysis*: *Passing mentions* in Chapter 4 and *Biographies* in Chapter 9.)

Filing rules

Theoretically it should be simple to list items in alphabetical (or alphanumeric) order, but it causes some of the biggest arguments in indexing. There are two main areas of disagreement: the basic filing rule to be followed (word-by-word or letter-by-letter); and whether the filing should be 'fiddled' to place entries where indexers think users are most likely to consult them.

We believe that rather than fiddling filing rules, indexers can serve users far better by agreeing on a standard approach to filing that can be used widely so that users become familiar with it. Any value that indexers lose by adhering to the simple rules can be retained by using double entry, a *see* reference, or a note to provide guidance about alternative access points.

Important decisions made about filing can be pointed out in an introductory note or other message to users. Even if users do not remember specific filing rules, it is important that they know that different rules exist, as this may encourage them to search more broadly when initial attempts fail.

See also *Subheadings* in Chapter 7.

Word-by-word versus letter-by-letter

The two main filing rules are word-by-word (nothing before something) and letter-by-letter. With word-by-word filing, a space files before anything else; with letter-by-letter filing, spaces are ignored. In word-by-word filing, *New York* files before *Newark*, because the space between *New* and *York* files before the 'a' in *Newark*. In letter-by-letter filing *Newark* files first because the 'a' in *Newark* files before the 'Y' in *New York*. Once you have set up your preferences, indexing software automatically files entries for you.

With word-by-word filing, similar terms are more likely to file together. Every phrase starting with the word *cat* will file before other words, such as *catalogue*, that start with *cat* but have no meaningful relationship to cats. *Cat naps* and *cats*, however, will be separated by the word *catalogue*. (As noted by Terri Hudoba, Index-L, 22 May 2006, this separation can be overcome by using *cat(s)* and ignoring the *(s)* in filing. Alternatively, a reference can be made from the singular to the plural form.) Because word-by-word filing provides useful groupings based on meaning, most authorities recommend it, including the *Style manual* (2002: 274).

With letter-by-letter filing, groups of related words are separated by unrelated words. For example, *cat food* and *cat naps* are separated by the terms *catharsis*, *cathedrals* and *catheters*. The advantage of letter-by-letter filing is that it ensures that words are not separated just because they use spaces or hyphens; thus *on line*, *on-line* and *online* file together, as do *A B A* and *ABA*. This is a useful feature. However, we believe the optimal solution is to use word-by-word for its useful conceptual groupings and then, if necessary, create references from any terms that will be separated because they contain hyphens or spaces (e.g., 'on line *see* online').

Commas in letter-by-letter filing

Strict letter-by-letter filing can separate entries for identical surnames, so it is often adapted by indexing to the first comma that indicates an inversion. The strict alphabetical method gives:

> Brown, Anna
> Browne, Bill
> Browne, Jenny
> Browning, F.
> Brown, Xavier

Indexing to the comma gives:

> Brown, Anna
> Brown, Xavier
> Browne, Bill
> Browne, Jenny
> Browning, F.

A similar approach is taken with inverted topical headings such as *chicken, Chinese-spiced*, which is alphabetised first to the first comma. The effect of this is to move the entry higher in the list, as it is filed initially by the first word only. When there are a number of inverted headings, the second word is then taken into account.

The rule of alphabetisation to the first comma applies only when the comma introduces an inversion, and never when the comma merely separates a list, for example, in *fennel, cabbage and carrot salad*.

See also *Index headings beginning with the same term*, below.

Punctuation, symbols, diacritics

In filing, punctuation marks such as apostrophes are treated as if they were not there, while hyphens, dashes, and slashes are treated as if they were spaces. Pat Booth (2001) suggests that for some subject words it would make more sense to give hyphens a null filing value and so ignore them. This means that *anti-estrogens* would file after *antidepressants*; this only matters in word-by-word filing.

Entries starting with symbols file at the beginning of the index, before numbers and letters, while symbols within entries are ignored. Symbols may be filed in ASCII order (en.wikipedia.org/wiki/ASCII) or order of appearance. Another method is to file them by their verbal equivalent; for example, '> (greater than sign), 99' is filed as 'greater than'. They may also be entered under both name and symbol. See the *Perl in a nutshell* index (www.oreilly.com/catalog/perlnut/inx.html) for a complex example of symbol indexing.

The ampersand (&) within entries is either ignored (being treated as a symbol) or filed as if it were written *and* in the language of the entry. Often double entry is needed, as users do not know whether a name contains an ampersand or the word *and*. This is common in library catalogues, where both forms are often entered.

Upper and lower case letters should be interfiled, although this does not happen automatically when computer filing using ASCII order is followed. In English-language indexes accented letters (diacritics, e.g., in *résumé*) are normally interfiled with the unaccented equivalents.

Numbers

AS/NZS 999 (section 8.3) says that headings beginning with arabic and roman numerals should be interfiled, in numeric order, before the main alphabetical sequence. It makes the exception that, when only a few headings begin with numerals, they may be arranged as if spelt out.

A more useful distinction is that when numbers are in the same category as other fully alphabetical headings, they can be arranged as if spelt out (Booth 2001: 163). Following this suggestion, you would not interfile the dates *1999*, *2000* and *2001*, but you could interfile the title *101 Dalmatians* (at '*One hundred and one dalmatians*', possibly doubled at '*a hundred and one*', filed at 'h'). The *Style manual* (2002: 277) says 'numerals are treated as if they were written as words'. Our preference is to index numbers first within the number sequence, and then, if necessary, with double entries as if spelt out.

There is more consensus about the filing of numbers in chemical names, and these are generally ignored in filing (but retained in the entry). Even here, there are exceptions, including cases where the chemical compound is well known by a name including the numbers. The herbicide *2,4-dichlorophenoxyacetic acid* is commonly known as *2,4-D*, and the neurotransmitter *5-hydroxytryptamine* is known as *5-HT* (and more commonly as *serotonin*). *2,4-D* and *5-HT* are therefore potential index terms.

Greek and Roman letters

There is no consistency in the filing of Greek letters, either between or within sources, indicating that features intrinsic to specific terms influence the decision (Browne 2005). In general, Greek letters should be considered in filing when:

- They are spelt out in the text, rather than written as letters.
- They are part of natural language, as in *alpha centauri*, *beta blockers* and *gamma globulins*.
- They are connected to the following word, as in *alpharetrovirus*; *betamethasone*.
- They have been incorporated into an acronym. For instance, alpha fetoprotein is abbreviated *AFP*, α-Tocopherol/β-Carotene Trial as *ABTC Trial*, and gamma amino-butyric acid as *GABA*.

Greek letters tend to be ignored in filing in indexes for works in enzymology and chemistry, but even if α-*glucose* and β-*glucose* filed under 'g', you would still have to file 'α–β isomerism' under 'alpha'. To put it only under 'i' ignores its specific meaning.

Greek letters may occasionally also be filed (or double entered) in the symbol section of an index, for example, in the term Δ-*E (delta-E) values* (the symbol for capital delta is a triangle).

Roman letters at the beginning of chemical names are generally ignored in filing but retained in the entry. *N-acetylglucosamine* would be filed at 'acetyl', and *p*-aminobenzoic acid at 'amino'. This does not apply when the letter stands for a distinct word, as in *mRNA* and *tRNA* which stand for *messenger RNA* and *transfer RNA* respectively (although Wellisch 1995: 20 states otherwise).

Initial articles

Filing of articles (*the*, *a* and *an*) is tricky because the rules vary according to the type of entry, the position of the article within the entry, and the authority you consult.

You should ignore (or invert) the article:

- at the beginning of the titles of articles, books, paintings etc.
- in names of corporate bodies (organisations and groups)
- in place names, e.g., Hague, The (if following *The Chicago manual of style*) or The Hague, filed at H (if following the *Style manual*) and Netherlands (not The Netherlands)

You should file on the article:

- within titles: in *Lion, the witch and the wardrobe, The*, you count the second and third *the*'s in filing, but not the first
- in place names: *The Northern Road*, *The Hague* (except if following The *Chicago manual of style* and the *Style manual*), *Den Haag* (including *The Chicago manual of style*, which treats articles in place names differently for non-English names)
- in indexes to first lines of poetry.

AS/NZS 999 (section 7.3.4.2) recommends inverting 'the' so that filing is explicit, and using a lower case initial letter for the second word in the entry;

this gives *hunting of the snark, The*. This looks strange to us (Alan Walker says it looks like *e. e. cummings*), so we capitalise the word that becomes the new entry point. Alternative approaches are to delete the initial article entirely, or to leave it at the beginning of the index entry but not file on it. Some indexers who leave it at the front claim this is essential as it is an integral part of the name. We find this logic strange, because if it is an integral part of the name surely they would retain it at the front and also consider it in filing.

Indexers often assume that the rules they follow are generally understood. However, when someone wrote to Index-L that 'most U.S. readers seem to know that in English, articles such as *a, an* and *the* are ignored in sorting', Pauline Sholtys (Index-L 19 December 2005) replied that a fellow musician had asked her why she was filing her music under the second word in the title. When Pauline replied that this was the standard, her friend was surprised. The rest of the choir – all college-educated professionals – was divided in opinion, and most seemed to think it was 'some exotic scheme' she was following because her occupation made her think strangely. They then asked her if she ignored *and, to*, and other 'little words'. Obviously a filing rule that many indexers take for granted is not universally known outside our field.

Because *the* is important in many names, because many users do not know that they should be disregarding some words in entries, and because most computer-generated lists do file on initial articles, we advocate double entry of terms at 'The', 'A', or 'An', or a note saying: 'The . . . for titles starting with *The* search on the second word' (Browne 2001b).

The NISO technical report on filing (Wellisch 1999) says 'An initial article in a heading should be treated as any other initial word', but it also adds instructions for inversion of articles if this is deemed necessary, for example, for library catalogues.

Another category of terms that is not covered by the rules is topical terms such as *the dead* and *the fantastic*. These are probably best indexed as inverted terms (*dead, the*) with a possible double entry under *the*. In the same vein, we have seen an index to a book on pregnancy with *the blues* filed under 't'.

'The' is prominent in Gary Larson's index to *Wiener dog art: a Far Side collection* (1990), which includes the entries:

> The one about accountants 96
> The one about alien biologists 102
> The one about the aliens 86

Filing Mt, St and Mc

In some indexes and lists, such as phone directories, *Mount* and *Mt* and *Saint* and *St* are interfiled as if the contractions are written in full, and names starting with *Mac*, *Mc* and *M'* are interfiled at *Mac*. This is done because people often do not know whether a word is written Mc or Mac, or St or Saint. Since the revision of filing rules in the 1980s, this is no longer recommended by any official indexing standard, although they do allow the practice where 'the nature, purpose, or tradition of a list requires arrangement as if spelt out in full'. Some indexers, especially in Scotland, continue the tradition.

The *Style manual* (2002) recommends: 'For ease of reference, names spelt differently but pronounced the same way should be placed together – a practice followed in telephone books.' It is not clear whether they mean this rule to be followed to its logical conclusion, in which case *Browne* should be filed with *Brown*; *Jermey* with *Germey*; and *Cripps* with *Kripps*.

The Chicago manual of style now accepts the filing of *St* as *St* (not *Saint*) and *Mc* as *Mc*, noting that this means they differ from the Merriam–Webster biographical and geographical dictionaries.

It is rare that filing something out of alphabetical order is good for readers, because you remove the entry from the right place to aid people who look in the wrong place! In addition, it can make browsing difficult. When searching for the name Macaraeg in a list such as the one below, it is necessary to keep imagining an extra 'a' in the Mc's to follow the alphabetical sequence:

McAnn-Smith
McAnulty
Mcardle
Mcarthur

It is far better to file everything in alphabetical order, and to use references and double entry to provide access from alternative entry points as necessary.

Filing, by importance

Indexers who use a subheading such as *mentioned* for passing mentions often file it at the bottom of a list, while they may force filing of an entry such as *overview* to the top. Using *about* for general content is a good alternative (for user groups who understand its meaning) as it nearly always files at the top of a list of subheadings.

William Collins (2001) wrote 'I once had an author present me with a list of "very important" terms that he wanted me to index out of alphabetical order, so that they'd appear at the beginning of the index, where everyone could find them right away.' The Russians would not find this so odd. Robert Dessaix wrote in his autobiography (*A mother's disgrace* 1994: 62) about his studies in Russia:

> the class paper we had to write on Dostoevsky was less 'free': it had to be couched
> in strictly Marxist literary terms and the bibliography had to begin with the letter
> L for Lenin, then go on to M for Marx, E for Engels and only then to A, B, etc.
> No one minded or thought it odd. We were just giving unto Caesar.

Index headings beginning with the same term

Filing becomes complicated when a number of headings start with the same term. For most book-style indexes this is not an issue, and the simplest approach is to index alphabetically, ignoring any punctuation within the terms. With long indexes such as browsable versions of collection indexes it can be intellectually useful and visually more appealing to group the terms.

According to AS/NZS 999 (section 8.5), index headings that begin with the same term should be filed in the following sequence: the term with or without subheadings; the term with a qualifier; and the term as the first element of a longer term:

> irrigation
>   costs of
>   implementation priorities
> *Irrigation* (report)
> Irrigation, Wendy
> *Irrigation options in the Murray–Darling Basin*

It is useful to file qualified terms together, so the user can easily see the options available. In lists of index terms in displayed collection indexes, the question is often whether you should index first to the end of the heading, and then file by subheading, or whether you should file alphabetically throughout. In the first option, you would have:

> Bile – congresses
> Bile Acids and Salts
> Bile Ducts – abnormalities
> Bile Ducts – surgery
> Bile Ducts, Intrahepatic

In the second you would have:

> Bile Acids and Salts
> Bile – congresses
> Bile Ducts – abnormalities
> Bile Ducts, Intrahepatic
> Bile Ducts – surgery

The first method can create useful groups, but it is somewhat arbitrary as it depends on choices that have been made about the syntax of headings. *Bile Ducts – surgery* could equally well have been written *Bile Duct Surgery*, and it would then have filed differently.

See also *Commas in letter-by-letter filing*, above.

Delivery of indexes to clients

Book-style indexes

Book-style indexers usually deliver indexes to clients via e-mail as RTF or Word documents with no layout except indents for turnover lines and subheadings, and bold and italic as required. Plain-text versions with coding tags for layout software and embedded indexes are becoming more common, and have to be negotiated with the client before indexing starts. See also *Markup languages* and *Embedded indexing* in Chapter 8.

AS/NZS 999 (section 6.4) recommends that 'the publisher should give the indexer an opportunity to check the proofs of a printed index before publication'. This seldom happens in practice, at least in Australia. AS/NZS 999 (section 6.4.4) also recommends that 'Publishers should offer indexers the opportunity to be named in the document.' In Australia, publishers who name some contributors on the verso of the title page usually also include the indexer. In our experience textbook publishers are more willing than trade publishers to acknowledge the range of professionals who have helped to create a book. If more indexers were publicly acknowledged, fewer people would say 'Oh, I thought indexes somehow just happened.' Occasionally indexers do not want their names on books which, because of time or cost constraints, are not up to their usual quality.

Collection indexes

Collection indexing is usually 'delivered' by direct entry into online templates – it may then wait in a provisional area until it has been approved by a supervisor for entry into the live database. In the past paper-based worksheets were completed. These were sometimes typed twice, and the versions compared to ensure total accuracy of data entry!

Typography and index design

Most decisions about the presentation of indexes are made by editors and designers, rather than by indexers, often simply following the house style.

An index usually uses the same typeface as the text, one or two points smaller in size. (A font is an assortment of type of one style, including bold and italic versions.) Ideally the type size should be at least eight point as some people, especially older and younger readers, find it difficult to read anything smaller. Sometimes small type is used to fit an index into a too-small space – this has been called 'five-point Myopia' font.

If there are two or more indexes, the more comprehensive one goes last because the index at the very end of the book is the one most likely to be found (Peters 2004: 275).

Most indexes start on a right-hand page and are presented in two columns, with more for larger pages. If too many columns are used there will be many turnover lines. Indexes are left-justified with a ragged right-hand side. When page numbers are right justified, indexes are hard to read, even with dot leaders. Do not use:

Asia Minor. 482
Assos. 550

Designers play an important role in fitting indexes to the space available. This includes choice of type size as well as changes in the spaces between lines, the width of margins, and so on. Designers also balance the length of columns, and deal with bad breaks, in which subdivisions are in the column following their main heading (jump entries). These can sometimes be dealt with by taking a few lines over to the next column; alternatively, 'continued' lines are used to indicate that an entry array has been split. AS/NZS 999 (section 9.4.1.5) says that if an index entry runs on to a new page, the index heading and any subheadings and subsubheadings should be repeated, followed by the word 'continued' . . . in parentheses, although this is rarely done in practice:

economic reform (continued)
    emphasis on growth 111–112

See *Subheadings: Indention, Cross-reference placement and format* and *Locators for special purposes* in Chapter 7.

Letter headings

Most indexes use a one-line space between each alphabetical section, sometimes adding a large capital letter to indicate the sequence that follows:

downshifters
dual-income households

E
economic liberalism

Most people find both of these formats acceptable – the advantage of using the space by itself is that it makes the index shorter and avoids clutter.

Occasionally indexes use bold-face for the first letter of the first word in each sequence, but this can be disruptive:

evening dress
event management
flower arrangement.

Quality Control and Interoperability

THIS CHAPTER COVERS general topics related to quality control and the sharing of indexing – evaluation, consistency, and interoperability. Markup languages are included as they facilitate the transfer and sharing of information, while embedded indexing allows the reuse of indexing information.

Evaluation

Indexing is a multi-step process. After entering terms to describe concepts, indexers spend time evaluating their entries and editing the initial terms to make the index into a coherent whole (*Term editing as you index* in Chapter 5).

When editors or other clients receive the index they have to evaluate it against the brief and check that the content has been covered adequately and the index is accurate. Book-style indexes may also be evaluated through peer review, by book reviewers, and when submitted for awards. Collection indexing is evaluated by editors, and sometimes in more formal large-scale studies. These are all discussed below.

Book-style indexing

> There must be a beginning of any great matter, but the continuing until the end, until it be thoroughly finished, yields the true glory.　　　　　Francis Drake

Editors need to evaluate indexes against the brief which was provided. Janet Mackenzie (2004) writes:

> Indexes are usually edited on screen. If the index is professionally prepared, the editor need only make a quick check to ensure that the indexer is competent and to correct typos and consistency with the text. Usually, though, the index is prepared by an amateur – the author. In most cases this is a false economy. An amateur index usually needs both substantive editing and copyediting.

An editor needs to:

- Check from the index to the book, to make sure that index entries lead to relevant pages.
- Spot check from the book to the index, to make sure that relevant sections of the book have been included in the index under appropriate topics, and that no major chunks are missing.
- Check the length.
- Check to ensure that cross-references lead to useful entries.
- Correct spelling errors and ensure that house style has been followed consistently: use of bold and italic, en rules in page spans, filing order.
- Check that page numbers are listed in ascending order.
- Check that there are no long lists of unanalysed page numbers – if there are, the editor asks the indexer to create subheadings.
- Spot check the coding, if any.
- Read through the index to ensure that the headings and subheadings describe their topics clearly and succinctly.
- If there are multiple indexes, check that the appropriate terms are in each.

The ASI site hosts a useful indexing evaluation checklist (www.asindexing.org/site/checklist.shtml).

Some indexers are acknowledged in book reviews and speeches at launches. This is important as it indicates the significance of indexes. Lists of positive, negative and mixed reviews of indexes are provided in the 'Indexes Reviewed' section of *The indexer*. Sometimes books are sent to reviewers before the index has been completed, in which case the review cannot comment on the index.

Awards for quality indexes are given by indexing societies (see their websites for details), and occasionally by specialist organisations such as the Society for Technical Communication in the United States (Wyman 2005).

Evaluation of periodical indexing shares characteristics with evaluation of both book-style and collection indexing.

Collection indexing

The quality of collection indexing is assessed in two ways – effective retrieval, and agreement with an optimum set of terms (that is, consistency with expert decisions).

Retrieval effectiveness includes both recall, the proportion of relevant items that are retrieved, and precision, the proportion of retrieved items that are relevant. Usually when searchers try to increase their recall – try to get more items – their precision decreases. Indexing aims to increase the proportion of relevant items that are retrieved.

Pertinence (usefulness) is also important, as a search may retrieve items that fit the search but are not actually useful for the searcher. This could be because the searcher already has similar information, because the items are too old, because they are in another language, and so on. These measures are used in the large-scale evaluations of automatic indexing systems (see *Collection indexes: Free-text searching and machine-aided indexing* in Chapter 5). When referring to search engine results, relevance usually means closeness of fit of the results to the search, and is given as a percentage. Search results (hits) can be ranked according to their relevance.

Collection indexing is evaluated by supervisors who may skim all of the output, often in printed format, and perform more detailed spot checks. The output can also be tested with real users and real searches, to ensure that the documents retrieved for searches on various terms are, in fact, relevant to the users of those terms.

Factors that influence quality are the experience of the indexer, including subject knowledge; vocabulary factors, such as the fit of the controlled vocabulary to the documents; document factors such as quality of writing, complexity, and variation between documents; process factors, such as rules and instructions; and environmental factors like noise and lighting.

Systems in which the thesaurus is integrated in the data entry process can automatically flag terms that are not in the thesaurus, thus preventing the entry of misspelt words and non-approved terms. Automatic error checking may also find anomalies – for example, you cannot be *elderly* and die of *Sudden Infant Death Syndrome (SIDS)*. The INIS database identifies items containing terms that are not usually associated with the classification code that has been applied, and flags them for manual checking.

Consistency

Book-style indexing

Consistency in book indexing includes the consistent selection of topics for inclusion, and consistent wording of those topics. It is relevant to indexes created by one indexer and, more importantly, to those created by teams.

Consistency in wording is achieved through indexers following standard rules about term creation, remembering the formats they have used previously, and checking for consistency at the editing stage. Team projects may use a thesaurus or other controlled vocabulary to ensure consistency.

Consistency is important in headings and subheadings. When similar wording is used for similar topics it is called parallel construction.

Consistency in the inclusion of topics is much harder to manage because it requires a judgement of the importance of each entry. Indexers maintain consistent levels of indexing through the use of informal or formal guidelines. For example, they might index a concept if it is written in bold-face; is discussed for at least a paragraph; is included in a word list; or if it offers an insight unique to the book. Decisions also have to be made about the inclusion of whole categories of terms such as names, places, and broad 'grouping' terms, such as *holiday locations* or *Mediterranean cooking*.

Given the variability in documents, indexers and users, it is inevitable that not every index will contain every term that may be useful for every user. Indexers can only do the best they can for the majority of users they envisage in the time and space allowed. Nonetheless, there should be a core of agreement on major concepts.

Consistency between indexers has been explored by Smith and Kells (2005) as they compare their thought processes and results when indexing the same book. On a similar note, Kari Kells (2004) has made available results from a workshop on indexing, in which a number of people indexed the same short text. The text, the indexes, and a comparison of the indexes are online. The comparison document shows entries from each of the indexes under broad headings such as 'Age, maturity and development' and 'Culpability of offenders'. The indexes vary widely: the differences include decisions about inclusion of categories of entry, such as place names; the wording of the entries (*adolescents*; *child offenders*; *juvenile offenders*; *minors*; *under eighteen year olds*; *young offenders*; *youths*); the use of a term as a subheading instead of as a main heading; and omission of a concept from the index.

Consistency is particularly important when many indexers work together on large-scale projects such as encyclopedia indexes. Issues to be considered are discussed in *Working for employers* in Chapter 1 and *Encyclopedias and other multivolume works* in Chapter 9.

Collection indexing

Indexing inconsistencies may occur with the same indexer over time, intra-indexer inconsistency; between indexers, inter-indexer inconsistency; and between systems, inter-system inconsistency – this is covered in *Interoperability*, below. Agreement is more likely with core subjects, and decreases as more terms are added. As the use of more terms increases findability, along with inconsistency, it may be that too much emphasis on consistency is counter-productive.

Inter-indexer inconsistency is difficult to achieve when:

- Topics are difficult to analyse, with different possible interpretations of their 'aboutness' (Chapter 4).
- No controlled vocabulary is used, or when there are no suitable terms in the thesaurus (Chapter 6).
- Indexers misunderstand the topic, or make mistakes in the application of thesaurus terms.

A book on multimedia indexing by Pauline Rafferty and Rob Hidderley (2005) was indexed by the British Library with the term: *Cataloguing of nonbook material* and by the Library of Congress with four terms: *Information storage and retrieval systems – Multimedia (Art)*, *Multimedia (Art) – Abstracting and indexing*, *Multimedia systems*, and *Semiotics*. While neither is obviously wrong, they have taken quite different approaches to the interpretation of the topic and the exhaustivity of indexing.

The closer the controlled vocabulary is to natural usage, the more likely it will be applied consistently by indexers and used naturally by searchers. When a controlled vocabulary does not match an indexer's way of thinking, or does not provide terms that are needed, selecting a term is like trying to fit a square peg into a round hole. In *MeSH (Medical Subject Headings)* the appropriate term for a book on gynaecology is *Genital Diseases, Female*, as the term *Gynecology* (in its American spelling) is reserved for books about gynaecology as a medical specialty. In practice, however, the term *Gynecology* is often wrongly used in catalogues to refer to diseases, as this is the way it is used in the titles of textbooks. See also *The malignant, mighty or maligned metatopic* in Chapter 4.

Similarly, the term *surrogate mothers* used to refer to women who nurtured other people's children (e.g., 'Hospital nurse as surrogate mother') – you could also have surrogate fathers. With developments in reproductive technology, however, the term shifted to mean women who actually bear children for other women. A number of indexing services, such as *Current law index* 1981–83 and *Psychological abstracts* to 1988, simply used the existing term to index both meanings.

Computer indexing is often praised for its consistency; however, while computers may apply algorithms (rules) consistently, they do not necessarily identify concepts consistently. Surely it is worse for a computer to consistently index bacterial cultures with the term *cultural life* than it is for them to use the correct term at least some of the time? See also *Collection indexes*: *Free-text searching and machine-aided indexing* in Chapter 5.

Interoperability

Interoperability in indexing refers to the ability of two systems to work together by exchanging information and using that information effectively.

Book-style indexing

Most book-style indexes are stand-alone products that will be used only with the item being indexed. This allows the indexer flexibility in indexing for the needs of that specific book and the audience identified for it. Some book-style indexes, however, will be reused in some way. The quality of the original indexing has a significant impact on the ease of reuse of indexes. Where possible, the person who created the original index should be the one to rework it.

Interoperability is important in two main areas:

- for entire indexes that will be edited for use with later editions of a book, or with updated versions of looseleaf services
- for portions of indexes that will be reused with portions of text, or for whole indexes that will be reused in different contexts.

When entire indexes will be edited for use with updated material, indexers have to consider the needs of future users as well as the needs of the current audience when they create the original index. Indexes for reuse usually have to be simpler than one-off indexes, so that the re-indexer can easily pick up the connections that have been made. They therefore rely more heavily on concepts that have been explicitly named in documents, and less on implicit concepts that are discussed but not named. Indexes for reuse should use *see* references rather than double entry, to make the synonyms explicit. With double entry, it is possible that the re-indexing will only be applied to one of a pair of terms. Alternatively, a controlled vocabulary can be used for synonym control.

For reuse of portions of books, or of whole books in different contexts, see *Custom-built publications* in Chapter 9 and *Embedded indexing*, below.

Collection indexing

Inter-system inconsistency occurs when more than one service indexes the same document. These inconsistencies are inevitable, as different services have different policies and controlled vocabularies. They become significant when:

- indexing information is to be shared to reduce duplicate indexing
- indexes are to be merged
- indexes are to be searched as one, although indexed and stored separately
- parts of an index are to be integrated into another system.

Interoperability is enhanced through the use of:

- shared standards for description and structure of data, including AACR2 and OAI-PMH
- Z39.50-compliant software for cross-database searching
- crosswalks to map fields within databases
- shared thesauruses or mappings between thesauruses.

These issues are discussed in a number of articles by staff from UKOLN and RDN, and in the journal *Ariadne* (Powell 2002; Guy 2004), as well as in *Standards* in Chapter 2, in *Digital libraries* and *Library collections* in Chapter 9, and in *Markup languages*, below.

Crosswalks map equivalent fields from one database to another to enable the transfer of data between them. The mappings are displayed as tables. They may be exact matches, for example from 'surname' to 'family name'; or they may be inexact, for example, from 'contributor' to 'author' and 'editor' and 'illustrator' (Haynes 2004: 158 and Gill *et al*. no date). The UKOLN site (www.ukoln.ac.uk/metadata/interoperability) lists crosswalks for translation between standards such as MARC, EAD, TEI, ISAD(G) and Dublin Core.

Relationships can be established between controlled vocabularies such as thesauruses to show terms that have equivalent meanings in each vocabulary. These are known as **mappings**. Mappings are created between professional and natural language thesauruses, between thesauruses of databases that are merging, and between thesauruses in different languages.

Problems with mappings can be minimised if thesauruses are developed to maintain consistency with related thesauruses. Government departments may all use one general records management thesaurus, and create their own supplementary thesauruses for terms relating to their specific functions (*Records and archives* in Chapter 9). The Chinese created a ten-volume general thesaurus in 1974, and in 1979 the standardisation committee suggested that all special thesauruses should consider establishing compatibility with the *Chinese thesaurus* (Zeng 1990).

When comparing two pre-existing thesauruses, it is not always possible to create one-to-one mapping. The draft British Standard *Structured vocabularies for information retrieval – guide part 4 (BS 8723)* provides examples of inexact mappings. For example *potted plants* may have to be mapped to *indoor plants*, even though the concepts are not identical; and the English word *skidding* is mapped to two different German words: *Rutschen*, which means skidding forwards, and *Schleudern*, which means skidding sideways.

When WilsonWeb introduced multifile searches, they had to make a major editorial effort to standardise the vocabularies across different indexes. The Wilson OmniFile Full Text project reconciles 'selected subject headings' from six Wilson indexes. Similarly, CASI has developed procedures for mapping terms assigned by other agencies using other vocabularies to terms in the NASA thesaurus, thus enabling easier sharing of records between the agencies (Lancaster 2003: 309).

The W3C SKOS (Simple Knowledge Organization System) Core Guide (W3C 2005) is a model for expressing the basic structure and content of controlled vocabularies such as thesauruses and taxonomies in RDF format, with a view to the sharing of data sources across the web.

Markup languages

Procedural markup refers to the instructions given to a typesetter about how to lay out text, for example, insertion of bold and italic type and different sizes. Most markup languages used today are for **descriptive markup**, in which codes indicate the type of content – for example, emphasis and chapter heading – but do not say how the content should be formatted. This makes for a more flexible system in which the same text can be output in different ways for different needs.

Markup languages such as **SGML (Standard Generalized Markup Language)** were initially developed to describe documents for layout and presentation. They are now also used to define metadata associated with documents. There is a wide range of markup languages for different purposes.

An attempt to standardise markup languages has led to the development of XML, discussed below. Although XML stands for eXtensible Markup Language, it is not a language at all but a set of rules specifying how markup languages are to be written. Within the XML system, users are free to devise their own terms and structures for the documents they are creating or editing.

Markup languages used for descriptive markup of documents include DocBook, and LaTeX. Using a markup language enables authors, editors and indexers to make information explicit so it can be used in data processing. For example, a small indent in an index normally prompts the reader to infer a first-level subheading. The indent may have been produced by paragraph style formatting, a tab character or several spaces. If the index is written in or converted into a markup language, however, the presence of a subheading is always indicated by the use of a particular 'tag' – for example, <index2>. This allows indexes from different sources to be combined automatically. When a printed or on-screen version of the index is required for human users, the <index2> tag can be converted to an indent in any of the ways described above. It could also be used to trigger a different colour or typeface, or a different tone of voice when the index is read aloud.

Marking up a book in this way requires the author or editor to identify text in the book which is in some way different from the norm. Chapter headings, stretches of bold or italic text, figure captions and citations might be tagged for later identification. Sections such as chapters are tagged as well. Within the index itself letter separators, main headings, subheadings and cross-references are tagged.

With a book marked up in this standard way an author, editor or publisher can routinely produce large-print copies for the visually impaired, extract tables of contents and first chapters for reviewers, collect together books with the same authors, arrange books in chronological order, check that a new book does not have the same title as an existing one, compile the book into a form suitable for reading on a hand-held computer, and so on. By promulgating and adopting world-wide standards for markup, this activity can be extended across the web and ultimately to the whole universe of books in print. This makes the considerable time and effort that is spent developing global standards for markup languages worthwhile.

Markup languages are also used to define the metadata used in documents, for use in the retrieval of documents. Examples are OAI-PMH (*Standards for records and archives* in Chapter 2) and TEI (below). The markup is important for retrieval and for harvesting of content. Standards for metadata content are discussed in Chapter 2.

Embedded indexing is also a markup ('tagging') process, with a number of different languages being used depending on the system. See *Embedded indexing*, below, and *Embedded indexing software* in Chapter 10.

XML (eXtensible Markup Language)

> You know what I want for Christmas? Markup Barbie. You pull a string and she says 'XML is tough'.
> Mark Pilgrim (diveintomark.org/archives/2004/07/06/tough, 23 March 2006)

XML, like HTML (hypertext markup language, the markup language used in most webpages), is a spin-off from the large and complex Standard Generalized Markup Language (SGML). The XML Working Group removed some of the less-used features of SGML and developed a relatively simple language that could be used by a wide variety of applications on the web.

XML provides for an open system in which to store all kinds of files – word processing documents, spreadsheets and database information. By breaking information down into tiny chunks and enclosing each of these in one or more 'tags', it allows an enormous amount of information to be represented. And because XML is text-based, it can be used on any platform and with almost any software, now and in the foreseeable future.

XML is similar to HTML in that the tags in XML are contained within angled brackets. XML tags, however, always come in pairs, so that an opening tag like <FIRSTNAME> has to be matched with a closing tag like </FIRSTNAME>. The only exceptions are empty tags, with no content, which are represented like this: <MIDDLENAME/>.

Within an XML document all the text is plain ASCII. The text represented on the screen in Microsoft Word as:

"I do not like that man, *señor*," she said.

might be converted into XML as

<SPEECH>I do not like that man, <ITALICS>se<SPECIALCHAR>
00F1</SPECIALCHAR>or</ITALICS>, </SPEECH>she said.

This could then be given to any word processing program with XML capabilities and restored to its original format.

Calling XML a 'language' is misleading. It is more like a grammar; that is, it can be used to construct languages but it has no vocabulary of its own. Anyone can use XML to construct their own unique tagging system: one user might use <I> for italics and another <IT>. Any XML document can be validated, that is, checked to see that it is syntactically correct.

XML is not meant for hand-coding or sight reading. XML documents are extremely large and complex, and are intended to be dealt with via compatible software. Some dedicated indexing software packages can already be adapted to produce XML documents, and Microsoft Office is moving towards XML compatibility for all its applications.

XML files can be viewed (but not edited) in a web browser. Here they appear as a colour-coded and indented sequence of elements that can be expanded to show their contents or 'rolled up' with a click of the mouse. A plug-in is available for Microsoft Internet Explorer that will also verify the correctness of XML. More complex formatting can be achieved through dedicated XML style sheets. Programs available for indexers working with XML include XMetal (www.xmetal.com/index.x), which has a downloadable demo version.

Cambridge University Press has adopted XML-based indexing for its books, but the markup is done in-house and the indexer is required only to add written numbers to the manuscript, and to use these, rather than page numbers, as locators when preparing the index (https://authornet.cambridge.org/information/productionguide/hss/indexing.asp#indexing_process).

DTDs and schemas

A DTD (Document Type Definition) is a collection of XML markup declarations written in XML Declaration Syntax that define the names that can be used for the different elements, what order they are to appear in and how they all fit together. A different DTD may be used for each type or class of document. By testing their documents against the DTD ('parsing'), indexers can tell if they have deviated from the rules that have been set down for structuring an index.

Schemas do the same thing as DTDs, but they are written in XML Document Syntax, which allows more extensive data-checking. This makes them more appropriate for e-commerce applications in which data validation is necessary. Schemas can be specified in a namespace, where schema-aware software should pick them up (xml.silmaril.ie/authors/schemas).

DocBook – for books

DocBook is a markup language that is most suited for books and papers about computer hardware and software, but has been used for books of all kinds. Using free tools along with the DocBook XSL stylesheets, you can publish your content as HTML pages and PDF files, and in many other formats (www.docbook.org/xml/5.0b3/index.html).

Fred Brown (2001) explains how to create an embedded index in DocBook using index elements. For example, to enter the main heading 'work experience' you would enter: <indexterm><primary>work experience</primary></indexterm>.

EAD – for archive pathfinders

Encoded Archival Description (EAD) is a markup language for archival finding aids. These are detailed descriptive access tools created by archival institutions to describe the original source materials they hold. EAD is maintained by the Library of Congress' Network Development and MARC Standards Office in partnership with the Society of American Archivists. It has a similar role for archives to MARC's for library records.

EAD has crosswalks to and from ISAD(G). Like ISAD(G), the EAD DTD emphasises the hierarchical nature of archival description and the inheritance of description – that is, everything that applies to a level higher in the hierarchy flows down to lower levels. Pitti (1999) has written an excellent overview.

LaTeX – for scientific and mathematical works

LaTeX is a document preparation (typesetting) system that has been developed by a collaborative users group and released under a public licence. It is available in both a Windows and a UNIX version. Markup in LaTeX is text-based; for example, index entries are preceded by a $\backslash i$ tag. Indexing in LaTeX allows for cross-references, substitution of terms and abbreviations. Although macros have been written for LaTeX indexing (linux.seindal.dk/item25.html), there are as yet no add-in programs as there are with Microsoft Word, Adobe FrameMaker and other commercial systems. John Culleton (2004) has written on indexing using the TeX typesetting suite (LaTeX is based on TeX).

RDF – for the semantic web and more

RDF (Resource Description Framework) is based on XML, and was developed under the auspices of the World Wide Web Consortium (W3C). RDF is designed to provide for the expression of semantic information (meaning). This will assist in interoperability of data, computer-understandable semantics for metadata, and better precision in resource discovery than can be achieved with full-text search. RDF can be used for resource discovery, cataloguing, intelligent software agents, content rating, description of intellectual property rights, electronic commerce, collaboration, and digital signatures (www.w3.org/RDF/FAQ).

At the core of RDF is the notion of a resource description. A resource could be a document, a book, a company or a person, or any other object or concept of interest. A description is a set of information which represents the resource.

Information is given in a resource description via defined properties. Only certain data count as properties, and these are specified through a list of valid property-types, called a schema. Property-types should be logically and practically appropriate to the type of resource. Thus 'weight' would be a valid property type for describing a vehicle, and 'CEO' would be a valid property type for describing a company, but not vice versa. Schemas are stored in namespaces.

The properties in a resource description are assigned values, of which the simplest are just strings of text – 'Harry Smith', '1200 kg' and so on. The value–property-type–resource triad is typically represented in plain English as 'value is the property-type of resource' or 'the property-type of the resource is value'; for example, 'Harry Smith is the CEO of Snibbo Enterprises'; 'the weight of the Toyota Camry is 1200 kg'. These triples are assumed to be logically independent assertions which are mutually compatible.

Values can be links to resource descriptions: thus 'Harry Smith' may have its own collection of values – thirty-eight years old, male, born in Berlin – which may in turn be called on by the person who wants to find out about Snibbo Enterprises. In plain English we can think of these as adjectives or subordinate clauses: 'Male, Berlin-born Harry Smith, 38, is the CEO of Snibbo Enterprises'. In RDF this involves a cross-referential structure, in this case from a collection of information about companies to a collection of information about people. This information can also be shown diagrammatically as a network of connections between nodes.

RDF syntax is a form of XML. In RDF no identifier (resource description) has more than one property, and all identifiers in a collection have the same property set. As in XML, each identifier must be declared before use, and in RDF this is done by providing a URI (Unique Resource Identifier) which identifies that resource.

URIs are obviously related to the URLs used to access websites, but RDF does not put any constraints on them other than that they are not duplicated: thus a URI could in principle refer to a library shelf list of physical books, a company's employee database, or any other unique way of locating a resource. If the resource of interest happens to be a webpage, the URI is identical with its URL.

Project Gutenberg, the free public domain e-book collection (www.gutenberg.org) is an example of a resource available in RDF format using qualified Dublin Core (www.gutenberg.org/feeds). See also *Topic maps* in Chapter 6.

SMIL – for multimedia presentations

SMIL (Synchronized Multimedia Integration Language) is recommended by the World Wide Web Consortium or W3C (www.w3.org/TR/2005/PR-SMIL2-20050927) for describing multimedia presentations using XML. It defines timing markup, layout markup, animations, visual transitions, and media embedding. A SMIL document contains layout and metadata information in a <head> section and timing information in a <body> section. It generally has combinations of two main tags: parallel (<par>) and sequential (<seq>). See also *Video* in Chapter 9.

TEI – for digital libraries (and bibliographies and indexes)

The Text Encoding Initiative (TEI) Guidelines (www.tei-c.org) is an international and interdisciplinary standard based on XML. It is used by libraries, museums, publishers and individual scholars to represent a variety of literary and linguistic texts for online research, teaching, and preservation. The TEI standard is maintained by a consortium of institutions worldwide. It includes 400 different textual components, which are expressed using XML (and previously SGML). These textual components include indexes and bibliographical references.

TEI uses the <DIV1> tag or a <DIV> tag to demarcate an index, and marks up the index itself as a structured list or table. An <INDEX> tag is provided for embedded indexing, and up to four levels of subheading can also be indicated (named LEVEL1, LEVEL2, LEVEL3, and LEVEL4). An index attribute associates the entry with a particular index, so multiple indexes are possible. TEI appears to make no special provision for cross-references within an index, but cross-references in general are supported through the use of a <REF> tag.

Embedded indexing

Embedded indexing is an important technique for enabling the reuse of index information. Tagged index terms are embedded (inserted) into the text to which they refer, and indexes are generated from the tagged text. Index terms travel with the content – if content is deleted or moved to another position, the index terms are deleted or moved to the new position too. No manual repagination is required, although new terms have to be created when new content is added.

For most indexers, embedded indexing means inserting index tags into text documents to create book-style indexes. It also includes:

- programs such as HTML Indexer, which embed index terms within the web-pages they refer to, for the creation of book-style web indexes
- online help indexes, in which index entries are attached to the help pages they refer to
- website and intranet metadata when it is stored in the <HEAD> section of webpages; in other cases metadata is stored separately in a database or content management system, so is not really embedded although many of the same principles of reuse still apply.

Software programs that allow embedding include FrameMaker and MS Word. These, along with specialised software that addresses some problems with embedded indexing, are discussed in Chapter 10. XML and markup languages can be used in embedded indexing, and are discussed above.

Uses of embedded indexing

Embedded indexing can speed up document preparation, because indexing can happen at the same time as editing and other tasks are finalised. It also allows reuse of content with its associated indexing either in different formats, or grouped with content from other sources. Before deciding to use embedded indexing it is important to decide what you hope to gain from embedding, and to ensure that the benefits will compensate for the extra costs.

Embedded indexing is common in publishing projects with a quick turnaround and numerous editions, and has been prominent in computer documentation. Publishing projects can be completed more quickly using embedded indexing, because index terms are added to the document and do not require final pagination or positioning before completion. A book indexer may index a book one chapter at a time as it is ready, and a website indexer can start indexing even if some pages will later move.

Although this provides benefits, it comes at a significant cost, as indexers do not see the whole book at once, and cannot easily edit the index. A significant amount of time is spent tracking the arrival and departure of documents. The process also requires a lot of care to ensure that embedded indexing terms are added only to the 'live' document – that is, the only one to which changes are allowed. If an editor and indexer work on different copies of the same document at the same time, the changes will be lost unless the two versions are merged. Even then there will be problems if the changes the editor has been making affect the index.

Embedded indexing is also important for single-sourcing, in which modular content is stored once and output as required in different formats or versions. This process is also known as multi-purposing. Thus, the same set of information might be used to create international, introductory and advanced materials in both RTF and HTML formats.

Content that is used in only some of the versions is called conditional text, and is tagged to show which versions it belongs in. Indexing terms are used in indexes for the different versions as appropriate. Manoj Bokil (2004) uses screenshots to show the creation of conditional text in RoboHelp.

Indexing single-sourced documents is more complicated than indexing stand-alone products, as the limitations and approaches of all of the different formats have to be taken into account. The index is optimised for the most widely used format and may not be ideal for the others. In a book you might refer to page numbers, but in an online help system you may want to link to the top of a topic, or to a specific heading within the topic. With a printed index you can control the display of subheadings, while with online help you are more dependent on settings within the software. For more information see the article by Kurt Ament (2003), *Online help* in Chapter 9 and *Microsoft Access* in Chapter 10.

With single-sourcing, documents are usually indexed with knowledge of the planned uses for the index, whether in a different format, or with just a portion of the book being used. A more complex situation exists, in which chunks of documents from different sources are gathered together for some purpose – often to provide a cost-effective compilation of documents (coursepack) for a specific course (see *Custom-built publications* in Chapter 9).

It is much more difficult to index effectively for this purpose, as the indexer has no control over the indexing of the other documents that will be integrated into the final package. The most effective approach is to index as simply as possible at the level of headings within the text. Because of the difficulties in combining index entries from different sources, coursepacks and other custom-published documents are often published without indexes, or with inadequate indexes.

Bill Johncocks (2005) has pointed out problems with the reusability claims of embedded indexing: 'Index reusability is one of the claims made for embedded indexing but the technique itself provides evidence that no human index can ever be divorced from its source document.'

When outputting different parts of the content for different books, the subject indexing for the larger book may not be appropriate for the subset. In a book on pharmaceuticals you might use the subheading 'in pregnancy' under drug names. If a smaller book is created containing only the drugs relevant in pregnancy, this subheading will apply to every entry in the index and will therefore be of no value.

Some work has been done on the use of unified topic maps in the selection of material for custom publishing, and in the creation of an index for the final product. The topic maps are created from all of the indexes, tables of contents and glossaries in the books that may be used – starting with a unified controlled vocabulary such as this should make the final index more coherent (Ogievetsky and Sperberg 2003).

Disadvantages of embedded indexing

While the benefits of embedded indexing can be great if properly implemented, there are some major drawbacks from the point of view of indexers:

- It is more tedious than standard indexing and takes longer.
- It is harder to view the index while it is being completed, thus keeping consistency throughout. Some programs have add-ons that make this easier.
- It requires knowledge of the program being used (MS Word, FrameMaker, proprietary software), or at least of special processes used by the specific publisher.
- It may have to be done onsite.
- If the embedded index is to be updated by the indexer or other people, it needs to be as simple as possible. For instance it should link to text headings where possible, and use the language of the text rather than potential language of the user.

Specialised Source Material: Formats, Subjects and Genres

MOST INDEXING PROJECTS follow general indexing rules, and most indexers can index standard works on most topics. Some projects, however, have special requirements. To analyse concepts adequately, indexers must understand the language of the subjects they are indexing and the typical needs of users of those documents or systems. For projects such as online help indexing, technical skills are also required.

Indexing societies maintain lists of indexers who are available for work. ANZSI Indexers Available (www.aussi.org/indexersavailable/subjects.htm) has about thirty-five categories for specialties, including *Arts and crafts*, *Business and economics* and *Health and medicine*. In the ASI salary survey (www.asindexing.org/site/SalarySurvey.shtml), the main areas of specialty noted were computer science (17%), medicine and surgery (14%), law (13%) and business and management (10%).

Both the Society of Indexers (UK and Ireland) and the American Society of Indexers publish books on a range of subject specialties. SI has published Occasional Papers (OPs) on indexing biographies, legal materials, the medical sciences, periodicals, and children's books (www.indexers.org.uk/InAvail/publications/oppubs.htm). This series has been discontinued, but similar material will be published in *The indexer*'s new Centrepiece feature.

ASI, through Information Today, has published books on indexing genealogy, history, law, medicine, psychology, and scholarly books (including economics, public policy, philosophy, law, and music), and one on cookbook indexing is planned. *Index it right* has chapters on philosophy, theology, biography, horticulture, art, encyclopedias, computer manuals and websites (www.asindexing.org/site/asipub.shtml). Many ASI SIGS link to useful information relevant to their specialty – follow links to individual websites at www.asindexing.org/site/sigs.shtml.

ASAIB has a range of publications, which include articles on specialties such as museum indexing, history and bibliography (www.asaib.org.za/publication.html).

This section examines selected formats (such as archives and e-books), genres (such as biography), and subjects (such as legal publications). These are interfiled alphabetically.

Annual reports

Annual reports of Australian Commonwealth government departments and instrumentalities must have an alphabetical subject index and a compliance index. Subject indexes give access to the general content of the document, with appendixes including financial statements indexed at a broad level only. Compliance indexes, which provide quick access to certain mandatory sections of the report, are usually brief and simple, and are often prepared by the editor. Annual report indexes can be based on those of previous years.

Lynn Farkas (2005) has reported on the evaluation of online annual reports, the accessibility of information within them (often poor), and the potential role of indexers in improving the quality.

Bibliographies

Bibliography is the study of books. Enumerative bibliography (sometimes called systematic bibliography) is the field most relevant to indexing, and refers to the listing of books according to some system, for example, by author, subject or date. Library catalogues and reference lists in books are bibliographies.

Topical bibliographies require careful selection of items for inclusion ('the chase'), as well as indexes for access by author, title and subject. Some bibliographies also include annotations that summarise or evaluate the content. Many countries – for example, South Africa (Theron 2002) – have a national bibliography that aims to list all the documents published in, and about, that country.

Bibliographies are collections, but published bibliographies are also finite, stand-alone documents, so their indexing has aspects of book-style and collection indexing.

Bibliography is one of those subjects that is difficult to search for using keywords, because the content about bibliography is swamped by the hits that are bibliographies.

Biographies

> Biography lends to death a new terror.
> Oscar Wilde

The main skill in indexing biographies is the ability to pick out key aspects of a person's life from the narrative thread (Bell 2004). In addition, there are three major issues to consider when indexing biographies, autobiographies, memoirs, diaries, letters, and some fictional works:

- name format
- indexing of the main character (the metatopic)
- passing mentions.

Indexing of names in general is dealt with in Chapter 4. In biographies indexers often add parenthetical qualifiers (glosses) to show the relationship of people in the index to the main character, for example, *King, Coretta Scott (wife)*, in a biography of Martin Luther King. Glosses should be used consistently and only when necessary to clarify relationships. In biographies abbreviations are often used for main characters in subheadings and should be made clear in an introductory note, for example, 'MLK = Martin Luther King'.

The metatopic (central topic) of a book is often used as little as possible in index entries. Carried to its extreme this means using no entries at all for the subject of the biography, and relying on specific entries such as *education*, *marriage* and so on. One disadvantage of this approach is that it is not always obvious what headings would be used. *Marriage* is a straightforward entry, but for personal relationships in general a user will not know which of the following headings to consult: *de factos, boyfriends, girlfriends, love affairs, significant others, friends, relationships*, and *sexual relationships*. These are more easily found under the subject's name, which provides a useful gathering point. Subheadings under names may be filed alphabetically, thematically, chronologically, or in page number order.

Passing (brief) mentions of minor characters may be of little weight when considered individually, but significant when gathered together. Some indexers advocate indexing all mentions, but not differentiating them with subdivisions that would suggest more importance than they possess. Others, with the view that saving the time of the reader is of primary importance, add subheadings to distinguish between the locators. A good compromise is to use a simple subdivision such as the year of occurrence, which divides up the long strings, but does not suggest that each entry carries great meaning.

Hazel Bell (2004) advises us: 'Tread softly on people's lives.' When indexing books about people indexers need to treat the topic sensitively, although in this they are largely dependent on the sensitivity of the text. They may also have to consider specific cultural requirements. When indexing documents about Aboriginal people, phrases such as *half-bloods* may be considered meaningless on the grounds that all humans have mixed blood, or derogatory. In addition, Aboriginal documents may be for use by men or women only, and so indexing and access may have to be restricted; this is most relevant in collection indexing. See also *Correspondence and diaries*, *Fiction* and *Library collections*, below.

CD-ROMs and DVDs

The approach to indexing a CD-ROM or DVD depends on the type of content (selected journal articles; images; an encyclopedia), the format of the content and the planned index interface. The client should provide details of their requirements, and if possible send a sample of a similar project. The types of indexing that might be required include:

- a simple list of keywords to be used for search and browsing
- an index adapted to the client's interface
- an index linked to the documents.

Linked indexes can be created for PDF documents, or using HTML Indexer or other programs for HTML documents. To prevent problems with 'browsing' back and forth between the index and the text, the index may be displayed permanently in a frame or sidebar at the edge of the screen. See also *Encyclopedias and other multivolume works* and *Multimedia (audiovisual) materials*, below.

Citations

Citation indexes provide access to published journal literature through names of authors who have cited a work, rather than through the subject of the work. If you have one good article on a topic, this is a way of finding other articles that are likely to cover the same subject. The citation principle is also used in bibliographic coupling, which links two articles that cite the same articles, and in co-citation, which identifies articles that have been cited together by other articles. Citation-based retrieval is independent of language and changing terminology, and it complements subject-based searches: both methods retrieve unique, relevant articles.

ISI publishes three citation indexes – *Science citation index*, *Social science citation index* and *Arts and humanities citation index*. Citation tracking is provided through Thomson ISI's Web of Science (back to 1900), Elsevier's Scopus database and Google Scholar, among others. Weina Hua (2001) has written on the Chinese Social Sciences Citation Index.

As the authors were reading about co-citation in Lancaster (2003), we thought it ironic that his book covers much the same topic as the collection indexing parts of this book, yet we have few citations in common. Why? Because his citations tend to be academic print publications, while ours tend to be practitioner-written web-accessible articles. We have something in common, though – we cite Lancaster, and he has cited us (Browne 2001a, cited in Lancaster 2003: 25, 357).

Correspondence and diaries

Indexing letters and diaries provides structured access to the minute detail contained in these documents. It can be difficult because:

- a numbering system for locators may have to be constructed; alternatively locators can be created using the date of writing, and names of the writer and recipient
- there will be many passing mentions

- the documents may be unstructured and inconsistent, often with misspellings and vague references; for instance 'our beloved aunt' has to be named
- there may be multiple authors
- the papers may be hard to read due to damaged paper and illegible handwriting
- research may be needed to identify family relationships, place names and so on (Jones 2000).

Douglas Matthews (2001) has written on the 'pleasures and pride derived from indexing volumes of published letters', including his own work on the letters of Charles Dickens. See also *Biographies*, above.

Custom-built publications

Custom publishers extract parts of documents from one or many sources, as requested by a purchaser, and put them together into one 'unified' product. Custom publishing can be a cost-effective way for users to get just the parts of documents that they think they will need. It is used in legal publishing and in the creation of 'coursepacks' for tertiary-level students.

Custom publishing has implications for the writing and indexing of books. It requires authors to write with the view that their book may not be read as a whole. This has always been true, but at least a reader who has access to the whole book can search any of it for clarification of a point. Now the reader must rely solely on the selected chapters, so authors cannot assume knowledge from other chapters.

Indexes are often omitted in custom publishing, or are cobbled together from existing indexing. Both of these options are unsatisfactory. Embedded indexing makes index terms reusable. If embedding is to be done, indexers have several choices:

- Edit index terms for each chapter as a separate unit, as well as editing the index as a whole. Those who buy the whole book should not be disadvantaged by the modular approach.
- Index to the level of the 'chunks' that might be purchased as individual units – this may mean indexing at a more granular (detailed) level.
- Index broad topics and avoid subtle analysis that may not merge well with index terms from other sources.
- Avoid cross-references, or keep a separate record of cross-references to be used as appropriate. For instance you would remove the reference 'cancer *see also* breast cancer' if the section on breast cancer is not included in the compiled book.
- Re-index identical text that is repeated throughout the document ('boilerplate' text) each time it appears.

When index entries from different sources have been combined, the complete index should be edited. A *Seybold Report* (1999) discusses the process of indexing in their custom publishing process, admitting that 'automatically creating an index of material from several separate sources is fraught with problems'. Copyright and the moral rights (Chapter 1) of the original indexers must also be considered.

More broadly, Jeffrey Garrett (2006) is concerned that accessing information through coursepacks and full-text searches on a 'just-in-time' basis rather than reading full works on a 'just-in-case' basis may significantly change the way we think and learn.

Data warehouses

Data from inactive records is often stored in 'data warehouses'. Data mining can automatically search these large stores of data for patterns of interest, using computational techniques from statistics and pattern recognition studies. Data from distributed and differently structured databases can be combined in a data warehouse, allowing a global overview and comprehensive analysis of data. Old sales records, for example, can provide information about retail trends or allow evaluation of specific customers. Human intervention is required to generate the hypotheses, to evaluate the findings, and to make decisions based on the trends that have been identified.

Digital libraries

Digital libraries are organised collections of electronic resources from a range of sources. They can include digitised portions of a library's collection and resources, paid for by subscription or licence fee, that are only available to a library's clients, but a digital library may be quite independent from any physical library. Resources are often harvested from approved providers. The term is used broadly, and it overlaps with the concepts of directories, subject gateways (hubs) and portals, which are also included here. See also *Organizing audiovisual and electronic resources for access* by Ingrid Hsieh-Yee (2006) and *Library collections*, below.

There are three levels of digital library interoperability (Arms 2002):

- **Federation (cross-database searching)**: Standardised protocols such as ANSI/NISO Z39.50 allow a user in one system to retrieve information from multiple remote repositories without knowing the search syntax used by those other systems. This approach is the most expensive for the network and the system.
- **Harvesting**: Each participant makes metadata about its collection available in a simple exchange format that can be harvested by service providers. For example, OAI-PMH (Chapter 2) allows for the collection of metadata from remote repositories, which is then stored and searched locally.
- **Gathering**: Publicly available metadata is gathered, as by search engines on the web. This is the cheapest option for data providers.

Roy Tennant (2004) experimented with OAI-PMH and pointed out that although using it 'was a breeze', the quality of the results depended on the effort that had gone into metadata creation by the providers. He found compatibility problems and inadequate detail. This is caused by the low threshold for participation; the basic level is very easy. It may eventually be remedied by the high ceiling – the potential to create much richer representations.

Libraries use a number of metadata standards for management and exchange of digital content:

- MODS (Metadata Object Description Schema, www.loc.gov/standards/mods/registry.html) is used by the Australian National Bibliographic Database to convert Dublin Core metadata records harvested through OAI-PMH (Chapter 2) into MARC format (Missingham 2004). MODS can be combined with other XML based standards such as METS.
- METS (Metadata Encoding and Transmission Standard) is used for the exchange of metadata on digital objects between libraries (www.loc.gov/standards/mets). Jacobs says 'packaging standards exist to create compound digital objects, integrating both files and metadata, including METS'. METS schema is a standard for encoding descriptive, administrative and structural metadata regarding objects within a digital library, expressed using the XML schema language.
- A Dublin Core/MARC/GILS crosswalk (www.loc.gov/marc/dccross.html) has been developed by the Library of Congress to convert metadata between MARC and other syntaxes.

Freely available resources are easier to manage than licensed ones, but there is no guarantee that they will remain on the web, or remain of the same quality. Projects such as Pandora (pandora.nla.gov.au), run by the National Library of Australia, are working to ensure the preservation of selected digital resources. The Internet Archive (web.archive.org) is working to preserve the web as a whole, to allow people to search for webpages at different times in their history.

Licensed resources are harder to manage than free ones, as they often require client log-ons, but while the licence is current their continued existence is assured. Compared to print resources they have the disadvantage that often a continual payment of licence fees is needed to access the resources, even back issues. There is some concern in the library community that the move to digital resources means the loss of control by librarians of library collections.

Several Australian universities have established institutional repositories to preserve and provide access to research articles (e-prints). Compulsory deposit requirements, along with author support, have led to high levels of content being contributed (Sale 2006).

Lorcan Dempsey (2006) has written about a program to build a digital library for education in science, mathematics, engineering and technology. The project depended on technical agreements about formats, protocols and security, content agreements about data and metadata, and organisational agreements about access, preservation and payment. They concentrated human effort on collection-level metadata, and used automatic methods to augment item-level metadata. Scalability required 'relentless' simplification.

Candy Schwartz (2005) lists some digital libraries and repositories for library and information science articles that may be of interest to indexers.

Directories

The Librarians' Index to the Internet (www.lii.org), the Open Directory Project (dmoz.org) and Yahoo (dir.yahoo.com and au.dir.yahoo.com) are examples of web-wide directories of resources, covering all topics. They provide a valuable service, giving quick access to selected information.

Subject gateways

Subject gateways (hubs) are web-based hierarchical directories of evaluated freely available websites relevant to specific subjects. They may link to external sites or harvest metadata (for instance using OAI-PMH, as above) to retrieve content from selected providers.

One place-based subject directory is Tasmania Online (www.tas.gov.au/tasmaniaonline), an early winner of the AusSI (now ANZSI) web index-ing prize, and an ongoing success. It indexes websites about Tasmania and by Tasmanians. It provides access via an alphabetical index (www.tas.gov.au/tasmaniaonline/SubjectIndex), broad categories, a search engine, popular hits, and an 'Ask a librarian' link, thus covering all bases. The Australasian Legal Informa-tion Institute (AustLII) provides access to Australian legislation and legal informa-tion (www.austlii.edu.au/au/legis/cth/consol_act) and also to international infor-mation through sites such as the World Law Index (Davis 2001).

The JISC-funded Resource Discovery Network (www.rdn.ac.uk) provides access to subject gateways including EEVL (engineering), HUMBUL (humani-ties), SOSIG (social sciences) and BIOME (health). The Renardus initiative funded by the European Commission provides a multilingual cross-searching facility across several European subject gateways (www.renardus.org).

Research has been done into the structuring of subject gateways using Dublin Core, RDF and topic maps (Tramullas and Garrido 2006). With wider adoption of metadata standards such as Dublin Core, it should be easier for web gateway providers to harvest relevant data for their databases of web resources. This poten-tial application may extend the range of the subject-based gateways in the future and possibly reduce the expense required to maintain them.

E-books

We use the term e-books (electronic books) broadly, to include all books avail-able in electronic format. It also has a narrower meaning, restricted to books specifically published for use on e-book reading devices. These often carry restric-tive rights and management controls that limit their usefulness. Readers may not, for example, be permitted to make copies to use on different reading devices or lend the book to friends, as they can do with a printed book. Most commercially produced e-books are fiction, although the number of non-fiction e-books is increasing. E-books are the publishing industry's fastest growing sector (www.idpf.org/pressroom/inthenews.htm).

Many textbooks are now supplied with a CD-ROM or DVD, which may contain the full copy of the book in electronic format. Sometimes this is supplemented by multimedia content (such as videos of surgical procedures and pronunciation guides for medical terminology) and related software.

Where the book has already been published in print, the electronic format usually reflects this; PDF format, for example, preserves page breaks, headers and footers, and other artefacts of the printing process. Thus a printed index can be reused for the electronic version, since the page numbering remains the same.

When e-books are released in other formats, indexes may be either omitted or recreated in electronic format. The latter usually involves the addition of hyperlinks from the index to the content. This is similar in practice to indexing a website (see below), and can be done using specialised software (Chapter 10).

An online version of the index to a book originally printed in 1878 can be found at gdl.cdlr.strath.ac.uk/smihou/smihouindexes.html. Page numbers have been replaced by hyperlinks, representing the way in which the book has been broken up into chapter-length files on a website.

E-books can be more readily updated and produced in different formats if embedded indexing is used. The second edition of our book *Website indexing* (Browne and Jermey 2004) is available for sale as an e-book in PDF format. We are considering embedding the index when we next update the book so that we can:

- make amendments to the text that change the pagination, without affecting the index
- present the book in different formats, e.g. A4 and A5 size
- provide live links from the index to the text.

Free-text searching of e-books is improved by the use of passage level indexing, a type of partitioning applied to full-text documents, which reduces spurious relationships and improves retrieval (Lancaster 2003: 190). Williams (1998) reports improved precision with a moderate decline in recall when full-text searches used 500-word overlapping window passages from the Computer Science Technical Reports collection of the New Zealand Digital Library (NZDL). Another project found improved access through e-book indexes that reorganised conceptually – that is, when the search was done, a subset of the index that was considered relevant to the search was presented to the user on one page, allowing them to browse all headings and subheadings from the index that had fitted the search criteria (Chi *et al.* 2004).

Some mobile phones now include e-book functions. While this may increase the use of e-books, it is hard to picture indexes playing a major role in information access on such small screens, although it is also difficult to picture effective full-text search.

Encyclopedias and other multivolume works

Printed encyclopedias usually include comprehensive indexes, either as a separate volume or included in the final volume. Electronic encyclopedias, including those on CD-ROM (see above), are sometimes structured with the view that browsing and searching can replace indexing. Well-structured browsing through broad categories can make for a pleasant afternoon's exploration, but does not always lead users to the specific information they are seeking.

Encyclopedia topic titles should all be indexed, reworded as necessary, often with a bold-face locator to indicate a major entry. It is handy to have a list of all of the topics even if all of the chapters are not yet ready for indexing, as this can help establish the structure of the index. The main topics can then be supplemented with specific entries from the text. There is a good discussion of encyclopedia indexing in *Facing the text* (Stauber 2004).

Encyclopedia indexing is different to typical book indexing because:

- The works are usually large, requiring many months' work by one indexer, or work by a number of indexers. The indexers have to remember (and document) a lot of decisions over a long period of time.
- The works are usually large, requiring complex locators. These include volume numbers (*III:217* for page 217 of Volume III) and occasionally the position within a page (*277b* for the bottom left of page 277).
- Separate indexes of names, subjects and places may be created.
- Encyclopedias are flat structures that deal with isolated topics one at a time, rather than in the context of a developing argument. Thus a lot of text is repeated to some extent throughout, and indexers have to be able to select the most all-encompassing discussion of each topic. Barbara Preschel, quoted in Lancaster (2003: 17–18) recommends for indexers of the *Funk & Wagnells Encyclopedia*: 'All textual information of a substantive nature should be indexed. "Substantive" is here defined as information that covers 8–10 text lines *or* that is *unique* or *outstanding* and will almost certainly not occur elsewhere in the encyclopedia.'
- It may require use of a thesaurus if more than one person is involved.

Wikipedia is a web-based, open-source multilingual encyclopedia (en.wikipedia.org). Anyone who registers can contribute to it and edit it. It does not have one alphabetical index, but various structural features enhance access to information. These include lists of broad categories (a type of high-level index) and links from terms to synonyms or alternative word forms (e.g., singular to plural). There are 'disambiguation' pages for homographs such as *Quetzal*, which is a bird, the Guatemalan currency and a computer file format. It also has numerous cross-references and internal links that lead to related topics, thus providing an alternative to the search system.

Team indexing

Encyclopedia and other multivolume indexes often require teamwork, or the consolidation of index terms created by a number of indexers over a period of time. When indexes are being consolidated, policies need to be decided about the source of terms, and the degree to which the consolidated index will be edited for consistency. When teams of indexers work on a project, standards need to be set for software, concepts to be included, and terms to be applied.

For team indexing to be effective, guidelines must be set and indexers trained in the requirements of the project. These may need to be expanded as specific issues are raised. Someone needs to take an overall role as project coordinator and quality controller, and this role needs to be budgeted for. Guidelines should cover:

- **The scope**: Whether, for instance, titles, names and places are indexed. If you are creating separate indexes you can gather entries for each index in a separate pass.
- **Non-text material**: Whether and how figures, maps and tables are to be indexed.
- **The level of indexing**: The number of entries per page, definitions of what makes something indexable, and so on.
- **The style of entries**: The specificity of entry, use of inversion, use of plural forms and so on.
- The **language** to be used.

Indexing work from all contributors should be combined and edited regularly to check for problems and inconsistencies. These may arise from alternative forms, spellings, abbreviations, and synonyms. It is usually easier to sort these out towards the beginning of the project.

At the simplest level, many projects use the index in progress as the controlled vocabulary. This can work reasonably well if it is kept up-to-date and if decisions have been made consistently. Large, long-term projects may take a formal approach to language control with the creation of a simple thesaurus. The thesaurus structure can be created ahead of time if the topic titles and chapter headings are known before indexing starts.

The project coordinator has to make sure that everyone is using compatible software. Even systems that should be compatible may have some problems that need to be ironed out; for instance, when transferring data from SKY Index to CINDEX we found we had to use 'dumb' quotation marks instead of inverted commas. A standard software template with all style requirements (such as style for locator ranges, filing order) should be set up and shared.

The memory of each indexer about decisions they have made has to be captured as well as possible and communicated to the other indexers. A mailing list for discussion of specific questions can be useful, as can memos by the project leader about major decisions.

Indexers should create cross-references when they think of them, either adding them to the index they are creating or to a separate subject list. These have to be checked and coordinated by the project leader, who also decides when to use *see* references and when to use double entry. Indexers should always use *see* references before the editing stage to avoid omitting locators at one synonym.

When consolidating contributions from a number of indexers the coordinator should check the individual parts before combining them. This includes spell checking, checking for completeness (no range of pages missing) and spot checks for accuracy. The files can then be combined and edited.

Editing time is significantly more than for a single-indexer project and could easily account for over 50% of the project time. Editing is easier if indexers create subheadings for all entries to save the editor from having to go back to the text for detail; these can then be shortened or omitted during the editing process if necessary.

The 'grouping' feature of indexing software can find topics spread throughout the index. One person might have used the term *soft toys*, another *plush toys*, another *stuffed toys*, another *toys, fabric* and another *fabric: toys made from*. By searching on *toys* you will find all these entries and can combine them as necessary. This feature is often used by indexers editing their own work, but is far more important when you do not know what terms other indexers have used. See also *Indexers*: *Working for employers* in Chapter 1.

Fiction

Indexes are created for fictional works for a number of reasons. For example, Thomas Mallon of the *New York Times* has said: 'I would be grateful for an index to *The Forsyte Saga* that listed, say, "determinism," in order that I might spare myself Galsworthy's grumblings upon the theme.'

As an indexer you are unlikely to be commissioned to produce an index to fiction, but it might make a nice addition to your portfolio. Hazel Bell (1992) has written on the indexability of serious fiction. There are a number of fiction indexes on the web including those by Mary Ann Chulick to a series of detective stories (www.levtechinc.com/Milan/Milan.htm), the Index to Literary Allusions in Jane Austen's Writing (www.pemberley.com/janeinfo/litallus.html), Encyclopaedia of Spells in Harry Potter (www.hp-lexicon.org/magic/spells/spells.html), the index of words in Joyce's *Finnegans Wake* (www.caitlain.com/fw) and a number of links at Tom Murphy's site (www.brtom.org/ind.html).

Agatha Christie kept 'plotting books' in which she planned her heinous crimes. At one stage she tried indexing them, but found it too difficult as notes for several stories were intertwined, and ideas for one book might be found spread through six different notebooks (Morgan 1985). See also the discussion of Dragon indexes in *Journals and magazines*, below and fiction collections under *Library collections*, below.

Genealogical and local history materials

Genealogical and local history indexes allow users to look up people's names and find information about the people and their family relationships. They often eliminate the need to access the source materials (e.g., cemetery inscriptions), thus saving time and helping to preserve the original materials. Local history indexes include places, buildings and events in addition to names.

Genealogical indexes are usually after-the-fact indexing projects, often done by volunteers through family history organisations. Few of the sources are in electronic format. There is a big demand for the results, but not much money to be made. Diane Jarvie (1998) described the establishment of a project for the indexing of school records in an article titled 'Is there an easy way to embark on an indexing project?' The answer appears to be no.

Genealogical sources that can be indexed include burial records, censuses, hospital records, monumental inscriptions, school admission registers, shipping indexes, newspapers and land records. Accuracy of transcription is essential, but can be difficult when old handwriting is unclear (Hicks 2005). The work may be initially written on cards and typed up later, especially if the indexers have to travel to view the records.

While most genealogical indexing is collection indexing, local and family history books are also an important source of information. In these nearly every name is indexed, no matter how little information is provided about the person. Research may be needed to determine some names and to clarify the relationships between people. The Geelong and District Book Indexing Project aims to provide wide access to local information through a volunteer-produced consolidated book index of the Geelong area (www.zades.com.au/geelong/gdbooks.htm). See also *Newspapers* and *Records and archives*, below.

Geographic materials

Indexes are created for maps, atlases, street directories and other cartographic materials, often by indexers with special skills or backgrounds in cartography or geography, using specialised software programs which can create indexes with geographic coordinates included. Jim Irvine (2005) has discussed HarperCollins' automated approach to atlas indexing.

Indexes to books on geographic topics may include place names, topics, historical details, and artistic features. Geographic indexes include many homographs which have to be qualified by the name of a larger place, for example, *Johannesburg (Kern County, California)* and *Johannesburg (Gauteng, South Africa)*. Individual maps in books and periodicals are also indexed, often with *map* as a subheading.

Indexes with a geographic component can be presented graphically. For example, in the index to Aboriginal languages in Western Australia you click on the part of the map indicating the area you are interested in (coombs.anu.edu.au/ WWWVLPages/AborigPages/LANG/WA/section1.htm#1.4). Access via the map is complemented by alphabetical indexes. See also *Geographic names* in Chapter 4.

Handbooks and manuals

This section covers various types of technical documentation and reports, including owners' manuals and operating instructions, service manuals for technicians, software and hardware manuals, standards, rules and regulations, catalogues and reports of corporations. Manuals that are packaged with appliances and equipment are used by many people, while technical and financial reports may have a limited audience. Terminology may vary depending on who has written each section, and in some cases there may not yet be words for all the actions performed. Wellisch (1995) points out that the operation of 'downloading' was being described before the word *download* was invented.

Manuals often use embedded indexing, as writing and rewriting continue after indexing has started, and revised versions are issued frequently. Manuals may use section or paragraph numbers instead of page numbers. Multiple indexes may be needed for equipment parts, software commands, symbols and so on.

Manuals produced on a tight budget or strict deadline often include automated indexes based solely on section headings. The quality of these indexes depends on the headings themselves, but they are usually poor. Larry Bonura (1994) and Max McMaster and Sue Woolley (2004) have written books on indexing aimed at technical writers. See also *Online help* and *Textbooks*, below.

How-to books
Indexes to how-to books have to provide access to specific task-oriented information – answers to questions, rather than information for its own sake – and make it directly available. It can be difficult to do this in the available space, and indexers may have to decide between providing more access points or better subdivisions for a smaller number of access points. Subject matter expertise still matters in apparently simple topics. Nan Badgett (2004) says 'Easy-to-read does not necessarily mean easy-to-index', and gives the example of a sewing index in which the indexer had confused *facing* and *interfacing*.

Computer books
High-tech companies such as those publishing computing books often pay better than traditional publishers, especially for embedded indexes. They usually also have stricter deadlines than other indexes. Some features of computer indexing noted by Lynn Moncrief (2000) are:

- direct contact with authors, usually technical writers
- no space limits
- indexing as documents are being written, requiring rework if content changes
- embedded indexes.

Content that requires indexing includes procedural information, GUI components, blocks of program code, tutorials and warnings. The index is often consulted by someone who has encountered difficulty with a program, but who has not read the whole book. The index therefore needs a wide range of entry points from the point of view of someone performing a task with the program, rather than just wanting general information about the program.

Computer books often have 'boilerplate' repetitions of chunks of text, which may be indexed each time they occur to preserve the context. Entries are often gerunds such as *formatting*. Acronyms are double posted unless they are used only in acronym form (e.g., *RAM*). Ideas for terms can be gleaned from competitors' documents, support hotline logs, and using the product yourself.

Cookbooks

Cookbooks can be easy to index because they contain familiar information and each topic has an obvious starting and stopping point. Nonetheless, important decisions must be made:

- categories to include: styles of cooking, main ingredients
- wording of entries: some indexers derive their index terms from recipe titles, while others reword them
- specificity of entries: *pasta*, or *linguini*, *macaroni*, *tagliatelle* and so on
- prioritising entries to fit in the available space.

Illustrations are normally indicated by an italic or bold locator, but when all the recipes are illustrated this is not necessary. Some cookbooks code special information within the index entries; for example, *eggplant lasagne (v)* indicates a vegetarian recipe and *rice cookies (gf)* indicates gluten free. This may be done as a shorter alternative to the creation of headings for these categories. The code should be explained in a note at the beginning of the index.

Cookbook indexers are eloquent about their art, and there are useful articles at the ASI Culinary Indexing SIG (www.culinaryindexing.org). The Cooks' Thesaurus (foodsubs.com) provides information on ingredients, their synonyms and their substitutes, for example, *black pasta* as a synonym of *squid-ink pasta* and *pasta nera*.

Images

Image indexing is important for historical, commercial and private collections. Images can also be important components of books and sometimes of periodicals.

The use of specific locators for figures in books is discussed under *Locators* in Chapter 7.

Image indexing has traditionally used general library and indexing techniques to provide word-based indexes for images, including entries for artist or photographer, medium, dimensions, period (e.g., baroque), and genre (e.g., landscape). A library subject heading may simply describe the milieu of the artist, for example, *Women Artists – Aboriginal Australian – Northern Territory – Tiwi Islands*. When indexing subjects, concrete terms are usually preferred to abstract terms – *weddings* rather than *marriage*.

This indexing has focused on what is explicitly shown in the image, known as the denotative level. A greater challenge is to index the implied meaning of the image, known as the connotative level. This is covered in *Multimedia (audiovisual) materials*, below. In an unusual instance of image indexing, Pro Hart used to place a DNA sample from his cheek cells in his paintings and record the exact position, along with the title of the work and the rightful owner, in a database (28 March 2006 www.news.com.au/story/0,10117,18629738–421,00.html). In theory this could be used as evidence in forgery cases.

Image databases on the web

There are many image databases on the web – a varied selection is introduced here.

Picture Australia (www.pictureaustralia.org) harvests images and metadata using OAI-PMH (Chapter 2). In early 2006 it collected images of Australia Day celebrations through the photo-sharing site Flickr (www.flickr.com).

The Centre for the Study of Cartoons and Caricature, University of Kent at Canterbury (library.kent.ac.uk/cartoons) offers a search facility with detailed indexing as well as transcription of all words within the cartoons.

Kids Click (www.kidsclick.org/ssearch.html) links to Picture Search Tools and to Sound Search Tools, which links to recordings of speeches, birdsong, and so on.

Getty Images (www.gettyimages.com) (not to be confused with the Getty Foundation) is an image database. It is indexed by:

- **Subject**: Keywords include nouns (*sky*), adjectives (*rusty*), verbs (*throw*), age groups (*elderly adult*), and locations, at different levels (*Left Bank, Paris, France, Europe*). These equate to the 'primary' or 'natural' subjects described in *Multimedia (audiovisual) materials*, below.
- **Style**: Keywords describe the image attributes as graphic elements. These include image orientation (*vertical*), colour (*sepia*), and other style keywords (*close-up, long shot, aerial, blur, soft focus, montage, cut out, digitally generated, three-quarter length, long exposure*).
- **Concept**: Keywords describe an overall idea generated by the image (*success, challenge, teamwork*). Images are also assigned broad subjects (*lifestyles, technology*). These equate to the 'intrinsic meaning or content' described in *Multimedia (audiovisual) materials*, below.

General Motors Media Archives project (Schroeder 1998) is an example of an internal company indexing project. Indexing covers subject (*1935 Chevrolet truck*) and style (*glamour, engineering testing*) as well as concept, which identifies what is unique or informative about the image. Kimberley Schroeder gives the example of a photo of the construction of General Motors' corporate headquarters in which horses were hauling the raw materials – trucks did not yet have the capacity to supply the materials for the headquarters of the world's biggest vehicle maker!

Thesauruses for image indexing

Thesauruses used for multimedia indexing include:

- Australian Pictorial Thesaurus, www.picturethesaurus.gov.au
- Thesaurus for Graphic Materials I: Subject Terms, www.loc.gov/rr/print/tgm1
- Thesaurus for Graphic Materials II: genre and physical characteristic terms, www.loc.gov/rr/print/tgm2 (examples of terms are *allegorical drawings* and *metalpoint drawings*)
- *Art and architecture thesaurus online*, from the Getty Foundation (www.getty.edu/research/conducting_research/vocabularies/aat), which is used for indexing, searching, and research in art, architecture, decorative arts, material culture and archival materials
- English Heritage's *Illustrated Thesaurus*, hitite.adlibsoft.com/intro.html, which includes ancient and historical monument terms, with sample photographs.

Content-based image retrieval (automated image retrieval)

Image search engines have been developed by commercial enterprises and research institutes. They retrieve images either by keywords, allocated as described above, or by features such as colour, texture and simple shape properties that can be automatically extracted from the images. This is known as content-based image retrieval. Automatic face recognition is one example. As yet, computer object-recognition systems can adequately handle only specific objects such as industrial parts that can be represented by precise geometric models, so human indexers are still required (www.cs.washington.edu/research/imagedatabase).

The ARTISTE project (www.cultivate-int.org/issue7/artiste) funded by the European Commission, translates metadata it finds into Dublin Core. It also uses content-based image retrieval techniques to analyse features such as colour and texture, and combines these with the textual metadata.

The Automatic Linguistic Indexing of Pictures website (wang.ist.psu.edu/IMAGE/alip.html) provides random samples of images with both human and computer-generated indexing terms. The program allocated the terms *ballet, doll, monument, indoor* and *plane* to two people wearing motorbike helmets in a ski-mobile, so there is something left that needs the application of human intellect! Nonetheless, the automatic indexing generates many useful entries.

Image-creation packages such as digital cameras attach their own metadata, including format and resolution information, to images. New software preserves the metadata attached to images when they are imported into other databases.

Web-wide image search engines

Google image search uses the text adjacent to images, filenames, link strings and ALT tags (the text labels that display when a mouse hovers over an image) to allow text searching, but also analyses properties such as colour. Research by Craven (2006) has found that many webpages contained images that did not have ALT tags, or had null ALT tags (with no content). Presumably they would be unlikely to be retrieved by search engines such as Google.

Information architecture

Information architecture (IA) involves the structuring of information in intranets and websites, primarily by the provision of useful categories for browsing. Clear labelling of webpages is crucial. IA is in many ways an extension of traditional library approaches. It uses categorisation (classification), indexing, cataloguing (metadata creation) and thesaurus (or taxonomy) creation skills, alongside new tools and processes such as wireframes and card sorting (e.g., using MindCanvas, www.themindcanvas.com). James Kalbach (2003) has compared the practice of information architecture and librarianship. Good sources of information on IA are iawiki.net and www.boxesandarrows.com. See also *Collection indexes: Metadata* in Chapter 5, *Taxonomies* in Chapter 6 and *Intranets and CMSs* below.

Intranets and CMSs

Content management systems (CMSs) create, modify, archive and remove information resources from organised repositories, usually websites (see below) and intranets. They include tools for publishing, format management, revision control, versioning, indexing, search and retrieval. They often include templates for the creation of certain types of information, such as procedures or forms. They can allow authorised people throughout an organisation to create content, rather than having a centralised documentation department. They may provide access to legacy data (pre-existing content in various formats) with varying degrees of structure.

In intranets information is accessed through the information architecture (browse hierarchy, see above), which may use a taxonomy (Chapter 6); and through search, which may rely on metadata (Chapter 5) and free-text terms. Social information sharing is also important (see *Knowledge management*, below).

Victor Lombardi (2004) has surveyed the problems people encountered when implementing content management systems. Apart from hardware and software, the four top problems were:

- migrating old content
- training authors and editors
- determining requirements
- structuring metadata.

Intranet projects that rely on decentralised contributions of content impose demands for writing and indexing on people who may not consider writing to be a part of their job. When content authors are expected to create metadata as well, they need to be trained in the principles of indexing, and their work has to be edited. Provision of pick-lists of approved terms and searchable thesauruses ensures more consistent metadata.

Folksonomies have been used in the corporate world to enable all staff to contribute terms according to their natural language and interpretations. These terms are then either mapped to thesaurus terms by metadata editors, or supplemented by other terms as needed (see *Websites*: *Collaborative tagging and folksonomies*, below). Yet other systems rely on automatic metadata creation and categorisation (see *Taxonomies*: *Automated categorisation and taxonomy generation* in Chapter 6).

When creating metadata for CMSs, indexers have to consider the use of the metadata by the search engine, as well as the quality of the metadata itself. Relevance ranking can be weighted to rely on a mixture of terms from titles, descriptions (abstracts), metadata keywords and free-text terms, and hit highlighting can emphasise search terms within result sets. A synonym list can ensure that a search for any one of a group of synonyms retrieves content containing any of those synonyms.

Clients may also have different priorities for the indexing, including: pure information access; personalisation, offering different content to different users; customisation, allowing users to adapt their view of the site for their needs; and branding, focusing on the image of the company that the site gives. In most cases information on recent developments is most sought for, so timing is crucial – it is no use indexing the announcement on bonus payments three weeks after it appears.

An intranet indexer normally cannot index everything fully, so must give special attention to the areas identified as most important to the company's goals. Sometimes the direct client and the ultimate client of the indexer are different, so good communication and written documentation are essential.

With an intranet, indexers can get to know the users to an extent not possible with a website; they can have both informal discussions and structured focus groups. The indexer can also examine search logs, the records of searches people have attempted, in order to identify popular searches and those which resulted in no hits.

Indexers working on intranets rely on team members for support in implementing technical requirements for metadata creation and search. They often have to tweak and evaluate systems until they are working optimally. Quotes for metadata work have to take into account the time that is spent in meetings and in seeking and incorporating feedback.

Fred Leise (2004) has written on metadata and content management systems. The StepTwo website provides a range of articles relating to knowledge and content management issues, including metrics to evaluate achievements (Robertson 2003). The Intranet Review Toolkit (www.intranetreviewtoolkit.org) includes heuristics (design principles) for assessing the quality of intranet projects.

Journals and magazines

Journal indexing differs from book indexing in several ways. Firstly, the index usually provides access only to the article, not to a smaller unit like a page, paragraph or sentence. Secondly, the content is usually by many authors, and there are a number of content types (e.g., news, articles, book reviews). Thirdly, the index accumulates over time; often the hardest part of journal indexing is smoothly integrating a new year's index into the existing accumulation. Finally, there are often author indexes or combined indexes including authors and subjects, and sometimes article titles.

The subject index usually identifies articles by main subjects only. Review-type journals are an exception, and are often released as monographs (stand-alone books) and journal issues at the same time. Subheadings of topics may be coined for the index, or may be the title of the article. Author indexes contain entries for first-cited authors with full citation details. They may include secondary authors either with a reference to the first author, or with citation details duplicated. Sometimes authors named fourth or later are omitted altogether (see *Collection indexing*: *Multiple authors in periodical indexing* in Chapter 3).

The content that is indexed depends on the nature of the publication and the reason for indexing. Some magazines are indexed selectively – for example, only recipes in a house and lifestyle magazine. Most indexes exclude advertising material – often ads from the front of a journal are removed before it is bound into yearly volumes. When magazines are indexed for historical reasons, parts of the publication such as advertisements are more likely to be included, as they offer information about the period.

Payment for journal indexing may be per hour, per article, or per issue. Per hour means that the length and content of each issue will not affect income, but also that earnings do not go up as you get faster. Per article is fair if all articles are roughly the same, but does not work when there are various types of content to be indexed. Per issue works well if issues are all roughly the same length, or if the rate has been worked out for an average length.

Retrospective indexing of old periodicals encounters problems of:

- incomplete sets
- poor quality paper or microfilm
- misspellings
- name inconsistencies

- outdated terminology (*wireless* for *radio*) and euphemisms
- difficulties with assigning authorship of articles

Language evolution affects choice of terms and cross-references. The *Women's Thesaurus* (ed. Mary ES Capek) was used for indexing *The Dawn: a journal for the household. Edited, printed and published by women* (Lee 1998).

Archival periodicals are important to many organisations, including colleges and schools. Alan Walker (2000a) discusses the problems with indexing names in school magazines. These include seniority numbering: when there were thirteen Cohens in the school they were named *Cohen 1*, *Cohen 2*, etc., instead of by forenames. When one Cohen left the school, the numbers of the others all moved up one. Other problems are reversals and pig-Latin terms: *Nehoc Sudnuces* for *Cohen Secundus* for *Cohen 2*.

Enthusiast indexes are created for a number of hobby-type magazines. There are quite a few indexes to *Dragon* and *Dungeon* magazines on the web (search 'Dragon index' to find them). It is interesting to see the different approaches that have been taken. Our son (Bill Browne, 2004, pers. comm.) indexed his magazines by 'prestige classes' and 'feats' – we would have used 'author' and 'title'. It is interesting that he capitalised all words and inverted the headings – something most professional indexers assume we should not do, but users seem comfortable with:

> Feat, General
>   Avoid Critical Hit
>   Dex 13+, Dodge, Skill Focus (Tumble), BAB +8 or more, ranks in Tumble, 292:114
> Feat, Kaiju
>   Battle Roar, 289:70
>   Improved Trample, 289:70

Carolyn Weaver (2002) has written a thorough overview of journal indexing. See also *Collection indexing* in Chapter 3 and *Newspapers*, below.

Knowledge management

Knowledge management (KM) captures and stores the knowledge an organisation holds and transfers it to those in the organisation who need it. It specifically includes tacit knowledge – knowledge that is held by individuals which has not been explicitly recorded, and is often considered impossible to record usefully. One part of knowledge management therefore involves connecting people to experts within an organisation.

The broad role of knowledge management includes issues to do with organisational culture, motivating people to share information, and setting up systems to make sharing easy, as well as mapping explicit and tacit sources of information within the organisation. It takes a 'whole of organisation' approach, requiring investment in support schemes, communities-of-practice (groups that form to share experiences about a discipline or problem), collaborative reward schemes, and so on.

The key technologies for knowledge management are online databases, document management systems and groupware (e.g., Lotus Notes), with corporate intranets (see *Intranets and CMSs*, above) the fastest-growing area. Information literacy is another key issue, and corporations need to teach employees to find and use information efficiently.

The role of knowledge manager has a narrower aspect, which includes synthesising and communicating information; it could be called knowledge integration. This role can be taken on by a technical writer, journalist, librarian or indexer. One specific task in knowledge management is the development of an online, organisation-wide thesaurus (see Chapter 6), which can be used for retrieval from knowledge repositories based on browsers and Lotus Notes.

Legal publications

It is likewise to be observed that this society [of lawyers] hath a particular chant and jargon of their own, that no other mortal can understand, and wherein all their laws are written, which they take special care to multiply.

Jonathan Swift, *Gulliver's travels*

Legal indexing includes bills, statutes, texts and case law. The documents and their indexing requirements can be complex, and the language is specialised. This is an area in which you probably should not work unless you have experience, or an editor or indexing colleague who will provide guidance.

Precise legal terminology is important; formal terms must be used exactly as given without paraphrasing or inversion, for example, *survival of actions, case at first instance* and *injurious falsehood* (which you would not index as *nasty lies*). Many of the words are derived from Latin and French (*ultra vires, in re, estoppel*). Legal definitions are important and may be gathered under a term such as *definitions*.

Other issues in legal indexing are:

- **Specialist indexes:** In addition to author and subject indexes, there may be tables of cases and tables of statutes, which are sometimes tagged and generated automatically. Even when these are simple lists of cases and legislation cited, they may require some special knowledge in the inversion and wording of entries.
- **Deep structure:** There may be many levels of classified entries.
- **Different user needs:** Judgement is needed to assess indexable concepts and entry points.

- **Special formats** such as looseleaf services: These require regular updating of text and index. Indexes to new content are provided as separate supplementary indexes until there is enough to warrant a consolidated index that merges old and new entries (see below).
- **Funding**: Subscribers to many legal services are charged on a per page basis, and indexing costs must relate to the budget based on expected sales for the pages of the index.
- **Specialist layout**: Bold-face may be used for main headings because the sub-headings may run for a number of columns. All locators may have to be attached to subheadings, with none attached directly to main headings.
- **Size**: Many legal publications are very large, although when someone talks about a 145-pound legal text they mean price not weight.

Reports of Royal Commissions and Inquiries, particularly long ones, are often indexed. See for example the indexes to the NSW Law Reform Commission reports (www.lawlink.nsw.gov.au/lawlink/lrc/ll_lrc.nsf/pages/LRC_reports).

Library collections

Library cataloguing involves:

- **Descriptive cataloguing**: Provides publication details such as author, title, publisher, pagination.
- **Subject cataloguing**: Provides terms for subject searching.
- **Classification**: Provides a broad subject grouping. Normally it is used to decide the order of items on the shelf, with similar subjects shelved close together.

Subject cataloguing is a form of subject indexing in its broadest sense, and shares many features with museum cataloguing and bibliographic database indexing. It is a major financial commitment: the Library of Congress spends $44 million a year on cataloguing (Marcum 2005).

Libraries generally use a controlled vocabulary from which most or all subject indexing terms must be selected, and a name authority list to ensure consistent formatting of proper nouns (names of people and organisations). Library cataloguing is at one extreme with respect to granularity of indexing. An indexer may create more index entries per page than a cataloguer does per book. Library catalogues may be enhanced by the inclusion of tables of contents and sometimes indexes, which provide access at a more granular level. Many library catalogues are now available through the web, either directly through their own websites or through links from Google searches to collections such as OCLC WorldCat and Libraries Australia.

Online catalogues have typically reproduced the information from card catalogues while allowing improved searching. The NCSU libraries have experimented with a new approach, using a faceted classification and Endeca software to provide enhanced browsing (www2.lib.ncsu.edu/catalog). Users can narrow results by selecting facets such as topic, format, genre, region, time, language and author from the left-hand side of the search screen. See also *Digital libraries*, above.

Fiction collections

Cataloguing works of fiction in library collections is important to give access to these items for literary scholarship and also for general readers. Collection indexing of fiction can cover:

- subject matter, e.g., horses
- readership, e.g., five- to ten-year-old boys
- frame, including time, place, and social environment
- author's intent or attitude.

Pattern matching allows people to find something similar to a book they have liked. Public libraries have traditionally done this by publishing lists of recommended books. Amazon.com does it automatically by letting searchers know the titles of other books that were chosen by people who bought the current book, and Library Thing (www.librarything.com) does it by enabling users to enter details of books with the keywords that describe them.

Names of people and places in library catalogues include a qualifier to indicate that they are fictional, for example, *Baggins, Frodo (fictitious character)* and *Middle Earth (imaginary place)*.

Interoperability

Q: How many cataloguers does it take to change a lightbulb?
A: Only one, but they have to wait to see how the Library of Congress did it.

Library catalogues are an extraordinary achievement in terms of teamwork. As the riddle above suggests, a large part of library cataloguing involves consistency with the practice in other libraries. Most libraries use copy cataloguing rather than original cataloguing where possible. This can involve adding a holdings statement (a note giving the location of the item in a specific library) to a pre-existing record in a shared database, or can involve downloading a record and adding it to a local catalogue.

Because so many libraries have to catalogue the same books, cataloguing rules and approaches have been developed by national and international bodies. With the exception of subjects of national interest, it is likely that cataloguers in New Zealand, South Africa and Scotland will use the same subject headings for the items they catalogue. For general subject headings, the most widely used tool is *Library of Congress Subject Headings (LCSH)*, while specialist libraries use other tools such as *MeSH (Medical Subject Headings)*. FAST (Faceted Application of Subject Terminology, www.oclc.org/research/projects/fast) is a faceted version of *LCSH* with simpler syntax for use in an online environment.

The two main classification schemes used worldwide are the Library of Congress Classification and the Dewey Decimal Classification; the latter is used in most Australian libraries. Specialist libraries may use specialist schemes. The Scorpion project at OCLC has experimented with the automatic application of Dewey Decimal Classification numbers to web-accessible text documents (www.oclc.org/research/software/scorpion/default.htm).

For descriptive cataloguing (bibliographic description or citations of publication details) most libraries use the *Anglo-American Cataloguing Rules* (*AACR2*). Most of the rules we use for indexing names have been derived from *AACR2*. The IFLA Section on Cataloguing has recognised the need for an international authority file to link authority records for personal names from the world's national bibliographic agencies, and OCLC is currently working on a pilot project with a German agency (O'Neill 2005). If successful, the project will be expanded to include corporate and geographic names, and records from abstracting and indexing services, archives, museums and publishers. Development of *AACR3*, incorporating major changes, is under way (www.collectionscanada.ca/jsc/index.html).

MARC (MAchine Readable Cataloging, ISO 2709, www.loc.gov/marc) is a communications standard for the exchange of bibliographic and other data between libraries. MARC tags identify the content that can be searched and the format used for display in online catalogues. To see MARC format, search for an item in the Macquarie University library catalogue (www.lib.mq.edu.au), click on the title, then click on 'Staff View'.

Federated search (cross-database searching) of library catalogues is possible using standardised protocols, such as ANSI/NISO Z39.50. These allow a user in one system to retrieve information from other computer systems without knowing the search syntax that is used by those other systems. The libraries searchable through the Library of Congress Gateway to Library Catalogs (www.loc.gov/z3950) comply with Z39.50. This protocol is being updated in a group of initiatives known as ZING – Z39.50 International: Next Generation (www.loc.gov/z3950/agency/zing).

The University of California Libraries has published a report (Bibliographic Services Task Force 2005) that suggests alternatives to the creation of standard cataloguing data for all library items.

An important development in bibliographic description has been the **Functional Requirements for Bibliographic Records (FRBR)**, a system for modelling bibliographic information associated with books, recordings and museum objects. This approach defines a resource as:

- **a work**: a distinct intellectual or artistic creation, such as *The Bible*
- **an expression**: an intellectual or artistic realisation of a work, such as *Good News for Modern Man*, a modern version of the Bible
- **a manifestation**: a physical embodiment of an expression of a work, such as hardback edition

- **an item**: a single exemplar of a manifestation, such as specific copy of hardback edition.

The common bibliographic elements of different expressions of a work can be catalogued once at the work level, and refined with additional fields that apply at the expression, manifestation and item levels. *AACR3 (Anglo–American Cataloguing Rules)* will use the FRBR data model.

AustLit, an online bibliography of Australian literature and literary criticism, was the first large-scale implementation of the FRBR model (www.austlit.edu.au/about/metadata.xml).

Looseleaf services

Looseleaf formats have traditionally been used for publications that require constant updating, particularly in law and accountancy, but also medicine, pharmacy, human resources, software, training manuals, directories and catalogues. The publications are kept in ring binders, and at regular intervals updates are sent out, with instructions for removing out-of-date pages from the existing publication. Most looseleaf services use paragraph numbering (*12.3.6.1*) for indexing, and flexible page numbering (e.g., chapter by chapter) to allow for the addition and removal of content.

Indexing looseleaf publications is tricky because although parts of the content change most of it stays the same, so a whole new index is not warranted. The solution is to create supplementary indexes for the new material issue by issue. When there is enough content in the supplementary indexes, a consolidated version, incorporating old and new entries, is published. It is only then that the entries for content that has been removed are removed from the index. A Dutch company has created WinGarb software to make the updating of looseleaf indexes more efficient.

When indexing looseleaf services you should be provided with redlines – files showing the original text and the changes that have been made. This is easier than trying to compare two versions and work out what is different.

Multimedia (audiovisual) materials

This section addresses general aspects of multimedia indexing in libraries, specialised databases and the web. The problems of indexing specific types of non-print materials are covered in this chapter under *Cartographic materials, CD-ROMs and DVDs, Images, Museum collections, Sound and music*, and *Video*.

Library indexing usually follows standard library rules, including bibliographic description following *AACR*, and sometimes specific thesauruses (see *Images*, above). Indexing collections of images, audio and video follows many of the general principles of indexing, although naming the topics is more complex when there is no textual description to rely on. Multimedia indexing is often done by people with subject knowledge rather than indexing knowledge, so training in indexing principles and quality control are particularly important.

Planning

The goals of multimedia indexing are to provide access to the information and to protect the materials. Quality indexing of vulnerable materials, especially the provision of digital copies for examination, can help preserve original materials, as they are not handled unless they have been selected. This is particularly important for old materials, such as glass negatives, which are very vulnerable. Indexing is also useful for research into items that are not stored locally.

Most museum and library catalogues index for the general community, while corporate databases may index for specific needs and uses. Organisations that sell images index them by all possible access points. Multimedia indexing may require special viewing equipment, and may depend on surrogates rather than the item itself. For example, the indexer may inspect music CD covers, first and last frames, or synopses, rather than listening to a CD or viewing a whole film.

Concept analysis and term selection

> Two experts, to explicate Meaning,
> Wrote a book called *The Meaning of Meaning*.
> But the world was perplexed
> So three experts wrote next
> *The Meaning of Meaning of Meaning*.
> Douglas Hofstadter*

Multimedia indexers provide publication details such as author or creator, title, publishing details, materials, and provenance, and they may have to create titles for unnamed works. The major challenge in multimedia indexing is identifying the meaning of a work. Erwin Panofsky (in Rafferty and Hidderley 2005: 13–15) identified three levels of meaning in images:

- **Primary or natural subject matter**, including factual and expressional subject matter. This is the generic level – e.g., a hard-working, studious child.
- **Secondary or conventional subject matter**: This is the specific level – a female figure may be Mother Teresa, and understanding it depends on cultural knowledge. This is called the iconographical level of art.
- **Intrinsic meaning or content**: This is the abstract, iconological, subjective, interpretative level. To analyse it the viewer uses information from the first two levels of meaning, along with information about the artist and the cultural background of production.

---

* When I e-mailed Douglas Hofstadter to ask permission to quote his limerick, he mentioned in his reply that a whole article in *The indexer* ('Marot, Hofstadter, index' v.21 n.1, 1998) had been devoted to his index to *Le Ton beau de Marot: in praise of the music of language*. Christine Shuttleworth had written: 'It may well be the most self-indulgent index ever published, but one can only admire its creator's industry as well as his inexhaustible exuberance and wit.'

The first two levels are denotative (that is, they denote, or show something). They are easier to identify than the third, although research may be needed. Indexing terms can include people, places, time periods, activities and events, and objects, as well as an overall description of the content (e.g., *landscape*). The third level is connotative (that is, it suggests a meaning but does not make it explicit). Interpretations will vary significantly, depending on the background of the viewer. It is possible to have a 'correct' name (perhaps with synonyms) for most items at the first two levels, but not at the third. For this reason Pauline Rafferty and Rob Hidderley (2005) have suggested using democratic indexing, in which viewers of an item can together construct the indexing for it.

The *Emotional dictionary* and *Emotional thesaurus* (www.writing.ws) are experiments that attempt to provide connotations for words as well as dictionary definitions. *Flamingo* and *Art Deco* have been identified as connonyms (synonyms through their connotations) because they both have underlying emotions of amusement and delight.

Web-wide multimedia search engines

Web-wide search engines such as AltaVista, Google and Yahoo provide audio, video and image search through individual tabs on the search page. MSN has image search but no audio or video. Dogpile is a metasearch engine that searches all of these. For a list of search engines with specific features see University at Albany webpage (www.internettutorials.net/choose.html). There are also specialist search engines such as Blinkx (www.blinkx.tv), which searches video and TV (especially news), and Singingfish (www.singingfish.com), which searches audio (including MP3 files) and video.

Museum collections

Museum cataloguing (indexing) has much in common with library cataloguing and multimedia indexing. Museum objects often do not have any accompanying text to describe them. Unless the curator has written a description, the cataloguer must write one and then allocate indexing terms. Information is recorded about the date of creation, source of the object, and function of the object. These elements fit well into the Dublin Core element set.

Museums are long-term collections that may have many cataloguers, so they need a thesaurus to organise the terms used for cataloguing. Because museum collections usually refer to items, rather than contexts, they often need more concrete terms than a general thesaurus. They may use the term *kitchen utensils* when a library catalogue might use *cooking*. Abstract terms such as *cooking* may be used to retrieve groups of objects, and should be included as related terms of the objects they are connected with. Museum indexing of old objects requires the use of terminology from the time of creation of the object.

The use of singular indexing terms is more common in museums than libraries, presumably because museums are cataloguing distinct items. They do not expect to have more than one penny-farthing bicycle, dress of Kylie Minogue's or stegosaurus fossil. Nonetheless, AS/NZS 999 (section 7.2.2.2) recommends the use of plural forms, and Leonard Will (1992) says that even if you only have one clock, the user's query is still 'What clocks do you have?'

Thesauruses used for museum indexing include the *Art and Architecture Thesaurus*, *Australian Pictorial Thesaurus*, and subject-specific thesauruses on topics such as railways and costume. *The Social History and Industrial Classification (SHIC)* published by MDA is a commonly used museum classification system in the United Kingdom (hilt.cdlr.strath.ac.uk/Reports/museumsreport.html). It groups objects under four primary headings: community life; domestic and family life; personal life; and working life. The MDA (previously Museum Documentation Association) also provides excellent fact sheets on indexing and cataloguing (www.mda.org.uk/catalog.htm; www.mda.org.uk/indexin.htm).

Collections Australia Network (CAN, incorporating AMOL, www.collectionsaustralia.net) searches more than 1500 museum, gallery, archive, and library catalogues throughout Australia. Herbariums, botanical gardens and zoos are also included in the site, making slightly strange bedfellows.

A Finnish group has developed a semantic web portal using seven domain ontologies (artefacts, materials, actors, situations, locations, times and collections) to allow multi-facet search. They transformed a thesaurus into an ontology using the (NT/BT) relationships as the basis (Hyvönen *et al.* 2005).

Naming artefacts

The local history museum in Mount Victoria, New South Wales, once had a machine at the front with a note asking people to identify it – we thought it looked like a taffy-maker, but it turned out to be a straw-stretcher used in hat-making. Military museums have similar problems, as there are many items that have precise names that are not generally known – for example, the average indexer may not know the distinction between *shot* and *shell*. Either an expert in the subject needs to be hired, or the indexer has to research the items. Similarly, when indexing images you may not know the names of either general or specific items (e.g., *ski-mobiles*, or *Sydney Harbour Bridge*). That is before you even grapple with the meaning of images, which is discussed in *Multimedia (audiovisual) materials*, above.

Newspapers

Newspaper indexes provide important leads to information about specific people, places and events, as well as general topics. A newspaper index can give a general idea of when an important event happened, so that users can then browse a limited section of a local newspaper.

When starting a newspaper indexing project you have to decide:

- **The newspaper(s)** to index and **the period**.
- **The source:** Some newspapers may be available only on microfilm.

- **The parts to be indexed**: You may exclude some material, such as advertisements and non-text items, or selectively index some material, such as editorials and letters.
- **The locators**: These can include title, source, date, edition, section, pages, column, and sometimes the length of the item (in column inches).
- **The indexing terms**: These need to be established and kept consistent.
- **Storage and access**: How will the content be stored and searched?

Headings are usually created for names of people, obituaries, places, local politics, sporting events, entertainment, major crime and social trends. Newspapers often change significantly over time, so an estimate of the work required should be based on samples from the period/s that will be indexed.

Barbara Semonche (2003) has written a thorough overview of newspaper indexing. Examples on the web include the indexes to *The Argus* (www.nla.gov.au/argus) and to the *Sydney Morning Herald* and related publications (www.sl.nsw.gov.au/infoquick/about.cfm). There are now many searchable full-text newspaper databases. Online news sources are automatically categorised by Google (news.google.com.au), so that a number of articles relating to the same topic can be retrieved together.

Often an organisation does not index a whole newspaper, but extracts articles of interest. For local history collections these include items on people and local events. For newspaper publishers they could include all substantial content. These were traditionally stored in vertical clippings files but now they are often held electronically, especially by the newspapers themselves. Vertical files are often organised using library-style headings, for example, *Music festivals – Blue Mountains*.

The problems of newspaper indexing are not all intellectual. Newspapers are bulky and need to be read on stands, while microfiche readers have to be placed near the computer used for data entry. The authors heard a talk by MP Govindaraj and HR Mohan (1995) on *The Hindu Index* database, based in Madras (now Chennai), which has been indexed since 1881. Our most vivid memory was one of the speakers throwing his hands up in dismay and saying 'But the dust . . . the dust!'

See also *Journals and magazines*, above.

Online help

Most major applications programs have an online help (applications help) system built in. This typically includes:

- **Contents**: The contents page lays out the major topics hierarchically in a more or less logical sequence.
- **Find**: A text-based search system searches for any word in the help documents.

- **Index**: The index is an alphabetical list of index terms (including subheadings) created by indexers. Users type in the first few letters of a keyword to jump to that location in the list.

Online help indexing may be done by professional indexers, by technical writers, or by a combination of these two. Even when an indexer is employed to create the index, other writers might maintain it.

Online help indexing is a form of embedded indexing, in which keywords and phrases that describe and give access to topics are 'embedded' or included within those topics. The indexer can only see the entries in context in the index when the project is built. Editorial changes are then made in the individual topics, and the index is built again.

Microsoft Office^{TM} programs use a compiled help system, where the help is created as a series of webpages and then compiled into a single file. Some software suppliers do not compile their help but keep the help system as a large set of HTML pages that can be accessed through any web browsing program. This makes it possible to prepare new help pages on the web which can then be incorporated seamlessly into the existing help system.

Estimating the time an online help index will take is difficult. One rule of thumb is to allow 10% to 15% of project resources for indexing: for example, twelve days for 300 topics.

Content needs to be analysed in the light of potential users' needs – these may be to complete tasks, to achieve goals, or to find conceptual information. Non-textual elements such as graphics, animation, video and sound should usually be indexed.

Many of the issues in the selection and wording of terms are the same as in other indexing projects. It is important to standardise style as much as possible before starting a project. Most normal style decisions have to be considered; in addition, punctuation at the beginning of terms is avoided as these symbols file before all letters; *PDF* is better than *.PDF* (that is, *dot PDF*). One of the most important issues is the form to be used for names of company products, which are often written inconsistently. A company style guide is useful if one exists.

As with all indexing you should consider alternative formats, including terms for novice and experienced users, acronyms and full terms, synonyms and competitors' terms. If double entry is used, the synonyms and alternative forms of terms should be noted to ensure that all topics requiring those terms are entered at all possible places. Alternatively, automatic methods of generating duplicate entries from a synonym table can be used. These save time and guarantee accuracy.

You may need to use more terms than you would for equivalent content in a book to make up for lack of browsing access. You may use both broader and narrower terms for the same topic. When the same index term has been used to index more than one page, the help system provides a 'disambiguator' box from which the user can select titles of interest – these titles offer another layer of information for topic selection. The size of the display window affects term choice – if the user can see only sixteen lines at a time and a topic has more than sixteen subheadings, the last ones may be missed. One way to avoid long lists of subheadings is to use more detailed main headings (e.g., *motorcycle accessories* rather than *motorcycles* with *accessories* as a subheading).

If possible, allow domain-specific indexing so that users can search just the relevant part of the index – for example, in an insurance company's help you could limit search to *Motor* or *Home* products as appropriate. This contrasts with book indexing, where one of the joys is the juxtaposition of content on the same topic from different areas of the book.

Online help can be context-sensitive, in which case the only information that is provided to a user is that which has been considered relevant to the user's location within the program. Many people are familiar with using the F1 button to access context-sensitive help.

Online help can be part of a single-sourcing documentation project. NRMA Insurance (a division of IAG) uses a proprietary authoring package based on SGML/XML that allows output in RTF, HTML and online help formats. The writing and indexing are done only once, but the information can be published in print form, on the web and in an online help system. The indexing is optimised for the online help version, which is the most important output format (Robertson 2001).

Future of online help indexing

Shane McRoberts from Microsoft said at a WritersUA (formerly WinWriters) conference that Longhorn Help will have no index feature as no-one uses them. Jan Wright (2005) pointed out at question time that no-one used Microsoft Help because 'Microsoft products had not exposed a real index for about five years in any of their mainstream products, and had therefore trained their users not to use an index.' McRoberts admitted that users of MSDN (the Microsoft Developers Network) used its index quite extensively. Gordon Meyer reported that Macintosh, on the other hand, is planning to introduce synonym rings in future help systems so users can fine-tune search. See also *Handbooks and manuals*, above.

Records and archives

Records are documents that have been generated as part of an organisation's day-to-day business. Their primary purpose is to provide evidence of, and information about, social and business activities. Record types include manual and electronic files of correspondence, sales documentation, financial documents, leaflets, e-mail and SMS messages and contracts.

Records management differs from librarianship in that its items tend to be originals, they fulfil legal requirements, and they are governed by a retention policy that determines their lifecycle from creation to disposal. Records may be made available to all staff within an organisation, or restricted to specific authorised users. Records management may use Electronic Document and Records

Management (EDRM) systems or Content Management Systems (see *Intranets and CMSs*, above). These work with central repositories of metadata, which identify when records are due for disposal, and what level of security is appropriate for them.

The indexing of records takes a functional approach, indexing primarily by originating group and function (purpose), rather than by subject. Whereas in a library catalogue the term *minutes* indicates a document about minutes, in records management it indicates documents that are minutes. Records are indexed using a keyword thesaurus (State Records NSW 2006):

- **Keywords**: Describe broad business functions and should reflect the organisational structure. Each keyword is followed by one activity descriptor.
- **Activity descriptors**: Describe business activities. Only keywords and activity descriptors that are linked in the thesaurus should be used together.
- **Subject (process) descriptors**: Describe subjects or topics that connect related business transactions. They are narrower terms than activity descriptors and give more details about the subject of the activities. Subject descriptors can be applied to any activity descriptor, and more than one can be used if appropriate. Free-text subject descriptors can also be used if desired.

To show how this system applies, an organisational function could have the keyword *managing human resources*; one activity descriptor is *recruiting staff*; a subject or process descriptor is *staff interviews*.

Many Australian agencies use the *Keyword AAA: Thesaurus of General Terms*, produced by the State Records Authority of New South Wales, in conjunction with a functional thesaurus for their own specific needs.

AGIFT (2005) is a three-level hierarchical thesaurus that describes the business functions carried out across Commonwealth, State and local governments in Australia. It was designed to provide standard terms for use in the 'Function' element of AGLS (based on Dublin Core; see Chapter 2) used for indexing government websites. The National Archives of Australia maintains the AGLS metadata standard, and promotes its use throughout Australian government agencies (National Archives of Australia 2002).

Although records management functions such as retention and disposal work best with the use of a functional classification, many staff and users prefer access through specific terms. Subject thesauruses (also called taxonomies) are used in records management to provide access to the specific subjects or concepts of interest to people. The subjects can be mapped to the functional classification. Taxonomies are often shared between organisations (*Records Management Society Bulletin* i.120, June 2004: 5).

Archives

Archives are inactive records that have been kept for their continuing value. They are of particular interest to historians and genealogists. Because they are likely to be old, they may have problems such as physical damage and illegible handwriting.

Indexing helps to preserve archives as it can remove the need to consult the original documents. Many archival records are indexed by volunteers, and some family history societies make money from index products (Hicks 2005). State Records NSW (2005) provides information for people planning to index State records.

Archives are arranged in the same order that was used by the person or organisation that accumulated them. Thus the original filing systems are preserved, even if sometimes they can be exasperating to use. Finding aids (pathfinders) are created to lead people to the appropriate groups of documents. They include names, functional titles, locations, dates or date ranges, record types (e.g., letters) and information about the content of record. This may be in the form of lists of key topics covered, and can be used as a source of index terms.

Subject enquiries about people and events may have to be translated into provenance enquiries, that is, finding out what functional area would have been responsible for that activity (there are good examples at www.archivists.org.au/pubs/brochures/understanding.html).

Max Downes (1996) has written on his development of a system for indexing historical data from the sealing industry, allowing access to the scattered records in logbooks, customs records and other sources. Contemporary words and place names are used, including *pipes of bread* (hard tack), *whalemen* (for the elephant sealers, as they shared the same skills and traditions as the whalers) and *Desolation* (the only name commonly used for Kerguelen).

The Australian Science and Technology Heritage Centre (www.austehc.unimelb.edu.au) hosts a range of archival records to do with Australian science and scientists. These employ Online Heritage Resource Manager (OHRM), a 'context-based resource discovery and access system that links creators, archival and heritage resources and published materials within the one system'. Name records follow ISAAR(CPF): International Standard Archival Authority Record for Corporate Bodies, Persons, and Families.

See also *Definitions* and *Standards for records and archives* in Chapter 2, *Markup languages*: *EAD* in Chapter 8, and *Genealogical and local history materials*, above.

E-mail

E-mail management is now an important part of records management, both for day-to-day operation of companies and for legal compliance. Organisations need e-mail policies to cover capture, storage, indexing, backups, privacy, retrieval, retention and disposal.

E-mail messages can be moved to an organisation's content repository directly from their e-mail client. E-mail metadata can be captured and automatically profiled and stored by threaded discussions, attachments, subject matter, or date. E-mail is now often combined with instant messaging (SMS), which also needs to be preserved.

The Australian government has published a standard for the use of metadata for e-mail storage (www.naa.gov.au/recordkeeping/control/agems.html). The standard describes the metadata that 'should be used by Australian Government agencies when transmitting electronic mail (e-mail) communications'. The tags to be used cover agent, rights management, message identifier, subject or title, keyword, history (date, time), relationship, message precedence and message importance.

Scholarly books

Scholarly books are complex academic documents with dense text on specialised topics. They usually appeal to a small audience, often of only a few hundred purchasers. Although they need indexes, they may not have adequate budgets for them. Scholarly works can be difficult to index as you have to pick up the threads of an argument as it develops. These books may also have complex structures, including tables, graphs and notes, and are more likely than most books to require an index of cited authors. Before taking on a scholarly index be sure that you have enough knowledge of the subject matter.

Scientific and medical publications

Science indexing is a specialised field because it requires subject knowledge and knowledge of scientific terminology. This section provides an introduction to the indexing of binomial Latin names, chemical names and names of pharmaceuticals. See also *Filing rules: Greek and roman letters* in Chapter 7. Although a basic principle of indexing is the use of natural language, in scientific works this includes scientific language, which is the 'natural' language in the field.

A recent publication edited by W Boyd Rayward and Mary Ellen Bowden (2004) brings together a wealth of papers of the history of scientific information systems. It covers specialised chemical databases that use a topological approach to searching, based on the molecular structure of the compounds (Fugmann 2004); the development of world-wide databanks of raw and evaluated data (Vickery 2004); and a history of developments in Australia (Middleton 2004).

Binomial Latin names

In the Linnaean taxonomy, all living things are placed within a scientific hierarchy that shows the closeness of their relationship to other living things. Within this hierarchy, binomial names indicate the genus (a bit like a surname) and species (a bit like a first name) of the organism; for example, red kangaroos are *Macropus rufus* and red-necked wallabies, which are in the same genus, are *Macropus rufogriseus*. In Latin *macropus* means 'big foot' and *rufus* means 'red'.

Binomial names are always in italic. They can be entered three ways: as a full name on each line; with the genus name as a heading, and the species name as a subheading; or with the genus name as a heading, and the genus abbreviated to its initial letter and the species name together as the subheading:

Staphylococcus aureus
Staphylococcus epidermidis
OR
Staphylococcus
   aureus
   epidermidis
OR
Staphylococcus
   S. aureus
   S. epidermidis

The advantage of the first method is that it treats each species as an individual. It can, however, get cluttered if there are long lists of names. The advantage of the middle one is simplicity; the last one shows the connection of the subheadings to the main heading if the list is continued in a new column.

In gardening books plants are entered in the form used in the text, with a reference from other names as appropriate. Common names may be ambiguous; where two species have the same common name, such as *black-eyed susan*, they must be qualified by the scientific name. There is a spell checker for botanical names in a Word dictionary at www.webindexing.biz/IndexingResources.

In field guides both common and scientific names should be used. Because scientists often call their subjects affectionately by their species names ('I saw three allotropis sunning themselves on the rock'), indexes to field guides often include entries by the binomial name in inverted as well as direct order. Thus *Ctenotus allotropis* should be indexed as such, and also as *allotropis, Ctenotus*.

Medical terminology

Medical indexes often include adjectival forms that are quite different from the related noun, such as *heart* and *cardiac*, *kidney* and *renal*. These can sometimes be grouped at one of the terms with a reference from the other. More often, terms have to be indexed with each starting word (*cardiac output* and *heart failure*; *renal medulla* and *kidney stones*), depending on the usage in the document. In this case a general reference such as 'kidney . . . *see also* renal . . .' is a signpost leading from all kidney entries to all renal entries.

Differences in US and British spelling may require double entries or references at terms such as *oesophagitis* and *esophagitis*.

Medical indexes and thesauruses often use the singular form for parts of the body. This works well for words such as *brain*, and is okay for *leg*, but is a problem for terms such as *alveolus* that are nearly always used in the plural (*alveoli*). General indexing practice uses the plural for all headings, but this looks strange with terms such as *brains* and *livers*. A compromise is to use the plural for body parts that we have more than one of (*alveoli*, *eyes*) and the singular for those of which we only have one (*brain*, *liver*). Terms such as *muscle* can be plural if you are counting them (*arm muscles*), but singular if you are thinking of them as a substance (*skeletal muscle*).

Medical databases generally use *MeSH (Medical Subject Headings)* or thesauruses based on *MeSH*. For broader coverage, and implementation in computer systems, the National Library of Medicine also provides UMLS (Unified Medical Language System, www.nlm.nih.gov/research/umls). Carolyn Weaver provides a list of health websites that are useful for medical indexers (www.weaverindexing.com/health.html).

Pharmaceutical names

Pharmaceuticals have generic names as well as brand names and chemical names. For example, *aspirin* is a generic name, *Aspro, Aspro Clear, Disprin* and so on are brand names, and *salicylic acid* is a chemical name. Generic names are more useful than brand names as they describe the drug itself, no matter who is marketing it. Most pharmacology indexes use the generic name, with either double entries or references from brand names. Brand names are capitalised and generic names are in lower case. This makes the brand names more prominent, but it cannot be avoided.

Software repositories

One of the goals of object-oriented programming is the reuse of the code base. To facilitate this, developers need to be able to search a repository to find specific components that can be used in a new product. Currently most repositories of software components are organised by product, to control and manage multiple versions of the code base, rather than to support search.

One example of online computer component indexing is the FSF/UNESCO Free Software Directory (directory.fsf.org). This is from the GNU Project site (www.gnu.org), which catalogues free software that runs under free operating systems, particularly GNU and GNU/Linux variants. It has categories for software development and system administration, and organises components by broad categories such as *live communication, audio, business* and *productivity*.

For optimal retrieval of software components, Joanne O'Dell (2004) recommends that each record should contain the following fields:

- author
- contact information
- component name
- operating system(s)
- version number of component
- source language
- byte size
- keywords to describe the functionality; from a thesaurus
- summary: a free-form textual description of the component

- unique identifier
- other required components (dependencies).

See also *Handbooks and manuals*, above.

Sound and music

Sound indexing includes music, sound effects and the spoken word, and is also part of video indexing. Music cataloguing includes descriptive cataloguing details such as title. In addition, some indexes include the style of music. Others try to allow searching by tune or rhythm: these are more experimental. Rarely, sounds are indexed by meaning.

Descriptive details include composer, title, key, opus number, form (e.g., concerto), instruments, conductor, and performers. The Tower Records website (www.towerrecords.com) allows refinement of initial searches through a range of facets provided at the left-hand side of the screen. J Stephen Downie (2003) has discussed the need for music information retrieval (MIR) systems to search for more than textual metadata to include facets such as pitch, temporal, harmonic, timbral, editorial, textual and publication details.

Kididdles (www.kididdles.com/mouseum/subject.html) allows search for children's songs through an alphabetical list, subject groups and search engine. It has a discussion list where you can ask about songs. The subject groups include traditional, learning (e.g., the alphabet), lullabies, silly songs, fun food, and so on.

The arrival of digital music has influenced music indexing in two ways: firstly, the unit of retrieval is likely now to be the track rather than the album; and secondly, modern music formats like MP3 allow indexing or cataloguing information to accompany the music file when it is copied or moved, making it relatively easy to search continually changing collections. The CDDB database is a free system, developed from user data, which is accessed by popular PC music-playing programs. When the user inserts a CD to play, the computer reads and stores the first few bytes of music. It then connects with the CDDB database on the web, sends off those bytes and receives in return a track list and details of the performer(s) and title of the CD. This is incorporated permanently into the user's own music catalogue, and it can be 'written into' any music files that are 'ripped' (copied in another format) from the CD. In the rare event that the CD has not yet been entered in the CDDB database, the user has the opportunity to do this themselves; the information they enter then becomes available on the web to anyone else with a copy of the same CD.

Pandora (www.pandora.com) is a website based on the Music Genome Project (www.pandora.com/mgp.shtml); do not confuse it with the library digital archiving project of the same name. The musical Pandora allows users to enter details of music that they like, and find music that is similar. Selections are made on a number of criteria. For example, if you type in *Green Day* it retrieves a number of tracks. If you then click on the image of an album cover (say, *Recognize* by

Jettingham) and select the question 'Why did you play this song?', it replies: 'Based on what you've told us so far, we're playing this track because it features hard rock roots, punk influences, a subtle use of vocal harmony, a vocal-centric aesthetic, and extensive vamping.' You can use the site to record preferences to make your own 'radio station'. It has worked well for members of our family who have tried it, though the number of tracks available is still fairly limited.

Another website searches for the rhythm you tap using the space bar on your keyboard (www.songtapper.com). We tried this with *God Save the Queen* and some other songs with some success, but it was baffled by more obscure tunes. We had no success with Query-by-Humming system (querybyhum.cs.nyu.edu) even when we had submitted the songs to the database.

As well as general search engines that search for music, there is also Singingfish (www.singingfish.com) which specialises in audio, including MP3 files.

An early experiment in sound indexing was done by Peggy Dowling at the Shell Film Unit. She classified sounds using the Universal Decimal Classification. The noise of turbines in electric power house, for example, had the number 621.313.12 (Collison 1972).

Cherrill Magee and Joann Keogh (2005) have written about the indexing of audio materials for a multilingual broadcaster, the Australian television station SBS. The audio files include songs in a number of languages. Another category is production music, short pieces that set a mood during voice-overs; a typical entry is *instrumental – world adventure – growing swells above light techno beat building dramatic tension and final hit*. A third group is sound effects, which have entries such as *footsteps – calm city environment – woman – high heels – continuous – slow*.

Recordings of the spoken word such as plays can be indexed or catalogued as the written original would be. Other recordings can be converted to text and the transcription indexed. See also *Multimedia (audiovisual) materials*, above, and *Video*, below.

Textbooks

Textbooks are often highly structured, with layout and typography indicating concepts that are important for students to know. These include the objectives at the beginning of chapters, lists of keywords to be learnt, review questions, and bold-face terms throughout the text. For children's textbooks, indexers should ensure that every question the children are asked can be readily answered using the index.

Indexers have to decide whether to index types of content as well as subjects, for example, headings for *exercises, case studies, review questions* and so on. The decision is made after consultation with the editor, and depends on the structure of the book and what the selling features are. Some textbooks have name indexes as well as subject indexes.

Successful textbooks are updated every few years, requiring re-indexing – this can be a good job if you were the initial indexer as you can work faster, and you have a chance to review the decisions you made originally. Sections of textbooks are sometimes provided in coursepacks through custom publishing (see above).

Video

Just as digital music allows individual tracks to be indexed or catalogued, so digital video allows action sequences to be broken down into segments. Segments can then be allocated keywords and users can enter these to jump directly to the relevant part of the video. A rudimentary indexing system is often seen on movie DVDs, but this can be extensively elaborated. Video recordings of material such as conference proceedings, legal actions, police interrogations, oral histories or committee meetings could support a relatively dense A–Z index, either individually or collectively.

Annodex is a file format for annotating (indexing) time-continuous bitstreams so that people can use text queries to search for video clips, then hyperlink to other video, audio or web content (www.annodex.net/specifications.html). The technology used is Continuous Media Markup Language (CMML).

SMIL is an XML-based markup language created by the W3C for creating rich multimedia content, integrating streaming audio and video with images and text for the web. It can link into the time code of audio and video materials, making it possible to index audio and video content. Some examples of videos indexed using SMIL are at the University of Texas site (www.gslis.utexas.edu/~l384k9/smil/smilindex.html).

MPEG-21 and MPEG-7 provide frameworks for the description of video content. Jane Hunter and Renato Iannella (1998) have written on a multi-level video indexing approach using RDF to contain both Dublin Core and MPEG7 descriptions of the same content.

Samuel Gustman *et al.* (2002) describe the indexing of videotaped oral histories from survivors of the Shoah (Jewish Holocaust). The indexing used speech-recognition software and volunteer labour. It provided passage-level metadata (details) as well as testimony-level metadata (for each interview). You can search the archive and view some testimonies at the USC Shoah Foundation Institute (www.usc.edu/schools/college/vhi). The authors discuss the need for a real-time cataloguing methodology, computer-assisted classification and categorisation, computer-assisted segmentation, and automatic summarisation to make the process feasible.

Web-wide video search engines

Tools such as Google's beta video search work by searching a program's closed captioning text (video.google.com). The search results simply provide an excerpt from the text and a single still image from the program. A search for 'platypus' on 20 December 2005 retrieved four videos, none on the subject of platypuses.

The hits were 'Platypus' by Reed Braden; 'Land mines (Satire)' by Duck-Billed Platypus of Death Productions; 'Google Current – Platypus' by Current TV, LLC; and 'Archive of American Television Interview with Fred Rogers Part 6 of 9' by Academy of Television Arts & Sciences Foundation.

A Yahoo Video search on the same day retrieved about 115 hits, many of which did contain video of platypuses. The program was, however, much slower, because it downloaded the complete files.

There are also specialist sites such as YouTube (youtube.com); Blinkx (www.blinkx.tv), which searches video and TV (especially news); and Singingfish (www.singingfish.com), which searches audio including MP3 files and video.

Web as a whole

People have attempted to index the web at three levels: the web as a whole, individual websites, and individual web documents. People have also indexed selected excerpts from the web – these are discussed in *Digital libraries*, above.

Search engines

The web as a whole is too big to be manually indexed, so search engines are necessary. Search engines are a form of database that provides access via free-text searches of the full text of documents. (A free-text search looks for words that occur in documents rather than for added metadata terms.) The found documents are ranked in order of relevance. 'Smart searching' uses information external to the page (e.g., the number of websites linking to it) to assist in relevance ranking.

Search engines give quick access to information through the use of inverted files – lists of all of the words in a document (except words such as *the* and *but* which have been designated as stop words) with the location at which they can be found. Inverted files used with bibliographic databases also provide details of the number of occurrences of each term.

Advanced search options, in which you can specify document type, date of updating, and so on, are a form of fielded search. Search engines may provide some rudimentary vocabulary control, with automatic suggestions of alternative spellings and the option to broaden a search to include synonyms. Search engines also allow 'query by example' searching; for instance, Google provides a 'Similar pages' link. Search engines inevitably suffer from the limitations of free-text search, including false drops. These can be manipulated by unscrupulous users who include names of competitors' products on their company's website.

Even the biggest search engines index only a portion of the web. Early search engines were limited in the formats that they could index, excluding, for example, PDF and Powerpoint files and content in the deep (hidden) web – that is, databases, and content that requires logins. Many of these disadvantages have been overcome, with a wide range of formats accessible. Tools such as Google Scholar (scholar.google.com) and Microsoft's Live Academic Search (academic.live.com) target scholarly material. Trudi Bellardo Hahn (1998) describes early developments in online searching, and Danny Sullivan (2006) has summarised his reporting on search engines over the last ten years.

Some non-commercial material is now accessible through the Creative Commons – a way of making material available while retaining some rights, such as the right to be acknowledged as author. Licences for use are embedded as metadata on the website using RDF. There are now Creative Commons search engines (creativecommons.org/find) and directories (commoncontent.org). For multimedia search engines, see *Images*, *Multimedia (audiovisual) materials*, and *Sound and music*, above.

Metadata and paid search

Subject metadata can enhance search on an intranet site, but very few web-wide search engines take it into account, as it has been abused by spammers trying to direct irrelevant traffic towards their site. Metadata fields such as titles and descriptions can still be important in search ranking, along with the words used in links leading towards the site. Quality material on a site can lead to an increase in its ranking as more people link to it.

Indexing aids on the web can be positive; see *Collection indexes*: *Metadata* in Chapter 5. They can also be negative: for instance, robots.txt tags tell a spidering robot not to 'index' content from that site.

Paid search provides a way of introducing metadata to the web. Advertisers select subject keywords that describe the services they offer. When people search on those terms, advertisers' details are provided in a separate 'sponsored' section. Advertisers set a price per keyword. If there is competition for the same keywords, advertisers can increase the price they pay per click to ensure a higher ranking on the site. Even paid search may be susceptible to fraud; for example, a company may click many times on a competitor's link to use up its daily advertising budget.

Information visualisation

Information visualisation is an important technique for presenting large quantities of information to allow users to identify patterns and trends. It may be used in association with web-wide search engines.

KartOO (www.kartoo.com) is a French metasearch engine that presents search results visually as a collection of nodes. Clusty.com, which uses Vivisimo software, provides a list of named categories. Visual Net software, produced by Canadian company Antarctica, creates large-scale browsable maps of information (www.antarctica.net). You can explore other visual displays of structured information at www.groxis.com, www.webbrain.com and www.inxight.com/map.

Semantic web

The semantic web is a project of the World Wide Web Consortium (W3C). It envisages replacing much human searching of the web with automated methods based on quality metadata. The semantic web depends on precise description of data to enable machine-processable transactions. Since computers find it difficult to understand the world, humans are now trying to describe the world in ways that are easier for computers to understand. Tim Berners-Lee, creator of the web and now with the W3C, considers the semantic web to be the next step in the optimal use of the web as a tool for performing tasks as well as discovering resources.

For the semantic web to work it requires the following (Hewlett-Packard 2006):

- A global naming scheme, sometimes called URIs – universal resource identifiers. In most cases URLs (universal resource locators) serve this purpose.
- A standard syntax for describing data. RDF, or Resource Description Framework lets you assert facts, e.g., 'Person X is named Shannon.'
- A standard method of describing the properties (attributes) of data, such as RDF Schema and other markup languages. RDFS lets you describe vocabularies and use them to describe things, e.g. 'Person X is an Australian resident.'
- A standard method of describing the relationships between data items (ontologies). An ontology lets you establish relationships between vocabularies, e.g., '"Visitors" in schema A are the same as "users" in schema B.'
- A way to support trust and security.

Examples of the tasks that a computer might perform for a user include selecting goods for purchase or booking medical appointments. For the latter the computer would need to know the person's health condition, regular medical practice, health fund requirements, specialist needs, schedule availability, transport timetables and so on. For this to work a lot of information has to be documented, including ephemeral items like a person's priorities – for example, is the choice of doctor or the time of the appointment more important?

See also *Markup languages*: *RDF* in Chapter 8 and *Topic maps* in Chapter 6.

Web documents

Stand-alone documents on the web may have book-style indexes, and sometimes indexes for print documents are mounted on the web. Book-style indexes are the most granular (detailed) information retrieval tool on the web; that is, they give access to specific chunks of information rather than whole webpages or websites. Some document indexes on the web are:

- Los Alamos National Laboratory Research Library Newsletter – library.lanl.gov/libinfo/news/newsindx.htm
- *The mathematica book* – documents.wolfram.com/v4/MainBook/Index
- *New frontiers in geriatrics research* – www.frycomm.com/ags/rasp/bookindex.asp
- *NSW Public Health Bulletin Subject Index* – www.health.nsw.gov.au/public-health/phb/Subject_Index_for_2002web.htm

- *Orders of magnitude* – www.informationuniverse.com/ordersmag/orders. htm
- *Technology in Australia 1788–1988* – www.austehc.unimelb.edu.au/tia/ bookindex.html
- *UNIX manual* – unixhelp.ed.ac.uk/index/index.html.

See also *Book-style website indexing software* in Chapter 10.

Websites

Websites as a whole can be indexed in the same way as web documents, except that maintenance has to be done if the sites are updated. The process then has some of the characteristics of collection indexing.

The main advantage of book-style indexes for websites is that they provide specific alphabetical access to the content of the site, without requiring users to browse through the hierarchy. They also provide subdivisions to show clearly what content can be expected in each location, and cross-references to lead users to alternative locations within the index.

The main disadvantages are the costs; the delay between creation of the resource and its addition to the index; the need for regular updating if the content changes; and the need for skilled indexers.

Some book-style indexes on the web are:

- American Society of Indexers – www.asindexing.org/site/backndx.htm
- FedStats (US) – www.fedstats.gov/cgi-bin/A2Z.cgi
- Indexing Society of Canada/Société canadienne d'indexation (ISC/SCI) – www.indexingsociety.ca/siteindex.html
- Penrith City Council quick index – www.penrithcity.nsw.gov.au/index. asp?id=634
- Queensland Environmental Protection Authority/Parks and Wildlife Authority – www.epa.qld.gov.au/site_information/site_index
- Society of Indexers (UK) – www.indexers.org.uk/site/index.htm (also available directly from the home page at www.indexers.org.uk)

The American Society of Indexers' Web Indexing SIG promotes the use of A–Z indexes on the web. It lists examples of indexes, resources, and indexers available for work (www.webindexing.org). The process of website indexing, as well as the pros, cons and alternatives, are considered in detail in our book *Website indexing* (Browne and Jermey 2004).

Alternatives to book-style indexing of websites include:

- site search engines, which search all words on the site
- subsite search engines, which search all words on a part of a site, e.g., a product catalogue
- site search engines with subject metadata (see also *Intranets and CMSs*, above)
- site maps, which display the structure of the site.

If a site does not provide any effective retrieval mechanism, web-wide search engines can be used to search specific sites. Typing 'site: www.webindexing.biz auslib' into MSN, Yahoo and Google retrieves pages within that site that contain the word 'auslib'.

Donna Maurer (2006) has discussed different approaches to information seeking and their implications for information access on intranets and websites.

See also *Book-style website indexing software* in Chapter 10.

Collaborative tagging and folksonomies

Folksonomy refers to the collective indexing of website or intranet-based content using freely chosen keywords. It is used on the following websites:

- www.43things.com, to label goals
- del.icio.us, to label social bookmarks
- www.flickr.com, to label photos.

Tags can be added by both the people who provide the content and the people who view the content. For non-text-based sites, some form of labelling is crucial. For photos the providers of the content are the best people to label the content, especially with respect to the denotative level (see *Images* and *Multimedia (audiovisual) materials*, above), but viewers can supplement the original tags. Groups of tags on sites such as *43 things* may be represented as cloud maps, in which terms that have been used more often to tag content are shown in larger type.

Collaborative tagging has been used in some intranets (Fitzgerald 2006). In some cases the tags are then added as entry points or preferred terms in the thesaurus, thus combining the enterprise-wide input of a folksonomy with the control of a thesaurus.

There is some debate about the need to 'tidy up' tags (Guy and Tonkin 2006). If someone tags a picture of a *platypus* as an *otter*, or a *747* as a *727*, should the tags be edited, or should they remain to show that person's viewpoint?

Jakob Voss (2006) compared the labelling and categorisation of pages in Wikipedia with folksonomies, library classification and indexing from a thesaurus. He concluded that the category system of Wikipedia 'is a thesaurus that combines collaborative tagging and hierarchical subject indexing in a special way'.

Memetic search allows small groups, such as people attending a conference, to agree on a unique tag for webpages about the conference so that all reports can be retrieved by searching for that tag (*Memetic search* 2005).

Collaborative tagging normally applies to individual websites. Wink is a specialised search engine that integrates results from tagged sources such as del.icio.us, dig, Furl, SlashDot, and Yahoo MyWeb.

See also *Collection indexes: Metadata* in Chapter 5.

World as a whole

Each of the sections in this chapter has dealt with the 'indexing', in a broad sense, of specific types of content. Here we consider the need to access information from a range of sources. This can involve sequential searching of different bits of content; bringing content of different types together using digitisation; and the use of human intermediaries, such as librarians and aficionados, with access to a range of sources.

Digitisation projects

Digitisation of paper-based materials and other physical formats has increased access to a wide range of content. Examples include:

- Distributed Proofreaders (www.pgdp.net/c/default.php) is a group of volunteers who digitise public domain texts for Project Gutenberg.
- Web-wide search engines Google and MSN aim to digitise a large number of print books to 'offer higher quality answers to web searchers' (Quint 2005). There is some controversy about the scanning of in-print books by Google without permission from the publishers. MSN Book Search plans to scan publicly available material, and in-copyright material in conjunction with copyright owners.
- Australasian Digital Thesis Program (adt.caul.edu.au/about/aimsoverview) aims to provide digital versions of theses produced by postgraduate research students at Australian universities on the web.
- Museum collections and art gallery pictures can often be browsed through digitised images on websites. The Tate Gallery (www.tate.org.uk) has digitised and indexed images of 65,000 artworks.
- National Library of Australia maintains a list of digitisation projects (www.caul.edu.au/org/nla-digitise.html).

Human assistance

Despite high-quality human indexing and brilliant search engine algorithms, there are still times when direct human intervention provides the best approach. There are a number of ways to get human assistance:

- Specialised web mailing lists such as Index-L.
- Targeted requests for information. For example, in probate genealogy, when all else fails researchers try the 'shotgun approach', writing letters to all people with the surname in question.
- At volunteer sites such as Wondir (www.wondir.com), you can ask any question and may get a range of answers, but no quality guaranteed. More specialised sites such as AbeSleuth (forums.abebooks.com/abesleuthcom) may provide better answers; the authors got an answer within hours to a request

for the title of a book of which we could only give a vague description containing some errors.

- At paid sites such as Google Answers (answers.google.com/answers) a screened researcher may answer your question for a price that you set.
- At *Ask a Librarian* sites you can get free answers from trained staff. Examples are AskNow, www.asknow.gov.au and AskUs, www.nla.gov.au/infoserv/askus.html.

Software and Hardware

L IKE MOST PROFESSIONALS, indexers use a wide range of software. Book and website indexers work with programs which allow them to enter index headings, sub-headings and page references, and which organise these into alphabetical or other orders. The programs also allow checking of cross-references and provide output to a formatted word processing file for final printing and sending to the client. Editing and other word processing work is an important part of an indexer's job.

Word processing software such as Microsoft Word and publishing programs such as Adobe FrameMaker and Adobe PageMaker allow users to embed indexing terms in a document and to generate indexes. Thus indexing can be completed before page numbers have been finalised, and index tags can move with portions of the document if they are reused elsewhere.

Indexes created for PDF documents can be automatically linked to the text they refer to. These indexes can then be incorporated into the PDF document or made available via the web.

'Indexing software' also includes programs that claim to analyse and index text automatically, without human intervention. These use structural features of the text (capital letters, words repeated several times) to try to make semantic judgements, identifying 'important' words and phrases and then listing these in alphabetical order with page numbers attached. The results are usually unimpressive for books and journals, but in large collection indexes automated programs may have a role to play.

Indexers in specialised fields also find a large and growing number of applications and utilities to make their working lives easier.

Here we discuss a range of software packages used in indexing, from the Big Three indexing programs (CINDEX, Macrex and SKY Index) and website indexing programs, to utility software such as macros that can make processes more efficient. Details of the software should be read in conjunction with the descriptions of types of indexing: for example, embedded indexing. The indexing software market is changing and growing all the time, and the details and descriptions given here are indicative rather than comprehensive.

The American Society of Indexers maintains a webpage listing indexing software at http://www.asindexing.org/site/software.shtml.

Hardware and occupational health and safety are covered at the end of this chapter.

Dedicated indexing software

The three most widely used dedicated indexing programs are CINDEX (www.indexres.com/cindex.html), Macrex (www.macrex.cix.co.uk) and SKY Index (www.sky-software.com). All are considered by their users to be excellent and essential programs. Demonstration versions are available for download so you can see which one suits your working style. A search of the Index-L archives will retrieve a number of messages comparing the packages, and Michael Wyatt (2000) has compared CINDEX and SKY Index.

CINDEX is the only one that has a Macintosh version. CINDEX and Macrex began as DOS programs but have produced Windows versions; SKY Index began as a Windows program.

The programs include features to speed up common indexing activities: flipping (rotating) a heading and subheading, copying an entry, adding one to the page number. They enable the use of macros, recorded sequences of actions that can be replayed with a single key, and acronyms, abbreviations that the program automatically expands.

All of them can produce output files in a variety of formats. The most commonly used format is probably RTF (Rich Text Format), a text-based format developed by Microsoft that represents formatting information as text codes. An RTF file can be opened for checking and editing in any word processing program. Other output formats are delimited text, HTML and XML. Output formats can be developed to support other requirements such as importing into Quark Xpress.

CINDEX™

CINDEX is produced by Indexing Research (indexres.com). It uses a 'card file' metaphor in its interface. Users can browse through the entries they have created and then 'open' one to view further details. Figure 1 shows a CINDEX screen.

CINDEX is available both for Windows and the Apple Macintosh. CINDEX for Windows comes in three editions: a Student Edition; a Standard Edition that provides a complete array of features for the professional indexer; and a Publishers' Edition that provides project managers with the capacity to supervise multiple projects in a networked environment. There is a CINDEX users mailing list (groups.yahoo.com/group/cindexusers/join).

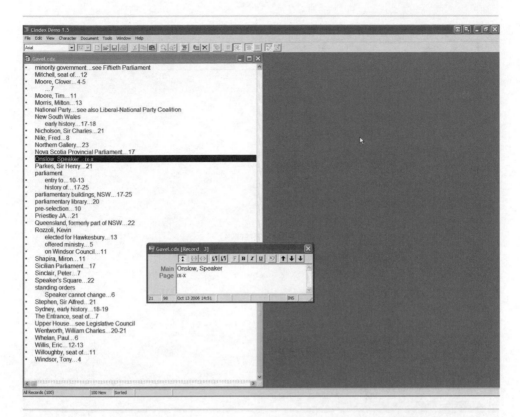

FIGURE 1 The CINDEX demonstration screen showing a 'card' display for one record.

Macrex™

Macrex (www.macrex.com) started as a DOS program. It now presents DOS features embedded in a window, allowing for some use of the mouse but remaining primarily key-driven. Figure 2 shows the Macrex user interface. A more Windows-like version is in planning (August 2006). Users who are familiar with a command-line interface work well with Macrex. There is a Macrex users mailing list (www.macrex.com/discuss.htm).

SKY Index™

SKY Index (www.sky-software.com) was written in Windows and uses an interface similar to that of a Microsoft Excel spreadsheet. It supports most standard Windows techniques such as drag-and-drop. Index entries are laid out horizontally across the screen, one per row; this makes them fast and easy to enter but can cause problems when the entries are particularly long or there are several layers of subheading. At the same time a panel on the upper section of the screen displays the index in its final form. Figure 3 shows the SKY user interface. There is a SKY Index users mailing list (groups.yahoo.com/group/skyindexusers) and a wiki to which everyone can add content at skyindex.pbwiki.com.

```
Macrex Version 8.06/TOA/LM: \\Ludwig\data\macnt\MACNTTEST          _ □ ×
Insert ON      0      : Ignore case/no wild  : 1625kb: Group (inactive)
Editing index \\Ludwig\data\macnt\MACNTTEST
Press <PgUp> or <PgDn> : F1 Menu : F4 Add Entries : Enter ?? for more help

1   air (Eng.) 189
2   air (Fr.) 189
3   Aristotle, debt to Plato 23, 46
4      literary criticism in 35, 74, 89-93, 101-97
5         on Aeschylus 101-4, 279
6         on Aristophanes 195
7         on Euripides 104-26, 187, 265-6
8         on Homer 103, 190-4, 206
9         on Sophocles 127-83, 275-7, 306, 309-10
10           Antigone 155
11           Oedipus Tyrannus 140-9
12      origins of tragedy, in epic 196
13         in revelry 197
14  Ave Maria (Gounod) 100
15  Ave Maria (Schubert) 101
16  Bag of bricks 206
17  Bagby, George 207
18  Bagshaw, Malcolm A 208
19  Bank of England 209
20  banking 210
21  bears 100, 217, 923
22      see also badgers; koala bears; polar bears; raccoons
23  Butler, Samuel (1612-1680) 71
24  Butler, Samuel (1835-1902) 73
25  Caligula 6, 13, 15, 1.14, 1.16, 1.36
26  Club 18-30 218
27  Club 21 219
28  Club 147 Fashions 220
29  emphasis 47, 49, 51-52
30  4-ethyl-[alpha]-picoline 217
31  3-ethyl-4-picoline 217
32  Finnbogadóttir, Vigdis see Vigdis Finnbogadóttir
33  illustrations (1) 112
34  internet providers, CIX 19
35  Livingstone, Ken 1.3, 1.97, 3.94
36  long numbers 100026-100027
37  Marlborough, John Churchill, first Duke of 66
38  milk, cows' 222
39     goats' 223
40  milk allergies 225
41  Les nourritures terrestres 108
42  Society of Indexers 3-5 passim
43  Society for the Preservation of Rural England 225
44  ten sixty-six 1066 and all that 213

Ready ==>
```

FIGURE 2 The Macrex user interface (from the demonstration program)

Microsoft Access™

A database is a collection of records, each made up of a number of fields relating to different properties of an individual item. These fields may hold simple, one-line text entries or large amounts of elaborate structured information, sometimes including links to graphics, sound or video files.

Databases save time on routine tagging; they are relatively easy to update; they allow automatic generation of double entries; and they give indexers control over features such as filing order. Large-scale indexes stored in databases are usually managed by IT specialists in conjunction with indexers. CINDEX, Macrex and SKY Index have built a special-purpose indexing application around basic database functionality, but sometimes an indexer has to bypass the special-purpose indexing features and work directly with a database file. This is common where the index is complex or has to be 'massaged' into a variety of different formats or styles.

Access is a relational database system. It can establish links between different sets of data so that information entered in one column of a table is connected to the

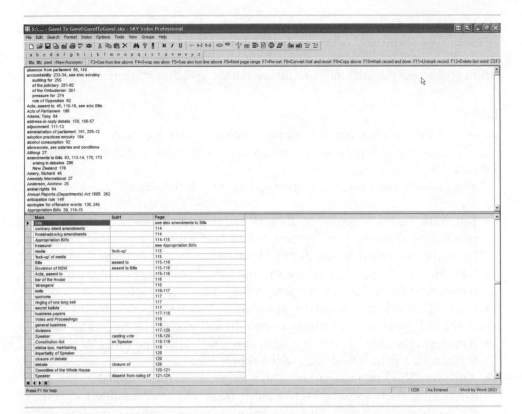

FIGURE 3   The SKY Index user interface with entry grid in page number order.

information in another table. For example, a list of affiliations in one table could be linked to an 'affiliation ID' field in a table of authors. In this case, firstly, only valid affiliation names could be entered; secondly, any change to an affiliation name in the first table would automatically change all the relevant author details; and thirdly, new affiliations could be added to the first table and immediately become available for use in entering author data. This kind of control is a powerful aid when setting up relationships between data.

The discussion below uses the example of an Access database that the authors created to facilitate indexing the NSW *Public Health Bulletin* (www.health.nsw.gov.au/public-health/phb/subauthindex.html). This print journal also appeared on the web, first as a PDF file and subsequently in HTML format. Our job was to produce a paper-based index for the issues of the magazine between 1990 and 1999, and thereafter to produce an ongoing yearly and cumulative index for new issues as they came out on paper, plus hyperlinked subject and topic indexes on the web. In addition to a topic index with a controlled vocabulary, we produced an index of authors and their affiliations, and at one time also put out an XML version of the index for each issue in order to link to the articles as they were loaded on to the PubMed system.

HTML and XML output can be created from an Access database, for example, by producing a report which includes the HTML tags as well as the fields in each record. Storage of indexing data in a database enables single-sourcing – the indexing is done once, and then the index terms are reused in different formats.

Tables

Tables are the data repositories within Access. Tables are broken down into records – one for each individual – which in turn are broken down into fields – individual items of data.

The *Public Health Bulletin* system included the following tables:

- **Journals**: This was optimistically included in case we needed to bring other publications into the same system, but in fact it was not needed. This table had only one record, giving details of the *Public Health Bulletin*.
- **Volumes**: This table showed the various annual volumes and supplementary issues, with fields showing the date, volume type and number.
- **Issues**: This table gave details of each of the 160 or so issues to date, linked back to the Volumes table so each issue could be assigned to the correct volume.
- **Articles**: This table had the title, page range, web URL and other information about each article, linked back to the appropriate issue
- **Authors**: This listed the names of all authors. Since these tended to recur, we used a drop-down look-up list to identify them wherever possible, rather than typing them in each time. Minor variations in names could be connected back to the same person: e.g., *Lynne V. Wallace* and *Lynne Wallace* both went in under the same heading.
- **Affiliations**: This table showed the organisation with which each author was affiliated. Because authors tended to change their affiliations over time, we had to maintain and update this list separately from the Authors table.
- **Subjects**: This listed all the allowable subject words under which to index the articles. These tended to be the same from one volume to the next, although we allowed for the addition of new subjects if necessary. The Subject table was also used to show cross-references to alternative headings, e.g., 'infectious diseases *see* communicable diseases'.

In addition to these, several linking tables connected the titles of articles with the names of their authors, etc.

Queries

A query is a set of parameters used to extract a particular set of records from one or more tables. The query controls which records are retrieved, the fields from each record that are retrieved, and the sequence of the records.

The queries created for the *Public Health Bulletin* collected material for the subject and author indexes in print, XML and HTML formats.

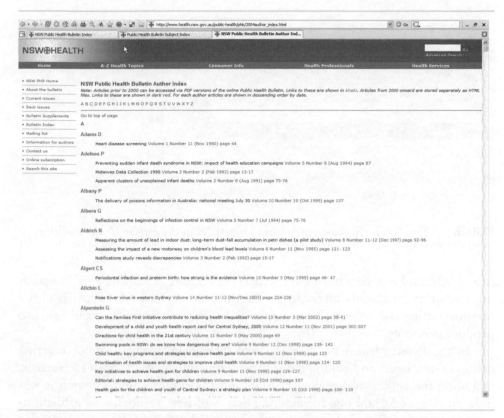

FIGURE 4   A section of an online HTML author index prepared for the *Public Health Bulletin* using Microsoft Access

Reports

Reports take output from tables or queries and 'pretty it up'; they allow text formatting and enhancements like lines and boxes to appear on the page, and control the filing sequence of the records. Reports are designed for print output, but they can be carried across into Microsoft Word and even, with some work, massaged into other formats like HTML for web display.

Our reports for the *Public Health Bulletin* included an author index and a subject index (for paper); an electronic XML report, and cumulative HTML author and subject indexes, each based on one of the queries described above. Figure 4 shows the author index. To view the finished product see www.health.nsw.gov.au/public-health/phb/2004subject_index.html (subject) and www.health.nsw.gov.au/public-health/phb/2004author_index.html (author).

Forms

Forms are used to control the entry of data into tables. In data entry mode they can be used to display drop-down lists, to check entries against a particular pattern

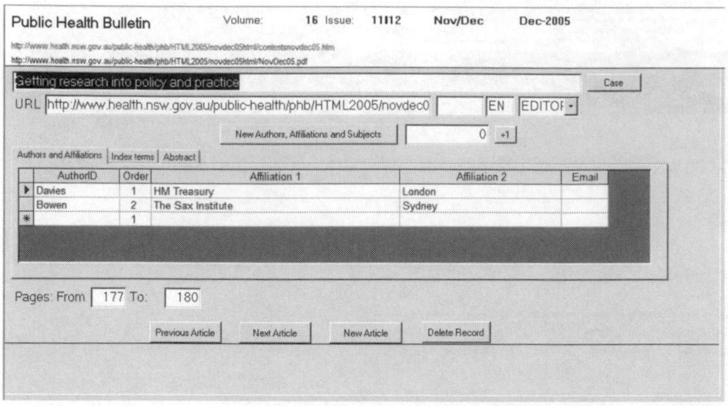

FIGURE 5   The Access database entry form for articles in the *Public Health Bulletin*

(e.g., credit card numbers must have sixteen digits), and to validate entries against other information already on the form. The use of forms to display records allows text formatting and colours, lines, boxes and other enhancements, and can also produce printouts.

In the *Public Health Bulletin* we used three main forms: one for entering details of new issues and volumes; one for entering information about each article, including the author and their affiliation and the subjects under which it was indexed (Figure 5); and one for entering details of new authors, new affiliations or new subjects. This third form was attached to a button on the second form so that it could be called up only when needed.

The system for the *Public Health Bulletin* took several weeks to construct, and we have continued to tweak it since then; in general it has functioned well and amply repaid the initial investment of time and trouble. Indexers who are confronted with complex projects should consider Access as a relatively user-friendly way of building up a sophisticated set of data-handling routines. Books on Access are readily available and there is a large selection of tutorials and other support material on the web. Anyone who is familiar with dedicated indexing software will have a head start in grasping the general concepts of database management.

Microsoft Excel ™

It is unfortunate that the Excel spreadsheet program was already well established before 1992, the year in which Access appeared; if Access had been around first, the number of people misusing Excel for data manipulation – including indexing – might have been smaller. Although in most cases Access does a much better job of indexing than Excel, Excel is still supreme in a few areas. As we move to electronic documents, the locators we need to use become more complex, expanding the role of data-manipulation programs like Excel. Bear in mind, however, that the maximum number of records in an Excel table is the maximum number of rows in a table – currently 65,536.

With an index in Excel, the user can perform limited database operations and also:

- sort records
- use string functions to convert upper to lower case, create an initial capital, etc.
- create customised macros and functions for reuse with different data
- move to and from other programs, allowing data to be massaged and re-formatted
- make occasional calculations, such as adding a fixed increment to a page number.

Embedded indexing software

Embedded indexing offers some benefits to publishers (see Chapter 8), but it makes indexing more difficult and time-consuming. Dave Prout (2004) comments: 'in a much-cited article, Nancy Mulvany reports that 95% of her respondents were not satisfied with embedded indexing programs. Although this informal survey did not try to imitate more rigorous studies like the Kinsey reports, many will suspect that the other 5% were probably lying.' Although the software packages in which indexers have to embed indexing terms have not improved much, a number of add-ons have been created (often by indexers) to make the process easier.

Embedded indexing is a key feature of various software packages for word processing, page layout and document preparation, as discussed below. It is also an integral component of some *Book-style website indexing software* (see below) and *Online help* systems (see Chapter 9). See also *Markup languages* and *Embedded indexing* in Chapter 8.

Microsoft Word™

Microsoft Word, like other major word processing programs, includes an embedded indexing feature. Phrases and words in document files are tagged, and later compiled to make an index. The indexing is embedded into the text, so if the index is recompiled, the page numbers in the index automatically change to reflect any changes to the page numbers in the document, and index entries are removed if the pages to which they refer are removed.

Relatively little professional indexing is done in Word because it is too complex for hobbyists and not powerful enough for full-scale publishing.

To mark up a word or phrase for the index, the user selects it and chooses Insert/Reference/Index and Tables/Mark Entry. This opens an entry marking dialog box, which can then remain open for ease of use as the indexer goes through the document to be marked up. Word indexing supports *see* and *see also* cross-references and one level of subheading. It also allows the user to vary the standard filing order; for example, *McKenzie* can be filed as *MacKenzie*. At the completion of marking up, an index can be generated through Insert/Reference/Index and Tables, and placed anywhere in the text of the document.

A paragraph marked up with Word's embedded indexing is shown below. The fields associated with the entry are shown, although in practice the user can choose to hide them.

> Linux{XE "Linux"} is an offshoot of Unix{XE "Unix:Linux as offshoot of"}, a popular operating system from the 1970s which was (and still is) widely used in tertiary education {XE "universities:Unix used in"}, {XE "tertiary education" \t "See universities"} environments. Unix in turn is closely related to C {XE "C (programming language)"}, the programming language which is used to construct nearly all the modules out of which Unix (and Linux) is made.

James Lamb (2005) has written on embedded indexing in Word, and there is a detailed tutorial at www.rdg.ac.uk/SerDepts/su/Topic/WordProc/WoP2Kind01.

Word can also be used to make concordances.

Microsoft Word add-ins

Because Word supports the standard programming language VBA (Visual Basic for Applications), developers can write large-scale macros that add functions to the Word program. Several such add-ins relate to indexing, some of which are described below.

DEXter is a Word template from the Editorium (www.editorium.com/dexter.htms), which contains macros to assist users in creating embedded indexes in Word documents. All the indexer has to do is go through the document highlighting blocks of text and pressing key combinations. At the final stage the familiar Word indexing codes are embedded into the document.

What distinguishes DEXter from the home-made macros that many indexers already use is that it sets up a second Word file – called the 'index document' – which contains a table showing all the index entries. Changes made to the index document are then carried back into the original when the Word indexing codes are embedded. Thus index entries can be filed, reviewed, edited and deleted on the fly, giving DEXter much of the functionality of a dedicated indexing program. DEXter can also be used to reverse embed entries that have been previously prepared in dedicated indexing software.

DEXter can be downloaded from the Editorium site and used free for forty-five days. It is available for versions of Word from 97 through to 2003 (2004 on the Macintosh).

WordEmbed, from JALamb.com Ltd (wordembed.jalamb.com) allows the user to take a free-standing index and make an embedded index out of it by copying the index entries into appropriate codes within a Word document. It begins by inserting temporary entries into the Word document at the appropriate locations and then substituting these for the locators in the finished index. The index can then be added to and modified until the indexer is ready for the final stage. Then the real index headings and subheadings are copied into the Word document in place of the temporary entries, ready for Word to compile an index that should be identical to the file you are working on. The WordEmbed manual can be downloaded from the website.

Indexing Toolbar for Word is an add-in that provides an extra toolbar and associated macros to automate the inclusion of headings, subheadings, cross-references and bookmarks for ranges. It is available from John Morrison: quiet.fusion@virgin.net.

IndexAssistant for Word loads itself into the Tools menu and operates via a dialog box and function keys. In addition to automating the insertion of entries and page ranges, it provides alphabetised lists of terms and an autocomplete function. It is difficult to evaluate this program from the demonstration version, which has most of the features disabled, but it appears to provide a useful interface for the Word indexing task. It is available from Jambient Software (www.jambient.com).

Reworx is not an indexing program, but it allows users to convert complex documents in Word format into HTML files, including cross-references in indexes and tables of contents. This may provide a short cut for Word users wishing to move Word material on to the web. A review of Reworx can be found at www.winwriters.com/articles/reworx, and the website for the program is at www.vmtech.com/reworx.htm. A demo can be downloaded for testing.

Adobe FrameMaker®

Adobe FrameMaker is a database program used for layout of technical documents. It supports tables and internal cross-references as well as a table of contents, index and other scholarly apparatus. The process of indexing is similar to that in Word, where the user inserts a special code at the point that the index locator will refer to. Multiple entries can be added at one location and subheadings can be included.

Adobe FrameMaker add-ins

Like Word, FrameMaker has several add-in programs that are designed to facilitate the embedded indexing process (Haskins 2004).

IXgen™ from Frank Stearns Associates (www.fsatools.com/ixmid.html) compiles the index entries in a FrameMaker file into a marker list. This can be viewed, changed, spell-checked and so on in one location, rather than working with markers scattered throughout the document. It can adjust capitalisation; generate some or all of an index from a set of keywords ('go' words); combine orphaned subheadings with the main heading; and flip (swap) headings with subheadings (*power supply, printer* becomes *printer, power supply*). Paragraph or character style tags can be used to generate index entries automatically, and one document can generate several indexes – for example, for names and topics.

Index Tools Professional from Silicon Prairie Software (www. siliconprairiesoftware.com) provides for embedded indexing. It includes a spell check option, and incorporates 'continued' lines in the output index. Index

Tools Professional can be used to produce a combined index to several book files in FrameMaker. Full documentation and a demo are available for download, but users will need to have FrameMaker to evaluate the program.

EmDEX (www.emdex.ca) allows index entries to be added, removed and formatted. It has special customised buttons for specific formatting requirements, and an autocomplete feature that automatically finishes off index entries that the user has typed before. It also allows index entries to be viewed as a group outside the document being marked up. IXgen and EmDEX both add menus and toolbars to the standard FrameMaker interface. They can be used in conjunction if necessary for the same document. A free demo is available for download from the site.

Sonar Bookends (www.virginiasystems.com/products_pc.html) is a family of programs that automatically generate concordance-style and proper name indexes from FrameMaker, InDesign, PageMaker and QuarkXpress publications. Free demos of the products can be downloaded from the site.

Adobe PageMaker®, Adobe InDesign® and QuarkXpress®

The Adobe page layout program PageMaker, and its successor InDesign, both have embedded indexing capabilities. Again, the indexing is carried out by inserting a code at the appropriate place in the document, and the resulting index is compiled at the end of the process and placed in a text frame that can then be added to the publication. A similar approach can be taken to mark up an index in QuarkXpress.

Sonar Bookends software (www.virginiasystems.com/products_pc.html) can also be used with these programs to automatically generate concordance-style and proper name indexes.

PDF indexing

The Portable Document Format (PDF) developed by Adobe is widely used as a medium for distributing electronic documents. This can be attributed to four factors:

- Because the Adobe Reader application for Windows and Macintosh has been distributed free, almost any computer user can open and view a PDF file regardless of the hardware or other software they are using.
- Because the document appears on screen exactly as in the print version, PDF guarantees that all users see essentially the same thing when they view a document, again regardless of platform.
- PDF files are difficult to change – indeed, this can be virtually impossible if the file is locked by its creator – and so the recipient of a PDF file can be reasonably sure that they are seeing the original version without editing or modification.
- Adobe has made the details of the PDF format public, allowing other developers to provide software which can create, edit or enhance PDF documents and viewers.

A range of indexing tools is available for PDFs, including TExtract (described below) and the popular Sonar series.

Sonar Activate for PDF documents

If you have a PDF document you can create links from the index to the text using Sonar Bookends Activate from Virginia Systems (www.virginiasystems.com). The program is an Adobe Acrobat plug-in, so you need the full version of Acrobat as well.

With the text of the book in one PDF file, the indexer exports the index to PDF and inserts it into the file for the book. The program automatically generates hyperlinks for each page number in the index and table of contents. It works by looking for a comma-separated list of numbers after text and some white space, for example, '*gorillas 5, 22, 96*'. It works only for one sequence of numbers, so if you have preliminary matter (e.g., pp. i–xii) you have to tell the program to ignore that section. You can add those links manually if needed.

A free demo of the program is available from the site.

Sonar Bookends

Sonar Bookends (www.virginiasystems.com/products_pc.html) is an automatic indexing program for PDF files. Unlike those described below, its claims are not extravagant: it can produce a concordance (a page number for every word); a list of proper nouns with page numbers; or an alphabetised list of words and phrases that you supply ('go' words) with the page numbers shown.

'Automated indexing' applications

Every few years a program appears which claims to provide 'automatic indexing'. The latest example is **TExtract**. TExtract takes a document, extracts some words and phrases, and creates an alphabetised list of these, without manual intervention. The document must be in PDF or plain text format and can consist of multiple files; the output is in RTF. It is claimed that the alphabetised list can be used as an adequate index to the document, although TExtract does allow further editing of the index once produced. A trial version of TExtract can be downloaded from Texyz at www.texyz.com/textract.

A review of TExtract (Shuter 2005) notes the limitations of this kind of tool. Some proper names are missed, others are not inverted; synonyms are not combined; some phrases are broken up inappropriately and at other times single words are combined into phrases. In addition there is no provision for subheadings. A new version of TExtract has been released since then, but it appears to suffer from the same problems.

IndDoc is a new automated book indexing tool for French texts that uses natural language processing and claims better results than previous methods.

Indexicon (reviewed by Browne 1996) and **Syntactica** (reviewed by Jermey 2003) have similar drawbacks. A lot of work has obviously gone into these programs and there are contexts in which they could be useful. It is unfortunate, however, that their creators market them with extravagant language. No doubt one day the semantic structure of natural language will be well enough understood to allow automatic indexing to work satisfactorily, but this day is still a long way off, and any claims made in this area for a particular program should be regarded with suspicion.

Sonar Bookends, discussed in *Embedded indexing*, above, is an 'automatic indexing' application which makes more moderate claims.

Automated collection indexing is discussed in various contexts throughout this book, including *Free-text searching and machine-aided indexing* in Chapter 5, *Automated categorisation and taxonomy generation* in Chapter 6, *Images: Content-based image retrieval* in Chapter 9, *Bibliographic database indexing decline* in Chapter 11 and *Thesaurus management software* and *Taxonomy management software*, below.

KWIC indexes

A KWIC (KeyWord in Context) index is produced from a list of titles, sentences or phrases. Each significant word is extracted and filed alphabetically, repeating each entry as many times as the number of significant words it contains. The entries for each word are then displayed in sequential order with a page number or other pointer to the original location. KWIC indexes have been used in current awareness services (listing all new journal articles published) and occasionally for other indexes (e.g., the index for the University of Bristol website at www.bris.ac.uk/index/full).

An example (from *Witness for the defence* by AEW Mason) is:

left to me." Mrs. **Thresk** meant no harm. She was utterly (143)
Prime-Ministers Henry **Thresk**, content with lower ground, was (152)
Bar in due time Henry **Thresk** was called; and when something did (154)
ed and killed old Mr. **Thresk**. From the ruins just enough was (156)
were made to Henry **Thresk**. But he was tenacious as he was (163)
in. So far then Mrs. **Thresk**'s stinging speeches seemed to have been (174)

A simple freeware KWIC-generation program can be downloaded from www.chs.nihon-u.ac.jp/eng_dpt/tukamoto/kwic_e.html.

Book-style website indexing software

You can create a website index using standard indexing software, but software is available that saves time, especially for an index that needs regular updating. The choice of software depends on your client's requirements and programming capabilities. Three options are discussed below.

HTML/Prep™

HTML/Prep from Leverage Technologies (www.levtechinc.com/ProdServ/LTUtils/HTMLPrep.htm) converts indexes that have been created using word processing programs or dedicated indexing packages into HTML files. Files need to be tagged before they can be converted. Tags indicate which lines are headings and subheadings, which ones are cross-references, and where the locator information starts. It is useful for single-sourcing, where a document has to be maintained in print and online formats. HTML/Prep has been used to create the index to the Society of Indexers (UK) website (www.indexers.org.uk/site/index.htm).

HTML/Prep automatically creates links from page numbers or other locators to webpages with those locators as names (e.g., *page 53* is linked to 53.htm). Within the index it links cross-references with the main headings to which they refer, and can generate an alpha bar (a hyperlinked line of initial letters) and a 'Return to Top' link. HTML/Prep can apply 'tips' that allow the user to hover over a subheading and see a popup box showing the heading structure above the current position in the index. This is useful when the display window is small, or headings have long displays of subheadings under them. You can see tips in the Yale Undergraduate Regulations Index (www.yale.edu/ycpo/undregs/pages/indexpage.html) and the Milan Jacovich detective series index (www.levtechinc.com/Milan/MilanHN.htm).

The program can also produce a separate document containing only main headings and cross-references, enabling browsing of just the main headings in a large index. Links from the main headings take the user back to the full index when more detail is needed. An example of a 'main heading index' can be seen in the BNA Labor Relations Reporter Index (www.bna.com/lrr/lrrindx.htm).

HTML Indexer™

HTML Indexer is a program from Brown Inc (www.brown-inc.com) for IBM-compatible computers that automates the clerical aspects of creating web indexes. It produces a back-of-book-style index. Users can select default entries or add their own, and can set various output options. HTML Indexer uses embedded indexing of metadata tags within the webpages themselves to store indexing information, thus making the indexes it produces easily updatable.

To create an index, the user begins with a set of webpages in HTML and creates a project file in the root directory of the website. This is used to record a list of pages to include. The pages are then brought in to the project, and every page title, level-one heading and named anchor point is given an entry in the index. Unwanted entries can be deleted and unwanted files removed. The user works through the headings, changing the text and adding subheadings if necessary. The file structure, with directories and subdirectories, is shown on the left of the screen. At any time an HTML file can be opened up for viewing in a browser to confirm what the index entry should be. The default is to have one index entry for each item, but users can add as many as they need. An alpha bar (a hyperlinked line of initial letters) is created, and various formatting options are available.

When the index is created, the details of each entry are saved in the Head section of the webpage as metadata. HTML Indexer can then draw on these entries to create an HTML index from any subset of pages on the site. This represents a version of embedded indexing in which the index entries are embedded in the HTML of the webpage.

One drawback of HTML Indexer is that it requires the indexer to access and work with the original pages on the site. If another user changes or deletes those pages, the index entries can be lost.

As well as producing HTML indexes, the program also allows the construction of compiled Windows Help and JavaHelp systems. A demo of HTML Indexer is available (www.html-indexer.com). It is fully functional except that indexing projects cannot be saved for updating, although the indexes created can be saved and used. More detail on HTML Indexer and HTML/Prep is given in *Website indexing* (Browne and Jermey 2004).

XRefHT32

XRefHT32, pronounced 'shreft', is a Canadian Windows-based tool for website indexing. It is available free at publish.uwo.ca/~craven/freeware.htm. Documentation is also available from the website.

XRefHT32 is similar to HTML Indexer; it creates HTML indexes with hypertext entries for use on the web. The indented structure of subheadings is displayed using bulleted lists. When used in conjunction with free thesaurus management software by the same developer, XRefHT32 adds hypertext cross-references to indexes automatically.

The interface is similar to that of the indexing tool SKY Index, whereby index entries and locators are entered into rows and columns. If your material is already in electronic form, you can extract page titles, headings at any level, or named anchors as the index entries, and the hyperlinks will be created automatically. The output can be in the form of a single file or as separate HTML files for each letter of the alphabet. A review of XRefHT32 by Heather Hedden is at home.comcast.net/~hhedden/XrefHT32_Review_KW2005_10–12.pdf.

Thesaurus management software

A thesaurus construction package should be powerful, flexible, cost-effective and easy to use. It should fit the project workflow, and allow access control at various levels. Specifically, it should allow you to input the fields and relationships you need, maintain them with minimum fuss, and output the thesaurus in various formats (including print and web). You should be able to transfer your data to another software package and to other people should the need arise. Although price is not the major consideration for most purchasers, some of these programs are now so cheap that they are affordable for small jobs – for example, as a way for indexers to maintain a controlled vocabulary for ongoing periodical indexing projects. The 'Check-list for thesaurus software' by Jochen Ganzmann, at the

Willpower Information site, is an excellent starting point for software evaluation (www.willpower.demon.co.uk/criteria.htm).

Three thesaurus construction packages commonly used for small to medium-scale projects are TermTree (www.termtree.com.au), MultiTes (www.multites.com) and WebChoir (www.webchoir.com) (Browne 2004). Cognatrix (www.lgosys.com/products/Cognatrix/index.html) is a thesaurus construction package designed for Macintosh computers.

MAIstro is a combination of Thesaurus Master and M.A.I., a rule-based, machine-aided indexing package (www.dataharmony.com). See a demonstration of M.A.I. using news content at www.newsindexer.com.

Taxonomy management software

Taxonomies are maintained and presented using a range of software products including:

- Word, Excel and Visio
- mind mapping software including Mindjet's MindManager (www.mindjet.com/us) and the open source software FreeMind (freemind.sourceforge.net/wiki/index.php/Main_Page, see an example at blog.outer-court.com/archive/2004_08_11_index.html#109222064061401876)
- specialised systems including SchemaLogic's SchemaServer (www.schemalogic.com), Wordmap (www.wordmap.com) and Protégé (mainly used for ontologies, protege.stanford.edu)
- modules attached to content management systems, sometimes used for automatic taxonomy generation (see Chapter 6)
- thesaurus management software (see above).

Non-indexing software

Indexers use a range of software packages to manage their businesses and to make their indexing procedures more efficient.

Security and backups

Losing an index can be disastrous for an indexer's income, schedule and reputation. Indexers need to ensure that they are equipped to deal with fire, flood, theft, crashing computers and misbehaving software. Essentials include:

- A long-term backup system – to CDs, DVDs or other external storage – which allows copied files to be stored somewhere physically separate from the originals. This should include essential applications programs as well as data.
- Regular use of current software to detect and remove viruses and spyware.

- Regular installation of newly developed security patches and upgrades for software such as Microsoft Office.
- A means of making reliable short-term backups while working on an index. Some users back up to floppy disks or flash memory; others upload material to storage areas on the web or send it to themselves via e-mail.

Accounting software

An indexing business requires software to manage invoicing, payments, work records and contacts. Each country has its own taxation laws and accounting standards, so the applications available for this vary from place to place. Australian businesses generally opt for MYOB or QuickBooks, both of which are adapted specifically to Australian financial systems and standards.

AutoHotkey

AutoHotKey, by Chris Mallett, is a freeware Windows macro system which sits between the keyboard and the computer. When triggered by a keystroke, it fires a sequence of keys, mouse clicks and other instructions. It is particularly useful for writing key sequences that involve interactions among two or more programs. It can be downloaded from www.autohotkey.com and added to the Startup folder so that it runs whenever the computer is switched on. When AutoHotKey is running, a small icon with a capital *H* appears in the tray at the bottom right of the screen.

To activate the program the user creates and save a text file called a *script*. The script consists of one or more sequences of commands written in a simple scripting language. The following script reproduces the keystrokes involved in typing the name 'Jon Jermey':

Send, Jon Jermey

Many macros can be included in one script, and the user can create different text files to be called up in different situations. Macros can be activated by Windows-key combinations, by other key combinations, or by a sequence of keys. Macros can include Ctrl, Shift and Alt key combinations as well as all the non-text keys like Home, End and Delete, and even mouse actions. Programming techniques like loops and conditional statements can be included. It also connects with the Windows API, giving it access to the clipboard, the registry, and the internal clock.

The help system is excellent, and the website provides a tutorial.

Voice recognition

Many indexers like to alternate key-based entry of terms with voice-based entry. The best-known programs for this are Dragon Naturally Speaking and IBM ViaVoice. Both can be trained to recognise one or more voices to a reasonable level of accuracy, and the programs are improving all the time, though they are still far from perfect.

Some indexers, however, have found it difficult to reconcile their way of working with the use of voice recognition software. These programs also require a quiet environment to operate successfully. There is a mailing list at groups.yahoo.com/group/DragonNaturallySpeaking.

Timekeep for Windows

Timekeep for Windows 2006 (www.the-indexer.com/timekeep.htm) is a business management program for indexers. It keeps track of indexing projects and allows the user to calculate their page rates, time taken per page, and so on. It can estimate index costs from sample information and process indexing invoices. A demo is available from the website.

Hardware

For efficient working a professional indexer should be prepared to invest in good-quality hardware:

- a Pentium 3 or better PC or equivalently powerful Macintosh
- a laptop if you want to work away from home, and as a backup system
- a large screen (monitor) with no glare
- a well-designed ergonomic keyboard
- a wireless mouse that can be used in a variety of positions, reducing the risk of wrist strain
- a microphone and headphones for indexers using voice-recognition software
- a fast broadband connection to the Internet through a reliable provider
- a comfortable work environment.

Health and safety

Indexing is a sedentary, computer-based occupation, so attention to the work environment is essential. Physiotherapist Nicola Ellis suggested at an SI conference that 'anyone wishing to pursue a sedentary lifestyle should first undergo a stringent health test to assess whether they are fit to withstand the inactivity'. Indexers have to set up an ergonomically appropriate workstation, or pay someone to do so. This includes:

- adequate space for working and storing materials
- a computer and desk set up so that your wrists and eyes are at an appropriate level with respect to the keyboard and screen
- an adjustable chair
- adequate lighting and, ideally, a pleasant view
- document holders, wrist rests, angle boards and footrests as required
- good lighting over the work surface
- a quiet, low-stress environment (see also *Indexers*: *Working from home* in Chapter 1).

You also need to ensure a safe overall environment for yourself and anyone such as couriers who may call at your workplace.

Indexers need basic typing skills – a touch typing course will save hours over the years. Indexers can reduce use of the mouse by using keyboard shortcuts or voice-recognition software and alternating keyboard-based work with other work. You need to take regular breaks (some say five minutes every hour), drink lots of water, do regular stretches and eye exercises, and breathe deeply.

Threats and Opportunities in Indexing

No one can foretell how the rooster will crow whilst it is yet in the egg.

Basuto proverb

THE INDEXING PROFESSION is threatened on many fronts. Activities in periodical and database indexing that were done by humans are being taken over by computers because they are cheaper, even though they may not index as well, and the increasing amount of material in electronic formats means that search engines have an ever-larger role to play in retrieval.

At the same time as the avenues for work appear to be declining, some of the existing work is being outsourced to countries other than the country of publication. This is putting downward pressure on indexing rates in traditional indexing countries, while at the same time offering new indexing opportunities in the countries taking on the work.

On the other hand, many indexers are busier than ever. Book indexing has not yet been passably replicated by a computer, and index quality can make a difference to sales, especially for textbooks where users have specific, easily defined needs. The indexing of high-importance databases such as MEDLINE is still mostly manual, with some automation. Many non-electronic documents from the past merit indexing. Corporate intranets and websites often use experts in metadata and thesaurus construction for large projects and ongoing consultancies. Finally, indexers need to be entrepreneurial and create information products of their own.

However much work we find, and however many indexers are employed in ten, twenty or thirty years' time, it is certain that the work of a future indexer will be vastly different to the work of an indexer of today.

Hopeless future

Stop, while ye may; suspend your mad career!

William Cowper, *Table Talk* (1781)

The main threats to indexers are the outsourcing of indexing work, the use of computers to replace human indexers, and the decline in the overall amount of indexing being done. User preferences play a role in the decline, as some people prefer to use a search function even when they may get better results using an index.

Outsourcing

Outsourcing of indexing work to low-wage countries has been causing concern to indexers, especially in the United States. There may be a natural limit to this, however. Already some overseas project managers are coming back to US indexers with job offers, although often at lower rates than a US-based client would offer.

Many indexers feel that indexing cannot be outsourced effectively because much understanding of works is culturally dependent. This does not appear to have deterred those making the change, nor does it stop Australian indexers accepting work from other countries. Although outsourcing is a strong negative to indexers in the countries doing the outsourcing, it is, of course, a great benefit to those in countries receiving the extra work.

Bibliographic database indexing decline

Indexes could be given heritage listing, like buildings and parks.

Elizabeth Drynan (2005)

Bibliographical database indexing has declined in Australia over the last few years because of government funding cuts, limited markets, high costs, the lack of interest shown by publishers and users, and competition from free-text searching of full-text databases. Michael Middleton (2004) has written on the development and decline of scientific and technological information services in Australia. In 1995, Lynn Farkas discussed the long-term viability of bibliographic database indexers. Although the number of online databases had increased significantly from 1984 to 1993, the proportion with indexing had declined. A number of databases had closed, including *Renewable Energy Index*, *Software Locator Database*, and *Science Index*. The emphasis in funding had moved from the assumption that governments would fund indexes as a public service, to the need for cost recovery. Since a large proportion of the costs of a database are for staff, indexing is one of the first things to be cut.

There are other strategies for cost effectiveness, which can also be applied in other types of indexing. They include:

- Find new sources of revenue. At this time sale of databases on CD-ROM was a significant revenue raiser.

- Seek other revenue generators: 'do once, package many times'; offer document delivery.
- Use cost-cutting technologies, such as direct data entry instead of worksheets.
- Reduce quality control.
- Reduce overheads: more than 80% of annual costs are staffing overheads, mainly for indexers or editors, so automation is often considered.

In 2000, Pamela Johnstone and Elizabeth Drynan noted the closure of *Australian Tourism Index* and *Taxindex*. In 2002 Elizabeth Drynan noted the closure of the Australian Mineral Foundation Library in Adelaide; this led to concerns about the future of its virtual representation, the Australian Earth Sciences Information System (AESIS), which had relied on it as a source collection for the index. In 2003, Nicole Manktelow wrote about funding cuts to specialist databases, including rural research and conservation databases such as Streamline and AESIS. Streamline has been somewhat resurrected as AANRO (www.aanro.net/page/home.html), and AESIS as AusGeoRef (a subset of GeoRef), so not all has been lost.

When describing the closure of the Australian Mineral Foundation Library, Drynan (2002) noted that Australian Library and Information Science Abstracts (ALISA), published by the Australian Clearing House for Library and Information Science at the University of South Australia, had a better chance of survival than other indexes because there were fewer primary resources in its field, and it was produced on a voluntary basis from donated resources. But in 2005, Drynan noted that ALISA was no longer being produced, due to cost of production, and because fewer publishers were sending resources to be indexed. She writes: 'for want of a nail, the shoe was lost, for want . . .?' Shelley Greenhouse (2000) has also discussed the future of database indexing.

The reasons for closure of these indexing and abstracting products are largely economic – either users have to pay the full running costs of the service, or they have to be subsidised by an organisation that promotes research in that field. The closure of a library, or lack of interest from publishers, can affect the service. The availability of many articles in full-text versions with keyword search capability has led some to decide that manually created indexes are unnecessary. The move of searching from specialist librarians to end users has also had an impact: librarians and expert users exploit the full capabilities of indexing based on a controlled vocabulary, while casual users may not, making the benefits of indexing less obvious.

No computer program has been created that can challenge a human as a book indexer, although work has been done in this area (Salton 1988). The situation is not as clear with collection indexing, however. Although some automated indexing approaches give inadequate results, approaches in which computer output is edited by indexers are claimed to provide quality indexing at a lower cost than purely human input.

It is ironic that while as indexers we bemoan the move of bibliographic database services towards the use of automatic indexing methods, researchers in that field consider they have been hampered by the reluctance of bibliographic database services to use automatic indexing methods. Karen Sparck Jones (2004) wrote:

> Operational bibliographic services were very reluctant to allow statistical methods any possible utility, especially given the tiny research experiments, and became substantially committed to the conventional boolean approach. The first Web engine builders had no such prior commitments and picked up the statistical idea . . . It thus took about twenty-five years for a simple, obvious, useful idea to reach the real world, even the fast-moving information technology one.

It now seems inevitable that more and more collection indexing tasks will be taken over by computers. What remains to be seen is the extent to which indexers remain central to the indexing process as vocabulary creators, planners and checkers.

See also *Collection indexes: Free-text searching and machine-aided indexing* in Chapter 5 and *Automated indexing software* in Chapter 10.

Periodical indexing decline

> The trouble with our times is that the future is not what it used to be.
>
> Paul Valéry (1871–1945)

The web is an excellent medium for publishing periodical literature: it is quick, requires no shelf storage, and is electronically searchable. Some electronic periodicals use a publish-ahead-of-print or print-concurrent model, while others are only available online. As indexes are considered a cost, not a revenue raiser, a number of publishers have dropped them, leading to loss of work for some indexers. Other periodicals have moved online but retained their indexes. Some publishers have decided to rely on the indexing done by aggregators, rather than indexing their own journals. Thus a medical publisher might feel that MEDLINE provides controlled vocabulary access to its journals without it having to make individual indexes.

There is always a flux in the periodicals being published, with some closing but new ones being created. Some indexers are finding work in newly established periodicals, or new projects to retrospectively index old issues. However, anecdotal evidence suggests that more journal indexing jobs are being lost than gained. Additionally, a long-term job usually pays better because the indexer has built up familiarity with the users, the content and the indexing language. Periodical indexing and database indexing often provide continuing work for indexers in the gaps between one-off jobs.

Book indexing decline

> Time, occasion, chance and change
> To these all things are subject.
>
> Percy Bysshe Shelley

Book indexing seems to be the healthiest of the three major areas of indexing. At this stage it is vulnerable to a decline in the number of indexable books being published and dependence on search in books available electronically.

Nancy Mulvany's analysis of US book production (2003) suggests a decline in the production of indexable books, even though production in some areas, such as juvenile literature and fiction, has increased. Martin Tulic's guest editorial in *The indexer* (2004) reports a decline in the proportion of hardcover non-fiction bestsellers that have indexes, from 73% in 1980 to 37% in 2000–03. He is also concerned at the trend towards the packaging of sections of books for university students, fearing that indexes will not fit this 'Wal-Mart' system of book sales (see *Custom-built publications* in Chapter 9).

The cost of books has a significant impact on reading levels in a country, and also on the potential for the production of more books. In South Africa, an anti-VAT campaign is fighting for the removal of the 14% VAT (sales tax) on books, claiming that this will improve education and literacy rates (Myburgh 2005). Some Australian publishing companies were badly affected by the introduction of the Goods and Services Tax. In addition, the importation of cheap goods from overseas pushes prices of many goods down, with the result that books are relatively expensive. Jeremy Fisher (2004), executive director of the Australian Society of Authors, suggests that under the US–Australia Free Trade Agreement 'writers will be faced with even fewer publishing opportunities'.

Some prominent books published recently – on the topic of communication! – have not had indexes. Although some reviewers have noted the lack, sales have still been high. Two examples are *Eats, shoots and leaves* by Lynne Truss and *Death sentence: the decay of public language*, by Don Watson.

Hopeful future

> Never let the future disturb you. You will meet it, if you have to, with the same
> weapons of reason which today arm you against the present.
> Marcus Aurelius Antoninus (121–180 CE), *Meditations*

Although there is much cause for concern for indexers, there is also hope. Printed books seem likely to require human-constructed indexes for a while yet, and as some opportunities in database and periodical indexing close, others are opening in fields such as taxonomy development and metadata creation. How happy indexers will be about future prospects depends on whether they feel that these new opportunities provide the intellectual satisfaction of the old.

Indexing opportunities will also be more dispersed, requiring marketing to a wider range of print and electronic publishers, corporations, government departments, individual authors and community organisations. Much more indexing work will be done by people who are not called 'indexers', but who are required to organise information in the course of their jobs. Networking with a wide range of people will increase indexers' chances of being involved in these projects.

Indexing jobs will require more commitment to technology, and more time spent learning programs and talking in meetings relative to actual indexing. Some jobs will involve training the computer, but not dealing with individual documents.

It is ironic that, while search engines have convinced some that manual indexing is not needed, in other cases search engine features such as Amazon's Search Inside the Book and Google's Book Search have exposed existing indexes far more prominently to the public. Perhaps indexers in ten years' time will be thanking search engines for bringing indexes into the limelight!

To do the best they can in the new information economy, indexers need the following skills:

- sound knowledge of basic indexing principles
- knowledge of the principles of metadata creation and search engine operation
- knowledge of the principles of taxonomy and thesaurus creation
- ability to evaluate and tweak automatic systems
- database design and management skills
- project management skills
- knowledge of usability issues and skills in user testing.

More of the same

> Let us prove to the world that good taste, good art, good writing [and good indexing] can be good selling.   adapted from Bill Bernbach

Johannes Schoeffer published an edition of Livy in 1518 with an announcement on the title page that it had an '*index copiosus*'. In the same year Venetian printer Aldus Manutius proudly claimed that his had an '*index copiosissimus*', and also named its compiler (Clough 1967).

Indexing, for all we complain to the contrary, is a highly respected skill, and indexes are a highly regarded tool. Just because many books are published without an index through ignorance or concern about costs, does not mean that no-one cares about indexes. We can expect that this respect will continue into the future, for as long as human-compiled indexes do make a difference.

Book indexing seems the most likely to continue strongly, as the granularity of the information (the importance of access to small details) makes it the hardest to automate. But periodicals and other documents for which efficient access to important information is required will also continue to require indexes. Because the nature of periodical publication is changing, with the focus now on the individual article rather than the journal, indexing may find a new role in pointing to the most useful articles from a less-cohesive publication structure than before.

Even bibliographic database indexing, which is threatened most by the availability of full-text documents, will continue in fields such as medicine and law where access to up-to-date information is crucial to the occupation, and in fields such as the humanities and social sciences, in which human indexers are sensitive to nuances of meaning that computers miss. Bibliographic databases are also important to the journal publishers whose products are indexed. Many libraries prioritise the purchase of journals that are indexed in major databases, so lack of indexing affects sale patterns. We also hope that the circle will turn, and that users who have noticed a reduction in access will fight for the reinstatement of indexing services that have closed.

More dispersed clients

Mulvany (2003) notes the decline in publication of indexable books, and suggests targeting the subject areas, such as business, that are growing or static, and also looking for work outside traditional publishing houses, including engineering reports and corporate training documents. Non-commercial publishers, including self-publishers, are responsible for 40% of all books, so indexers should market in these areas. Printers and packagers are also doing many of the things that publishers used to do, including commissioning indexes.

Outsourcing and export

There are both threats and opportunities from globalisation of indexing, depending where you live and what special skills you have to offer. Many indexers have worked for overseas clients with no difficulties except a pay cheque in a different currency. For the average indexer in the United States or the United Kingdom, the impact of outsourcing is likely to be negative. Australian computer specialists have both lost and gained work from globalisation, and the same may prove true for Australian indexers. For indexers in India and the Philippines, outsourcing has been a golden opportunity.

India has a strong tradition in information retrieval research, being home to Ranganathan (creator of the Colon Classification) and the first national standard on indexing. In 1994, though, Garry Cousins (1995) found that most locally published books had no indexes – perhaps because of the oral tradition which required sequential access – and that there were no professional indexers. There is now an Indian branch of the Society of Technical Communicators (STC) with an interest in indexing (www.stc-india.org).

Globalisation also allows the exploitation of specialist skills, no matter where the indexer lives. Groups of indexers can work jointly on projects using e-mail and web-based data entry – qualifications for the job are more important than geographical location.

An increase in Australian works being sold into overseas markets, including China, could balance some declines in Australian book purchases, although if these books are translated they will need Chinese-speaking indexers. Nicholas Jose (2005) writes about China: 'There is interest in biography and non-fiction, especially when it exposes China's past or speculates on its future.' Professor Li Tao, China's senior translator of Australian literature, says: 'the limited budget for supporting the introduction of Australian culture into China is used not very well'. Nonetheless, a Chinese translation of Germaine Greer's *The female eunuch* sold 10,000 copies.

More software-dependent work

The development of dedicated indexing software for book indexers, and computerised systems for collection indexers, have provided a great benefit to indexers and publishers in the last two decades. More recent developments such as the increased use of embedded indexing, while providing some cost and efficiency benefits to publishers, in general make the indexing process more difficult and time-consuming, without always a commensurate increase in payment to indexers (see also *Embedded indexing* in Chapter 8).

When new editions of books with embedded indexes are published, it will be interesting to see whether authors can work with the embedded data, and whether the indexes do prove to be readily reusable and updatable.

Work done by non-indexers

> If you wish your merit to be known, acknowledge that of other people.
>
> Oriental proverb

Information access is part of the work of many professionals, including computer specialists and information architects as well as librarians and indexers. Many of the basic principles of information science are being reinvented by other groups, and the roots of these ideas are not always acknowledged. Philip Resnik and Gary Adams (1996) have written: '"Conceptual" is something of a recent buzzword in the information retrieval business . . . for example, a search involving "agriculture" might do well to turn up documents about "farming".' It is strange to hear of something so fundamental being called a 'recent buzzword'. Indexers and librarians have been indexing concepts for centuries.

Metadata and thesaurus creators for content management systems are as likely to be editors, journalists, computer specialists and subject specialists as they are to be indexers. In some cases the indexer's role is as occasional consultant with others doing the day-to-day work.

New venues for indexes

> Weep not that the world changes – did it keep
> A stable changeless state, 'twere cause indeed to weep.
> William Cullen Bryant

While book indexes should continue to be created for their own sakes, there will also be ways in which they may expand their usefulness.

One step in this direction is the display of indexes in Amazon's Search Inside the Book feature; a similar approach is taken with Google's Book Search, which also provides the option to browse the indexes of online books.

When the same indexer creates the index to a second edition of a book, it would be relatively easy to generate a subset of the new index that contains only entries that are in the later edition but not in the earlier edition. This is a marketing tool and an aid to users who buy the second edition and are especially keen to identify the new content.

When the same indexer creates the indexes to a number of books with similar content for the same publisher, they could follow a standard approach for all the indexes, and then generate a combined index for the whole collection. This is a marketing tool and an aid to users who have bought a number of the books; e-book aggregators or libraries could provide it to enable people to select the best book or books to answer their queries.

New fields for indexers

When the railway business declined in the 1960s, Theodore Levitt famously asked 'What business are you really in?' He suggested that the railways got into trouble because they assumed they were in the railroad business when they were really in the transportation business, and therefore let others take customers away from them. To find out what business you are really in, you need to ask:

- what need your product or service satisfies
- whose need is satisfied
- how the need is satisfied
- when the need is satisfied
- what 'satisfied' means.

Indexers too may find that they have to reinvent themselves and apply their skills in new areas. Jobs that use some indexing skills include:

- metadata creation
- topic map, ontology, thesaurus and taxonomy construction
- information architecture design
- content management system implementation
- DTD (document type definition) creation and tagging
- training and checking machine-aided indexing systems
- implementing automated indexing and categorisation systems
- research
- technical writing.

Working with the enemy

When someone on Index-L asked: 'What is MAI?' Shelley Greenhouse replied: 'A pox on the indexing world!' MAI (machine-aided indexing) is taking work away from indexers, who sometimes feel they are left with a smaller role for less money, cleaning up the mess the system has generated. Nonetheless, requirements testing, interface design, MAI implementation, and the editing of output from MAI systems is likely to be a growth area in collection indexing as the use of fully manual systems declines.

Some of the new work in these areas will be with individual bibliographic databases, while other work will be with aggregators who consolidate indexing for hundreds or thousands of journals.

Catching up with the past

While many new publications are available in electronic format from the time of creation and are therefore easily searchable, most old documents are on paper, so manual indexing or scanning is necessary if access is to be improved. Retrospective indexing is therefore one area of possible work. In general there is lots that can be done, but not always any money to pay for the work. Volunteers are crucial in this area, although consultants might be paid to oversee the work.

The National Library of Australia lists a wide range of retrospective indexing projects including newspapers, magazines and serial fiction (National Library of Australia 1993).

Making our own products

It has been said that the best way to predict the future is to invent it. Some indexers have attempted to make money by creating index products, including indexes to the manuals for Osborne computers, and genealogical after-the-fact indexes. Mini 'webliographies' which index and link to key articles on specific topics could be sold on the web.

The WineDiva website (www.winediva.com.au) was created by an indexer who saw it as a way of using her indexing and organisational skills to create a product. The profit comes from advertisers who pay for more than a basic entry, and from other commercial ventures such as the sale of books through the site.

The small markets and the feeling that 'information wants to be free' mean it is difficult to make money from indexing products, although the development of effective micropayments systems on the web and the problems people face with information overload may make it easier in future. Although people do not like to pay for data, they may pay for selected quality data, interpretation and convenience.

Conclusion

The oyster defends itself against an intruder and produces a pearl. The information world is our oyster – whether it turns out to be a toxic heavy-metal-laden mass, or home to a pearl of great beauty, is yet to be seen. This book points to the pearl.

References

All URLs were accessed in May 2006 unless otherwise noted. Most are also available through the Internet Archive (www.archive.org). Some of the topics covered in this book have been dealt with in more detail in articles we have written. Online versions of these are accessible at www.webindexing.biz/articles.

AACR2 (Anglo-American cataloguing rules). 2nd edn. 1988 revision. Eds Michael Gorman and Paul W. Winkler. Ottawa: Canadian Library Association; Chicago: American Library Association; London: Library Association. 3rd edn currently under consideration.

Abrahams, Marc 2006. 'Where the' *Annals of improbable research* July–August, p. 7, improbable.com/pages/airchives/paperair/volume12/v12i4/WhereThe-12-4.pdf.

AGIFT (Australian governments' interactive functions thesaurus) 2005. 2nd edn, www.naa.gov.au/recordkeeping/thesaurus/index.htm.

Aitchison, Jean, Gilchrist, Alan and Bawden, David 2000. *Thesaurus construction and use: a practical manual.* 4th edn, Chicago: Fitzroy Dearborn Publishers.

Albrechtsen, Hanne 1993. 'Subject analysis and indexing: from automated indexing to domain analysis' *The indexer* v.18 n.4, pp. 219–224.

Ament, Kurt 2003. 'Indexing single-source documents', www.winwriters.com/articles/indexing/index.html.

Anderson, James D 1997. *NISO-TR02, Guidelines for indexes and related information retrieval devices*, www.niso.org/standards/resources/tr02.pdf.

—— and Perez-Carballo, J 2005. *Information retrieval design: principles and options for information description, organization, display and access in information by retrieval databases, digital libraries, catalogs, and indexes.* St Petersburg, FL: Ometeca Institute, www.scils.rutgers.edu/~carballo/ird2005.html.

Anglo-American cataloguing rules see *AACR2*.

ANSI/NISO Z39.19:2005 Guidelines for the construction, format, and management of monolingual controlled vocabularies, www.niso.org/standards/index.html. Equivalent international standard: ISO 2788.

References

Arms, William Y. *et al*. 2002. 'A spectrum of interoperability: the Site for Science prototype for the NSDL' *D-lib magazine* v.8 n.1, www.dlib.org/dlib/january02/arms/01arms.html.

AS/NZS 999:1999 (ISO 999:1996) Information and documentation – guidelines for the content, organization and presentation of indexes. Homebush, NSW: Standards Australia; Wellington, New Zealand: Standards New Zealand.

Australian governments' interactive functions thesaurus see *AGIFT*.

Badgett, Nan 2004. 'Lick the needle, not the thread: a how-to guide for how-to books' *Key words* v.12 n.4, pp. 127–129.

Bagheri, Mansoureh 2005. 'Indexing education in Iran', in *Indexing: engage, enlighten, enrich: proceedings from the ANZSI conference*. Melbourne: Australian and New Zealand Society of Indexers, pp. 13–18.

Bagheri, Masoumeh 2005. 'Development of thesauri in Iran', in *Indexing: engage, enlighten, enrich: proceedings from the ANZSI conference*. Melbourne: Australian and New Zealand Society of Indexers, pp. 19–24. Reprinted with minor variations in 2006 in *The indexer* v.25 n.1, pp. 19–22.

Baker, Victoria 2005. 'Interview: Victoria Baker, indexer of *Indexing Books*, 2nd edition' *i-torque* i.25.

Barnum, Carol, Henderson, Earvin, Hood, Al and Jordan, Rodney 2004. 'Index versus full-text search: a usability study of user preference and performance' *Technical communication* v.51 n.2, pp. 185–206.

Bates, Marcia J 1989. 'The design of browsing and berrypicking techniques for the online search interface', www.gseis.ucla.edu/faculty/bates/berrypicking.html.

—— 1998. 'Indexing and access for digital libraries and the Internet: human, database and domain factors' *JASIS* v.49, pp. 1185–1205, www.gseis.ucla.edu/faculty/bates/articles/indexdlib.html. A previous online draft without figures at dlis.gseis.ucla.edu/research/mjbates.html was dated 1996.

Beghtol, C 1986. 'Bibliographic classification theory and text linguistics: aboutness analysis, intertextuality and the cognitive act of classifying documents' *Journal of documentation* v.42 i.2, pp. 84–113.

Bell, Hazel 1992. 'Should fiction be indexed? the indexability of text' *The indexer* v.18 n.2, www.aidanbell.com/html/hkbell/SFBI.htm.

—— 1997–2000. 'History of indexing societies, Parts I to VII', www.aidanbell.com/html/hkbell/samplearticles.htm (scroll down to links).

—— 2004. *Indexing biographies and other stories of human lives*. 3rd edn. (Society of Indexers Occasional Papers on Indexing, No. 1.) Sheffield: Society of Indexers.

Bennett, Denise and Williams, Priscilla 2006. 'Name authority challenges for indexing and abstracting databases' *Evidence based library and information practice* v.1 i.1.

Bibliographic Services Task Force, the University of California Libraries 2005. 'Rethinking how we provide bibliographic services for the University of California: final report: December 2005. Libraries, digital resources and interoperability', libraries.universityofcalifornia.edu/sopag/BSTF/Final.pdf.

Bokil, Manoj 2004. 'Conditional Text in RoboHelp HTML vx4' *Indus* July, www.stc-india.org/indus/072004/tooltime.htm.

Bonella, Irene 2003. 'A century of pay inequity: is the end in sight?' *Australian library journal*, pp. 313–325.

Bonura, Larry 1994. *The art of indexing*. New York: John Wiley.

Booth, Pat 2001. *Indexing: the manual of good practice*. München: KG Saur.

Borko, Harold and Bernier, Charles L 1978. *Indexing concepts and methods*. New York: Academic Press.

Bridge, Noeline 2003. 'Verifying personal names on the Web' *The indexer* v.23 n.3, pp. 149–156.

Brown, Fred 2001. 'DocBook (SGML/XML)' *Allegro time!* September, www.allegrotechindexing.com/news014.htm.

Browne, Glenda 1992. 'Scope notes for *LISA subject headings*' *Online review* v.16 n.1, pp. 3–16.

—— 1996. 'Automatic indexing and abstracting', presented at: Indexing in the electronic age conference, Robertson, NSW, 20–21 April, www.aussi.org/conferences/papers/browneg.htm.

—— 2001a. 'Indexing Web sites: a practical guide' *Internet reference services quarterly* v.5 i.3, pp. 27–41.

—— 2001b. 'The definite article' *The indexer*, v.22 n.3, pp. 119–122.

—— 2004. 'Thesaurus construction software: parts 1 and 2' *Online currents* v.19 i.3–4, www.webindexing.biz/Articles/ThesaurusConstruction.htm.

—— 2005. 'The alpha and the omega – filed at the beginning and the end' *ANZSI newsletter* v.1 n.10, pp. 5, 7.

—— and Jermey, Jonathan 2004. *Website indexing: enhancing access to information within websites*. 2nd edn. Adelaide: Auslib Press 2004. Also for sale as an e-book through RMIT Informit (www.informit.com.au) and as a PDF at www.webindexing.biz and Lulu (www.lulu.com).

BS 8723: *Structured vocabularies for information retrieval – guide* Part 4 Draft version.

Builder.com 2003. 'Understanding information taxonomy helps build better apps', builder.com.com/5100-6374-5055268.html.

Burger, Marlene 1999. 'Indexing traditional African musical instruments' *The indexer* v.21 n.4, pp. 169–172.

Carroll, JM and Rosson, MB 1987. 'The paradox of the active user', in JM Carroll, ed. *Interfacing thought: cognitive aspects of human-computer interaction*. Cambridge, MA: MIT Press, faculty.ist.psu.edu/rosson/Papers/Paradox.pdf.

Cauchi, Simon 2000. 'The problem of the "passing mention", in *The August indexer: proceedings from the second international conference, 1999, Hobart, Tasmania*, ed. Margaret Findlay, Melbourne: Australian Society of Indexers, pp. 41–47.

Chi, EH, Hong, L, Heiser, J and Card, SK 2004. 'eBooks with indexes that reorganize conceptually', in *Proceedings of the human factors in computing systems conference (CHI2004) conference companion, Vienna, Austria*, www.clsp.jhu.edu/research/malach/pubs/JCDL2002MALACH.pdf.

Chicago manual of style see *Indexes: a chapter from the Chicago manual of style*.

Clough, Cecil H 1967. *Machiavelli researches*. Napoli, p. 87. In: *The indexer*, v.18 n.2, p. 86.

References

Coates, Sylvia 2001. 'Term selection: putting Humpty Dumpty together, at last' *Key words* v.9 n.5, pp. 145–147, www.asindexing.org/site/coatesarticle.pdf.

Collins, William L 2001. 'The lighter side of indexing' *A to Z: the newsletter of STC's Indexing SIG* v.4 n.1, pp. 1–4.

Collison, Robert L 1972. *Indexes and indexing*. 4th rev. edn, London: Ernest Benn.

—— 1981. 'The future of indexes and indexing' *The indexer* v.12 n.4, pp. 171–172.

Colton, Caroline 1996. 'The indexer's tale' *Blue pencil: newsletter of the Society of Editors (NSW)*, p. 4.

Column 8 1994. *Sydney morning herald* 16 February.

Cousins, Garry 1995. 'In search of indexers in South India', in *Indexers – partners in publishing, proceedings from the first international conference*, Marysville, Vic. [Melbourne]: Australian Society of Indexers.

Craven, Tim 1997, last updated 2002. *Thesaurus construction*. London, Ontario: University of Western Ontario, Graduate School of Library and Information Science, instruct.uwo.ca/gplis/677/thesaur/main00.htm.

—— 2006. 'Some features of *alt* texts associated with images in Web pages' *Information research* v.11 n.2, informationr.net/ir/11-2/paper250.html.

Culleton, John 2004. 'Open source indexing' *The indexer* v.24 n.2, pp. 58–60.

Davis, Madeleine 2001. 'Building a global legal index: a work in progress' *The indexer* v.22 n.3, pp. 123–127.

Deacon, Prue 2003. 'Changes in the *Health and Ageing Thesaurus* and reindexing in HealthInsite', presented at: Indexing the World of Information: International Conference of AusSI, Sydney. Published in *AusSI newsletter* v.27 n.10, www.aussi.org/conferences/papers/deacon.htm.

Deerwester, S, Dumais, ST, Furnas, GW, Landauer, TK, and Harshman, RA 1990 'Indexing by latent semantic analysis' *JASIS* v.41 n.6, pp. 391–407, www.si.umich.edu/~furnas/Papers/LSI.JASIS.paper.pdf.

Diakoff, Harry 2004. 'Database indexing: yesterday and today', *The indexer* v.24 n.2, pp. 85–96.

Diodato, Virgil 1994. 'Duplicate entries versus see cross-references in back-of-book indexes' *The indexer* v.19 n.2, pp. 83–87.

Dixon, Geoffrey 1991. 'The indexer replies' *The indexer* v.17 n.4, p. 268.

Downes, Max 1996. *Indexing sealers' logbooks from Heard Island*. Kingston, Tas.: Antarctic Division.

Downie, J Stephen 2003. 'Music information retrieval' *Annual review of information science and technology* v.37, pp. 295–340, music-ir.org/downie_mir_arist37.pdf.

Drynan, Elizabeth 2002. 'Indexes in danger' *Online currents* v.17 i.2. Also archived at pandora.nla.gov.au.

—— 2005 'ACHLIS and ALISA bow out' *Online currents* v.20 i.9. Also archived at pandora.nla.gov.au.

Farkas, Lynn 1995 'Economics and the future of database indexing', in *Indexers – partners in publishing, proceedings from the first international conference*, Marysville, Vic. [Melbourne]: Australian Society of Indexers.

—— 2005. 'Evaluating online annual reports: an indexer's experience', in *Indexing: engage, enlighten, enrich: proceedings from the ANZSI conference*. Melbourne, Vic: Australian and New Zealand Society of Indexers, pp. 33–40.

Farrow, John 1995. 'All in the mind: concept analysis in indexing' *The indexer* v.19 n.4, pp. 243–247.

Fetters, Linda K 1996. *Handbook of indexing techniques: a guide for beginning indexers*. Rev. edn. Port Aransas, TX.: FimCo Books. There is also a 3rd edn. published by Fetters Infomanagement Co. in 2001.

Fidel, Raya 1994. 'User-centered indexing' *JASIS* v.45 n.8, pp. 572–576, www.ischool. washington.edu/fidelr/RayaPubs/UserCenteredIndexing.pdf.

Fisher, Jeremy 2004. 'Free trade?' *Australian author* August, pp. 32–33.

Fitzgerald, Michael 2006. 'Essential technology: the name game' *CIO magazine* April 1, www.cio.com/archive/040106/et_main.html.

Flath, Tordis 2005. 'Journal indexing: further discussion and ideas', in *Indexing: engage, enlighten, enrich: proceedings from the ANZSI conference*. Melbourne: Australian and New Zealand Society of Indexers, pp. 50–54.

Foskett, AC 1982. *The subject approach to information* 4th edn. London: Clive Bingley.

Fugmann, Robert 2004. 'Learning the lessons of the past', www.chemheritage.org/pubs/ pub-nav3.htm.

Gaffney, Gerry 2003. 'The myth of the stupid user', www.infodesign.com.au/ articles-presentations/articles/themythofthestupiduser.asp.

Garrett, Jeffrey 2006. 'KWIC and dirty? human cognition and the claims of full-text searching' *Journal of electronic publishing* v.9 n.1, hdl.handle.net/2027/ spo.3336451.0009.106.

Gerhart, Susan L 2004. 'Do Web search engines suppress controversy?' *First Monday* v.9 n.1, firstmonday.org/issues/issue9_1/gerhart/index.html.

Gill, Tony, Gilliland, Anne and Woodley, Mary (no date). *Introduction to metadata: pathways to digital information*. Online edn., version 2.1, ed. Murtha Baca, www.getty.edu/research/conducting_research/standards/intrometadata.

Gould, AM 1974. 'User preference in published indexes' *JASIS* v.25 n.5, pp. 279–286. In: Hans H Wellisch, 1993. 'More on inverted headings, subheadings and function words' *AusSI newsletter*, v.17 n.5.

Govindaraj, MP and Mohan, HR 1995. '*The Hindu Index* database', in *Indexers – partners in publishing, proceedings from the first international conference*, Marysville, Vic. [Melbourne]: Australian Society of Indexers, pp. 174–180.

Greenhouse, Shelley 2000. 'The future of database indexing' *Key words* v.8 n.4, pp. 125–126, 132, mysite.verizon.net/vze2bpts/ASIkwarticle.htm.

GSA 2005. 'Efficient and Effective Information Retrieval and Sharing (EEIRS) Request For Information (RFI) response analysis December 2005' *Federal CIO Council website*, www.cio.gov/documents/EEIRS_RFI_Response_Analysis.pdf.

Guidelines for alphabetical arrangement of letters and sorting of numerals and other symbols see Wellisch 1999.

Guidelines for indexes and related information retrieval devices see Anderson 1997.

References

Guidelines for the construction, format, and management of monolingual controlled vocabularies see *ANSI/NISO Z39.19.*

Gustman, Samuel, Soergel, Dagobert, Oard, Douglas, Byrne, William, Picheny, Michael, Ramabhadran, Bhuvana, and Greenberg, Douglas 2002. 'Supporting access to large digital oral history archives' *JCDL02* 13–17 July, pp. 18–27, mi.eng.cam.ac.uk/~wjb31/ppubs/jcdl02malach.pdf.

Guy, Marieke, Powell, Andy and Day, Michael 2004. 'Improving the quality of metadata in eprint archives' *Ariadne* i.38, www.ariadne.ac.uk/issue38/guy.

Guy, Marieke and Tonkin, Emma 2006 'Folksonomies: tidying up tags?' *D-lib magazine* v.12 n.1, www.dlib.org/dlib/january06/guy/01guy.html.

Hahn, Trudi Bellardo 1998. 'Text retrieval online: historic perspective on web search engines' *ASIS bulletin special section* April–May, www.asis.org/Bulletin/Apr-98/hahn.html.

Hartnett, Sonya 2004. 'The colour of success' *Australian author* v.36 n.3.

Haskins, Lucie 2004. 'Indexing in FrameMaker without tearing your hair out' *Key words* v.12 n.4, asicolorado.org/members/lhaskins/IndexingKW1204.pdf.

Haynes, David 2004. *Metadata for information management and retrieval.* London: Facet Publishing.

Healy, Benjamin 2004. '*The Atlantic Monthly's* "proper-name index"' *The indexer* v.24 n.2, pp. 68–70.

Hearst, Marti A 2006. 'Clustering versus faceted categories for information exploration' *Communications of the ACM* v.49 n.4, bailando.sims.berkeley.edu/papers/cacm06.pdf.

Hedden, Heather 2006. 'Software for HTML indexing: a comparative review' *The indexer* v.25 n.1.

Heery, Rachel and Patel, Manjula 2000 (modified 2004). 'Application profiles: mixing and matching metadata schemas' *Ariadne* i.25, www.ariadne.ac.uk/issue25/app-profiles.

Hewlett–Packard 2006. 'Introduction to semantic web technologies', www.hpl.hp.com/semweb/sw-technology.htm.

Hicks, Shauna 2005. 'Indexing archives for access', pp. 72–77. In: *Indexing: engage, enlighten, enrich: proceedings from the ANZSI conference.* Melbourne: Australian and New Zealand Society of Indexers. Also published in *The indexer* v.24 n.4, pp. 200–202.

Hlava, Marjorie M 2002. 'Automatic indexing: a matter of degree' *Bulletin of the American Society for Information Science and Technology* v.29 n.1, www.asis.org/Bulletin/Oct-02/hlava.html.

Hsieh-Yee, Ingrid 2006. *Organizing audiovisual and electronic resources for access* Westport, Conn: Libraries Unlimited, 2006.

Hua, Weina 2001. 'The development of the *Chinese Social Sciences Citation Index*' *The indexer* v.22 n.3, pp. 128–129.

Hunter, Jane and Iannella, Renato 1998. 'The application of metadata standards to video indexing', archive.dstc.edu.au/RDU/staff/jane-hunter/ECDL2/final.html.

HURIDOCS: Human Rights Monitoring and Documentation Series v. 5, 2001. *How to record names of persons.* Versoix, Switzerland, www.huridocs.org/popnames.htm.

Hutchinson, H *et al.* (no date). 'How do I find blue books about dogs?: the errors and frustrations of young digital library users', hcil.cs.umd.edu/trs/2005–27/2005–27.htm.

Hyvönen, Eero *et al.* 2005. 'MuseumFinland – Finnish museums on the semantic web' *Journal of web semantics (preprint submitted to Elsevier science)*, v.3, n.2, www.seco.tkk.fi/publications/2005/hyvonen-makela-et-al-museumfinland-finnish-2005.pdf.

Indexes: a chapter from The Chicago manual of style 2003. 15th edn. Chicago: University of Chicago Press.

Information and documentation see *AS/NZS 999.*

Irvine, Jim 2005. 'Creating indexes for world atlases at HarperCollins Publishers' *The indexer* v.24 n.3, pp. 119–122.

ISO 999:1996 see *AS/NZS 999.*

Jarvie, Diane 1998. 'Is there an easy way to embark on an indexing project?' *AusSI newsletter* v.22 n.4, pp. 31, 34, 38.

Jermey, Jonathan 2003. 'Syntactica – an "intelligent text analysing service" that fails the IQ test', *AusSI newsletter* v.27 n.2, www.aussi.org/anl/2003/02march/syntactica.htm.

Johncocks, Bill 2005. 'The myth of the reusable index' *The indexer* v.24 n.4, pp. 213–217, www.theindexer.org/files/24-4-johncocks.pdf.

Johnstone, Pamela and Drynan, Elizabeth 2000. 'The value/future of bibliographic indexing and abstracting' *Online currents* v.15 i.6. Also archived online at pandora.nla.gov.au.

Jones, Clodagh 2000. 'Indexing journals: the journal of Annie Baxter Dawbin', in *The August indexer: proceedings from the second international conference, Hobart, Tasmania, 1999*, ed. Margaret Findlay, Melbourne: Australian Society of Indexers, pp. 77–81.

Jörgensen, Corinne and Liddy, Elizabeth 1996. 'Information access or information anxiety? – an exploratory evaluation of book index features' *The indexer* v.20 n.2, www.theindexer.org/files/20-2-jorgensen.pdf.

Jose, Nicholas 2005. 'Jumping puddles' *Australian author* August, pp. 8–11.

Kalbach, James 2003. 'IA, therefore I am' *Bulletin of the American Society for Information Science and Technology* v.29 n.3, www.asis.org/Bulletin/Feb-03/kalbach.html.

Kells, Kari 2004. 'Advanced/Intermediate Seminar, IASC/SCAD conference 3 June 2004', Index West, www.indexw.com/IASC.

Klement, Susan 2002. 'Open-system versus closed-system indexing: a vital distinction' *The indexer* v.23 n.1, pp. 23–31.

Lamb, J. A. 2005. 'Embedded indexing' *The indexer* v.24 n.4, pp. 206–209, www.jalamb.com/publications.html.

Lancaster, F. Wilfred 2003. *Indexing and abstracting in theory and practice*. London: Facet Publishing.

Lathrop, Lori 1999. 'Index usability test questions (for online indexes or printed indexes)', www.indexingskills.com/usabhtml.html.

Lee, Elizabeth 1998. 'Challenges in indexing nineteenth century periodicals: *The Dawn* and automatic indexing' *AusSI newsletter* v.22 n.11, pp. 91, 104–105.

Leise, Fred 2004. 'Metadata and content management systems: an introduction for indexers' *The indexer* v.24 n.2, pp. 71–74.

References

Levick, George RT 1993. 'Comments on: "Inverted headings and subheadings" by Kingsley Siebel' *AusSI newsletter* v.17 n.1, pp. 7–8.

Lider, Brett and Mosoiu, Anca 2003. 'Building a metadata-based website' *Boxes and arrows*, www.boxesandarrows.com/view/building_a_metadata_based_website.

Lombardi, Victor 2004. 'Managing the complexity of content management' *Boxes and arrows*, www.boxesandarrows.com/view/managing_the_complexity_of_content_management.

Mc – *names starting with* Mc *are filed at* Mc *not* Mac.

Mackenzie, Janet 2004. *The editor's companion*. Melbourne: Cambridge University Press.

Magee, Cherrill and Keogh, Joann 2005. 'Indexing sound (English and other languages) within a multilingual broadcaster', pp. 109–117. In: *Indexing: engage, enlighten, enrich: proceedings from the ANZSI conference*. Melbourne: Australian and New Zealand Society of Indexers.

Mallon, Thomas 1991. 'The best part of every book comes last' *New York times* 10 March late edn. – final, Section 7, p. 1.

Mallory, Michael and Moran, Gordon 1994. 'Scholarly search for the truth, and problems associated with indexing/abstracting' *The indexer* v.19 n.2, pp. 99–101.

Manktelow, Nicole 2003. *Sydney morning herald* 22–23 February.

Marcum, Deanna 2005. 'The future of cataloging', www.loc.gov/library/reports/CatalogingSpeech.pdf.

Matthews, Douglas 2001. 'Indexing published letters' *The indexer* v.22 n.3, pp. 135–141.

Matthews, P and Bakewell, KGB 1997. 'Indexes to children's information books' *The indexer* v.20 n.4.

Maurer, Donna 2006. 'Four modes of seeking information and how to design for them' *Boxes and arrows* 14 March, www.boxesandarrows.com/view/four_modes_of_seeking_information_and_how_to_design_for_them.

McGuinness, Deborah 2001. 'Ontologies come of age', www-ksl.stanford.edu/people/dlm/papers/ontologies-come-of-age-mit-press-(with-citation).htm).

McMaster, Max 2005. 'Mentoring scheme in Victoria: concept and development', in *Indexing: engage, enlighten, enrich: proceedings from the ANZSI Conference*. Melbourne: Australian and New Zealand Society of Indexers, pp. 105–108. Also published as 'Mentoring scheme in Australia' *The indexer* v.24 n.4, pp. 189–191.

—— and Woolley, Sue 2004. *Indexing for technical communicators*. Melbourne: Monarch Computing Services.

Memetic search 2005. www.memography.org/index.php/Memetic_search.

MeSH (Medical Subject Headings) 2006. National Library of Medicine, www.nlm.nih.gov.

Middleton, Michael 2004. 'Drops in the ocean: the development of scientific and technological information services in Australia', www.chemheritage.org/pubs/pub-nav3.htm.

—— 2006. 'Controlled vocabularies resource guide' sky.fit.qut.edu.au/~middletm/cont_voc.html.

Milstead, Jessica and Feldman, Susan 1999. 'Metadata: cataloguing by any other name . . .' *Online* January, www.cbuc.es/5digital/1.pdf.

Missingham, Roxanne 2004. 'Reengineering a National Resource Discovery Service: MODS Down Under' *D-lib magazine*, v.10, n.9, www.dlib.org/dlib/september04/missingham/09missingham.html.

Moncrief, Lynn 2000. 'Indexing computer-related documents', in *Beyond book indexing: how to get started in web indexing, embedded indexing, and other computer-based media*. Diane Brenner and Marilyn Rowland, eds. Medford, NJ: Information Today, in association with ASI, pp. 13–24.

Morgan, Janet 1985. *Agatha Christie: a biography*. London: Collins, 1984.

Mulvany, Nancy 2003. 'The numbers, please: US book production, 2002' *i-torque* i.6.

—— 2005. *Indexing books*. 2nd edn. Chicago: University of Chicago Press.

Myburgh, Sue 2005. 'The fight to remove VAT on books in South Africa' *inCite* May.

National Archives of Australia 2002. '*AGLS*', www.naa.gov.au/recordkeeping/gov_online/agls/summary.html.

National Library of Australia 1993. *Towards Federation 2001: Linking Australians with Their Heritage review meeting, progress reports 1994–1996. Section C – Working Group on High Priority Cross Sectoral Projects 1993*, www.nla.gov.au/niac/meetings/c1.html.

Nielsen, Jakob 1994. 'Ten usability heuristics', www.useit.com/papers/heuristic/heuristic_list.html.

NISO-TR02 see Anderson 1997.

NISO-TR03 see Wellisch 1999.

O'Dell, Joanne 2004. 'Indexing software components: a proposal for enabling reuse using "novel" techniques' *Key words* v.12 n.2, pp. 59–60.

Ogievetsky, Nikita and Sperberg, Roger 2003. 'BookBuilder: content repurposing with topic maps' *XML conference and exposition 2003*, 7–12 December, Philadelphia PA, www.idealliance.org/papers/dx_xml03/html/abstract/05-04-05.html.

Olason, Susan 2000. 'Let's get usable! usability studies for indexes'. *The indexer* v.22 n.2, pp. 91–95, www.theindexer.org/files/22-2-olason.pdf.

O'Neill, Ed, with the assistance of Rick Bennett 2005. 'VIAF: the Virtual International Authority File' *ACOC Seminar, Sydney, 31 January 2005*, www.oclc.org/research/projects/viaf.

Osgood, Martha 2004. 'Peer reviewer guidelines' *Key words* v.2 n.4, p. 119.

Oyinloye, Ajibola Maxwell 2000. 'The Nigerian experience: indexes, indexers and indexing' *The indexer* v.22 n.2, pp. 78–80.

Perlman, Janet 2001. *Running an indexing business*. Medford, NJ: Information Today, in association with ASI.

Peters, Pam 2004. *The Cambridge guide to English usage*. Melbourne: Cambridge University Press.

Pinker, Steven 1999. *Words and rules: the ingredients of language*. London: Weidenfeld & Nicolson, pp. 270–275.

Pirolli, Peter and Card, Stuart 1999. 'Information foraging', *Psychological Review*, i.106, pp. 643–675.

Pitti, Daniel V 1999. 'Encoded Archival Description: an introduction and overview' *D-Lib magazine* v.5 n.11, www.dlib.org/dlib/november99/11pitti.html.

References

Powell, Andy 2002. 'RDN interoperability and standards framework. Version 2.1', www.rdn.ac.uk/publications/interop-standards.

Prout, Dave 2004. 'Why embedded indexes are different, not better' *Key words* v.12 n.4, pp. 134–136, 142.

Quint, Barbara 2005. 'Microsoft launches book digitization project— MSN Book Search' *Information today* 31 October, www.infotoday.com/newsbreaks/nb051031-2.shtml.

Rafferty, Pauline and Hidderley, Rob 2005. *Indexing multimedia and creative works: the problems of meaning and interpretation.* Aldershot, Hants: Ashgate.

Rasmussen, Lisa 1992. 'Selected linguistic problems in indexing within the Canadian context' *The indexer* v.18 n.2, pp. 87–91.

Rayward, W Boyd and Bowden, Mary Ellen 2004. *The history and heritage of scientific and technological information systems.* Medford, NJ: Information Today, Inc, on behalf of ASIST and the Chemical Heritage Foundation, www.chemheritage.org/pubs/pub-nav3.htm.

Resnik, Philip and Adams, Gary 1996. 'Multilingual issues in WWW indexing and searching: position paper for the W3C Distributed Indexing/Searching Workshop', www.w3.org/Search/9605-Indexing-Workshop/Papers/Resnik@Sun.html.

Robertson, James 2001. 'Online help publishing solution for NRMA Insurance Limited', www.steptwo.com.au/papers/nrma/index.html.

—— 2003. 'Metrics for knowledge management and content management' *KM Column* February, www.steptwo.com.au/papers/kmc_metrics/index.hml.

Robertson, Michael 1995. 'Foreign concepts: indexing and indexes on the Continent' *The indexer* v.19 n.3, pp. 160–172.

Ryan, Christine Nelsen and Henselmeier, Sandra 2000. 'Usability testing at Macmillan USA' *Key words* v.8 n.6, pp. 198–202.

Saigh, Robert 2004. 'Index or perish' *Key words* v.12 n.4, pp. 123, 129.

Sale, Arthur 2006. 'Comparison of content policies for institutional repositories in Australia' *First Monday* v.11 i.4, www.firstmonday.org/issues/issue11_4/sale.

Salton, G 1988. 'Syntactic approaches to automatic book indexing' *Proceedings of the 26th annual meeting of the Association for Computational Linguistics*, pp. 120–126. New York: ACM, citeseer.ist.psu.edu/salton88syntactic.html.

Schroeder, Kimberly A 1998. 'Layered indexing of images' *The indexer* v.21 n.1, pp. 11–14.

Schwartz, Candy 2005. *LIS scholarly research – indexes & bibliographies*, web.simmons.edu/~schwartz/lis-indexes.html.

Semonche, Barbara 2003. 'Newspaper indexing policies and procedures', parklibrary.jomc.unc.edu/indexing.html. Excerpted from: *News media libraries: a management handbook*.

Seybold Report 1999. 'RRD Provides Thomson with custom textbooks and web-enabled archives' *Seybold report on publishing systems January 1*, www.seyboldreports.com/SRPS/subs/2808/html/rrd.htm.

Shirky, Clay 2005. 'Ontology is overrated: categories, links, and tags', shirky.com/writings/ontology_overrated.html.

Shuter, Janet 2005. 'TExtract [review]' *The indexer* v.24 n.4, pp. 250–251.

Siebel, Kingsley 1991. '*The indexer*'s indexes' *The indexer* v.17 n.4, pp. 267–268.

—— 1993. 'Inverted headings and subheadings' *AusSI newsletter* v.17 n.1, pp. 3–7.

Simkin, John 2005. 'AusSI: aspirations and achievements since 1976', in *Indexing: engage, enlighten, enrich: proceedings from the ANZSI conference*. Melbourne: Australian and New Zealand Society of Indexers, pp. 131–135.

Smith, Jeanette 2004. 'Learning indexing: the way through the woods' *Key words* v.12 n. 2, pp. 50–53.

Smith, Sherry L and Kells, Kari 2005. *Inside indexing: the decision-making process*. Bend, Oregon: Northwest Indexing Press.

Soergel, Dagobert 1985. *Organizing information: principles of data base and retrieval systems*. Orlando: Academic Press, p. 229. In: JD Anderson and J Perez-Carballo, 'The nature of indexing: how humans and machines analyze messages and texts for retrieval. Part I: research, and the nature of human indexing' *Information processing and management* v.37 n.2, pp. 231–254.

Sparck Jones, Karen 2004. 'IDF term weighting and IR research lessons' *Journal of documentation* v.60 n.5, www.soi.city.ac.uk/~ser/idfpapers/ksj_reply.pdf.

Spencer, Dawney 1998–2004. 'Indexing', suite101.com/articles.cfm/indexing/more.

State Records NSW 2005. 'Indexing projects', www.records.nsw.gov.au/archives/indexing_projects_4566.asp.

—— 2006. 'About keyword classification', www.records.nsw.gov.au/recordkeeping/about_keyword_classification_431.asp.

Stauber, Do Mi 2004. *Facing the text: content and structure in book indexing*. Oregon: Cedar Row Press, www.domistauberindexing.com.

Steckel, Mike 2002. 'Ranganathan for IAs' *Boxes and arrows*, www.boxesand-arrows.com/view/ranganathan_for_ias.

Stephenson, Mary Sue 2005. 'Indexing resources on the WWW', www.slais.ubc.ca/resources/indexing/database1.htm.

Structured vocabularies for information retrieval – guide (BS 8723) Part 4 Draft version.

Style manual: for authors, editors and printers 2002. 6th edn. Revised by Snooks & Co. Milton, Qld: John Wiley & Sons.

Sullivan, Danny 2006. 'My decade of writing about search engines' *Search engine watch* 17 April, blog.searchenginewatch.com/blog/060417-130526.

Swan, Elizabeth 2003. 'A passionate searcher's view of indexing and indexes' Presented at: Indexing the world of information: international conference of AusSI, Sydney, www.aussi.org/conferences/papers/SwanPassionateSearcher.htm.

Taylor, Arlene 1999. *The organization of information*. Englewood, CO: Libraries Unlimited, pp. 138–139. In: JD Anderson and J Perez-Carballo, 'The nature of indexing: how humans and machines analyze messages and texts for retrieval. Part I: research, and the nature of human indexing' *Information processing and management* v.37 n.2, pp. 231–254.

Tennant, Roy 2004. 'Metadata's bitter harvest' *Library journal* 15 July, www.library-journal.com/article/CA434443.html?display=Digital+LibrariesNews&industry=Digital+Libraries&industryid=3760&verticalid=151.

Theron, JC 2002. 'Indexes to *A South African bibliography to the year 1925*' *The indexer* v.23 n.2, pp. 58–62.

Thorn, Michael 1993. *Times educational supplement* 1 Oct.

Tramullas, Jesus and Garrido, Peidad 2006. 'Constructing web subject gateways using Dublin Core, RDF and topic maps' *Information research* v.11 n.2, informationr.net/ir/11-2/paper248.html.

Triffitt, Geraldine 1999. 'Crosscultural terminologies: politics enters indexing', in *The August indexer: proceedings from the second international conference, 1999, Hobart, Tasmania*, ed. Margaret Findlay, Melbourne: Australian Society of Indexers, pp. 120–131.

Tulic, Martin 2004. 'Editorial' *The indexer,* v.24, n.2.

Vickery, Brian 2004. 'Recent developments in electronic access to the data of science', www.chemheritage.org/pubs/pub-nav3.htm.

Vitiello, Giuseppe 2004. 'Identifiers and identification systems: an informational look at policies and roles from a library perspective' *D-lib magazine* v.10 n.1, www.dlib.org/dlib/january04/vitiello/01vitiello.html.

Voss, Jakob 2006. 'Collaborative thesaurus tagging the Wikipedia way', arxiv.org/ftp/cs/papers/0604/0604036.pdf.

W3C 2005. 'SKOS Core Guide W3C Working Draft 2 November 2005', ed. Alistair Miles and Dan Brickley, www.w3.org/TR/2005/WD-swbp-skos-core-guide-20051102.

Walker, Alan 1995. 'Maintaining indexing principles while breaking the rules of thumb', in *Indexers – partners in publishing, proceedings from the first international conference*, Marysville, Vic. [Melbourne]: Australian Society of Indexers.

—— 2000a. 'Indexing for school archives: school magazines and historical records', in *The August indexer: proceedings from the second international conference, Hobart, Tasmania, 1999*, ed. Margaret Findlay, Melbourne: Australian Society of Indexers, pp. 132–142.

—— 2000b. 'Impressions of the Dalian Conference of the China Society of Indexers' *The indexer* v.22 n.1, pp. 21–22.

Warner, Amy 2002. 'A taxonomy primer', www.lexonomy.com/publications/aTaxonomy-Primer.html.

Weaver, Carolyn G 2002. 'The gist of journal indexing' *Key words* v.10 n.1, pp. 16–22, www.asindexing.org/site/keypast.shtml.

Weinberg, Bella Hass 2000a. 'ASIS '99: a filtered summary for indexers' *Key words* v.8 n.1, pp. 12–19.

—— 2000b. 'Book indexes in France: medieval specimens and modern practices' *The indexer* v.22 n.1, pp. 2–13.

Wellisch, Hans H 1993. 'More on inverted headings, subheadings and function words' *AusSI newsletter*, v.17 n.5.

—— 1996 (c1995). *Indexing from A to Z*. 2nd edn. Bronx, New York: HW Wilson Co. (1st edn 1991).

—— 1999. *Guidelines for alphabetical arrangement of letters and sorting of numerals and other symbols. NISO-TR03*, www.niso.org/standards/resources/tr03.pdf.

Whitton, Evan 1997. 'Pros and cons of Wood's enquiry [Royal Commission into police corruption in NSW]' *Weekend Australian* 30 August.

Will, Leonard 1992. 'Thesaurus principles and practice', www.willpowerinfo.co.uk/thesprin.htm.

Williams, Michael 1998. 'An evaluation of passage-level indexing strategies for a technical report archive' *LIBRES: library and information science research* v.8 i.1, libres.curtin.edu.au/libre8n1/williams.htm.

Willinsky, John and Wolfson, Larry 2001. 'A tipping point for publishing reform?' *Journal of electronic publishing*, v.7, i.2, www.press.umich.edu/jep/07-02/willinsky.html.

Wilson, Michael and Matthews, Brian 2002. 'Migrating thesauri to the semantic web' *ERCIM News* n.51, www.ercim.org/publication/Ercim_News/enw51/wilson.html.

Wittmann, Cecelia 1990. 'Subheadings in award-winning book indexes: a quantitative evaluation' *The indexer* v.17 n.1, pp. 3–6.

Wright, Jan 2005. 'WritersUA thirteenth annual conference' *Key words* v.13 n.2, p. 57.

Wyatt, Michael 2000. 'Review of CINDEX for Windows 1.5 and SKY Index Professional 5.1 (revision)' *AusSI newsletter* v.24 n.9, pp. 81, 84–87, www.aussi.org/resources/software/review.htm.

Wyman, Pilar 2005. 'Judging indexes' *A to Z: the newsletter of STCs indexing SIG* v.8 n.1, pp. 14–18, www.stcsig.org/idx/articles/judge.pdf.

Zeng, Lei 1990. 'An overview of the abstracting and indexing services in China' *The indexer* v.17 n.2, pp. 99–107.

Appendix

Selected websites

43 things tagging site	www.43things.com
AANRO	www.aanro.net/page/home.html
AbeSleuth book queries	forums.abebooks.com/abesleuthcom
Aboriginal languages in Western Australia	coombs.anu.edu.au/WWWVLPages/ AborigPages/LANG/WA/section1.htm#1.4
AGIFT thesaurus	www.naa.gov.au/recordkeeping/thesaurus/ index.htm.
AGLS (Australian Government Locator Service)	www.naa.gov.au/recordkeeping/gov_online/agls/ summary.html
aliaINDEXERS mailing list	alia.org.au/alianet/e-lists/subscribe.html
Allegro time! technical indexing newsletter	www.allegrotechindexing.com/news014.htm
Amazon books	Amazon.com
Annodex file format	www.annodex.net/specifications.html
ANSI/NISO Z39.19:2005	www.niso.org/standards/index.html
Antarctica	www.antarctica.net
ANZSI (previously AusSI)	www.aussi.org, to be www.anzsi.org
The argus	www.nla.gov.au/argus
Ariadne	www.ariadne.ac.uk/
Art and architecture thesaurus online	www.getty.edu/research/conducting_research/ vocabularies/aat
ARTISTE project	www.cultivate-int.org/issue7/artiste
Arts Law Centre of Australia	www.artslaw.com.au
ASAIB	www.asaib.org.za
ASI (American Society of Indexers)	www.asindexing.org
ASI – Colorado branch	asicolorado.org/members/lhaskins/ IndexingKW1204.pdf
ASI Culinary Indexing SIG	www.culinaryindexing.org

ASI Web Indexing SIG — www.webindexing.org

ASI Web Indexing SIG mailing list — groups.yahoo.com/group/web-indexing.

Ask Now research service — www.asknow.gov.au

Ask Us research service — www.nla.gov.au/infoserv/askus.html.

AustLit database — www.austlit.edu.au/about/metadata.xml

AusSI (now ANZSI) — www.aussi.org, to be www.anzsi.org

Australasian Digital Thesis Program — adt.caul.edu.au/about/aimsoverview

Australasian Legal Information Institute (AustLII) — www.austlii.edu.au

Australian Bureau of Statistics — www.abs.gov.au

Australian National Health Data Dictionary — www.aihw.gov.au/publications/hwi/nhdd10

Australian Pictorial Thesaurus — www.picturethesaurus.gov.au

Australian Society of Archivists — www.archivists.org.au/pubs/brochures/understanding.html

Australian Word Map — www.abc.net.au/wordmap/default.htm

AutoHotKey keyboard macros — www.autohotkey.com

Automatic Linguistic Indexing of Pictures — wang.ist.psu.edu/IMAGE/alip.html

Blinkx video search engine — www.blinkx.tv

BNA Labor Relations Reporter Index — www.bna.com/lrr/lrrindx.htm

Boxes and Arrows journal — www.boxesandarrows.com.

Bulletin of ASIST — www.asis.org/Bulletin/

Business Entry Point — www.business.gov.au

Cambridge University Press — https://authornet.cambridge.org/information/productionguidehss/indexing.asp#indexing_process

Canadian Heritage Information Network Data Dictionaries: User Guide — www.chin.gc.ca/English/Collections_Management/Humanities_Dictionary/user_guide.html

Carolyn Weaver — www.weaverindexing.com/health.html

Categories for the Description of Works of Art — www.getty.edu/research/conducting_research/standards/cdwa

Centre for the Study of Cartoons and Caricature — library.kent.ac.uk/cartoons

China Society of Indexers (CSI) — www.cnindex.fudan.edu.cn

CINDEX software — www.indexres.com/cindex.html

CINDEX users mailing list — groups.yahoo.com/group/cindexusers/join

Clay Shirky's writings about the Internet — shirky.com/writings/ontology_overrated.html

Clusty.com search engine — clusty.com

Content management systems wiki — www.cmswiki.com/tiki-index.php?page=Ontology

Cognatrix thesaurus construction software	www.lgosys.com/products/Cognatrix/index.html
Collections Australia Network (incorporating AMOL)	www.collectionsaustralia.net
Collections Canada	www.collectionscanada.ca
Content-based image retrieval database	www.cs.washington.edu/research/imagedatabase
Controlled vocabularies resource guide	sky.fit.qut.edu.au/~middletm/cont_voc.html.
Cooks' Thesaurus	foodsubs.com
Creative Commons directory	commoncontent.org
Creative Commons search engines	creativecommons.org/find
Cybrary: National Library Catalogues Worldwide	www.library.uq.edu.au/ssah/jeast
Cyndi's list (genealogical information)	cyndislist.com
Data Harmony MAI software	www.dataharmony.com
Del.icio.us tagging network	del.icio.us
Deutsches Netzwerk der Indexer (DNI)	www.d-indexer.org/welcome.html
DEXter software	www.editorium.com/dexter.htm
Digital Object Identifiers	www.doi.org
Distributed Proofreaders for Project Gutenberg	www.pgdp.net/c/default.php
D-lib magazine	www.dlib.org.
DocBook markup language	www.docbook.org/xml/5.0b3/index.html
DragonNaturallySpeaking mailing list	groups.yahoo.com/group/DragonNaturallySpeaking
Dublin Core	dublincore.org
Dublin Core/MARC/GILS crosswalk	www.loc.gov/marc/dccross.html
EdNA Metadata Standard	www.edna.edu.au/metadata
Embedded indexing tutorial	www.rdg.ac.uk/SerDepts/su/Topic/WordProc/WoP2Kind01.
EmDEX	www.emdex.ca
Emotional dictionary and *Emotional thesaurus*	www.writing.ws
Encyclopaedia of Spells in Harry Potter	www.hp-lexicon.org/magic/spells/spells.html
English Heritage's *Illustrated Thesaurus*	hitite.adlibsoft.com/intro.html
Faceted Classification mailing list	finance.groups.yahoo.com/group/facetedclassification
FacetMap	facetmap.com/index.jsp

FedStats (US)	www.fedstats.gov/cgi-bin/A2Z.cgi
Finnegans Wake index	www.caitlain.com/fw
First Monday	www.firstmonday.org
Flamenco code at sourceforge	flamenco.berkeley.edu
Flickr image collection	www.flickr.com
Formal contracts for indexing	members.aol.com/indexarts/samplecon.htm
	pages.prodigy.net/jeanmidd/contract.html
	www.wellchosenword.com/indxctrt.htm
Free Software Directory	directory.fsf.org
FreeMind free mind mapping software	freemind.sourceforge.net/wiki/index.php/ Main_Page
Geelong and District Book Indexing Project	www.zades.com.au/geelong/gdbooks.htm
Geoscience Australia Place Name Search	www.ga.gov.au/map/names
Getty Images	www.gettyimages.com
Getty Thesaurus of Geographic Names	www.getty.edu/research/conducting_research/ vocabularies/tgn
GNU Project	www.gnu.org
Google Answers	answers.google.com/answers
Google News	news.google.com.au
Google Scholar	scholar.google.com
Google Video	video.google.com
Government of Canada Core Subject Thesaurus	en.thesaurus.gc.ca/bib_e.html
Groxis search software	www.groxis.com
HealthInsite	www.healthinsite.gov.au
The history and heritage of scientific and technological information systems	www.chemheritage.org/pubs/pub-nav3.htm.
HTML Indexer (Brown Inc)	www.html-indexer.com
HTML/Prep (Leverage Technologies)	www.levtechinc.com/ProdServ/LTUtils/ HTMLPrep.htm
HURIDOCS	www.huridocs.org/popnames.htm.
IA-Peers get-togethers	IAwiki.net/CocktailHours/Sydney
IDPF report on e-books	www.idpf.org/pressroom/inthenews.htm
IEEE Learning Technology Standards Committee	ieeeltsc.org/wg12LOM
IFLA (International Federation of Library Associations)	www.ifla.org
Indecs e-commerce framework	www.indecs.org/action.htm
Index to Literary Allusions in Jane Austen's Writing	www.pemberley.com/janeinfo/litallus.html

Index Tools Professional (Silicon Prairie Software)	www.siliconprairiesoftware.com
Index usability test questions (Lori Lathrop)	www.indexingskills.com/usabhtml.html.
The indexer: the international journal of indexing	www.theindexer.org
Indexing definitions	www.webindexing.biz/Webbook2Ed/ glossary.htm.
Indexing Society of Canada/Société canadienne d'indexation (ISC/SCI)	www.indexers.ca
Index-L mailing list	indexpup.com/index-list/faq.html
IndexPeers mailing list	finance.groups.yahoo.com/group/ IndexPeers
Information Architecture wiki	iawiki.net
Information research	informationr.net/ir
Information Today newsbreaks	www.infotoday.com/newsbreaks
Informit e-Library (RMIT)	www.informit.com.au
International Children's Digital Library	www.icdlbooks.org
International Good Practice website	www.aboutindexing.info
Internet Archive	web.archive.org
Internet Movie Database	www.imdb.com/title/tt0108052
Internet Review Toolkit	www.intranetreviewtoolkit.org
Introduction to metadata	www.getty.edu/research/conducting_research/ standards/intrometadata/
Inxight software	www.inxight.com/map
IRS Tax Map using topic maps	www.missouribusiness.net/irs/taxmap/ tmhome.htm
IXgen (Frank Stearns Associates)	www.fsatools.com/ixmid.html
Jambient Software	www.jambient.com
James Lamb publications	www.jalamb.com/publications.html
Journal of electronic publishing	www.press.umich.edu/jep, hdl.handle.net
Justice Sector Metadata Standard	info.lawaccess.nsw.gov.au/lawaccess/ lawaccess.nsf/print/jsms
KartOO search visualisation	www.kartoo.com
Kididdles	www.kididdles.com/mouseum/subject.html
Kids Click	www.kidsclick.org/ssearch.html
KWIC-generation program	www.chs.nihon-u.ac.jp/eng_dpt/tukamoto/ kwic_e.html.
Last words of fictional characters website	www.geocities.com/Athens/Acropolis/6537/ fict-a.htm
LaTeX indexing	linux.seindal.dk/item25.html

Lexonomy's taxonomy primer	www.lexonomy.com/publications/ aTaxonomyPrimer.html.
Librarians' Index to the Internet	www.lii.org
Library Journal	www.libraryjournal.com
Library of Congress – Gateway to Library Catalogs	www.loc.gov/z3950
Library of Congress – Name Authorities	authorities.loc.gov
Library Thing	www.librarything.com
LIBRES: library and information science research	libres.curtin.edu.au/libre8n1/williams.htm.
Los Alamos National Laboratory Research Library Newsletter	library.lanl.gov/libinfo/news/newsindx.htm
Lulu e-book store	www.lulu.com
Macquarie University library catalogue	www.lib.mq.edu.au
Macrex (UK & US)	www.macrex.cix.co.uk www.macrex.com
Macrex users mailing list	www.macrex.com/discuss.htm
MAIstro MAI demonstration	www.newsindexer.com.
MARC (MAchine Readable Cataloging)	www.loc.gov/marc
Mark Pilgrim	diveintomark.org/archives/2004/07/06/tough
The mathematica book index	documents.wolfram.com/v4/MainBook/Index
MDA (previously Museum Documentation Association)	www.mda.org.uk
MeSH (Medical Subject Headings)	www.nlm.nih.gov.
Metadata for e-mail storage	www.naa.gov.au/recordkeeping/control/ agems.html
METS (Metadata Encoding and Transmission Standard)	www.loc.gov/standards/mets
Microsoft's Live Academic Search	academic.live.com
MindCanvas remote research tool	www.themindcanvas.com
Mindjet's MindManager	www.mindjet.com/us
MiTAP global monitoring system	mitap.sdsc.edu/about.html
MODS (Metadata Object Description Schema)	www.loc.gov/standards/mods/registry.html
Montague Institute Review site indexes	www.montaguelab.com/Public/indexes.htm
Moving Picture Experts Group	www.chiariglione.org/mpeg
MultiTes thesaurus construction software	www.multites.com

Mura catalogue, AIATSIS	mura.aiatsis.gov.au
NCSU libraries faceted classification	www2.lib.ncsu.edu/catalog
Nederlands Indexers Netwerk (NIN)	www.indexers.nl
New frontiers in geriatrics research index	www.frycomm.com/ags/rasp/bookindex.asp
Newspaper indexing policies and procedures	parklibrary.jomc.unc.edu/indexing.html
NISO (National Information Standards Organization)	www.niso.org
NLA list of digitisation projects	www.caul.edu.au/org/nla-digitise.html
NSW Knowledge Management Forum	groups.yahoo.com/group/NSW-KM-Forum-Announce
NSW Law Reform Commission reports	www.lawlink.nsw.gov.au/lawlink/lrc/ll_lrc.nsf/pages/LRC_reports
NSW *Public Health Bulletin Subject Index*	www.health.nsw.gov.au/public-health/phb/2004subject_index.html
NZGLS (New Zealand Government Locator Service)	www.e.govt.nz/archive/standards/nzgls
OCLC – FAST (faceted LCSH)	www.oclc.org/research/projects/fast
OCLC – Scorpion (DDC for web indexing)	www.oclc.org/research/software/scorpion/default.htm
OCLC – VIAF (international authority file)	www.oclc.org/research/projects/viaf
ONIX at Editeur	www.editeur.org/onix.html
Open Archives Initiative	www.openarchives.org
Open Directory Project	dmoz.org
Orders of magnitude index	www.informationuniverse.com/ordersmag/orders.htm
Pandora (Music Genome Project)	www.pandora.com
Pandora (NLA)	pandora.nla.gov.au.
Penrith City Council quick index	www.penrithcity.nsw.gov.au/index.asp?id=634
Perl in a nutshell index	www.oreilly.com/catalog/perlnut/inx.html
Picture Australia	www.pictureaustralia.org
Pro Hart's cheek cells (article)	www.news.com.au/story/0,10117,18629738-421,00.html
Project Gutenberg	www.gutenberg.org
Protégé ontology software	protege.stanford.edu
PsycInfo database	www.apa.org/psycinfo/about/sample.html.
PubMed database	www.ncbi.nlm.nih.gov/entrez
Queensland Environmental Protection Authority/Parks and Wildlife Authority	www.epa.qld.gov.au/site_information/site_index

Query-by-Humming system	querybyhum.cs.nyu.edu
Renardus subject gateway initiative	www.renardus.org
Resource Discovery Network	www.rdn.ac.uk
Review of XRefHT32 (Heather Hedden)	home.comcast.net/~hhedden/ XrefHT32_Review_KW2005_10-12.pdf
Reworx software	www.vmtech.com/reworx.htm
SchemaLogic's SchemaServer	www.schemalogic.com
Scholarly research – indexes & bibliographies	web.simmons.edu/~schwartz/lis-indexes.html
ScienceDirect database	info.sciencedirect.com/content/journals/china
Search Tools Consulting	www.searchtools.com/info/classifiers.html
SearchEngineWatch blog	blog.searchenginewatch.com/blog/060417-130526
Shoelace tips website	www.fieggen.com/shoelace/shoelacetips.htm
SIGCR-L mailing list	mail.asis.org/mailman/listinfo/sigcr-l
SIGIA-L mailing list	mail.asis.org/mailman/listinfo/sigia-l
Singingfish (audio and video search)	www.singingfish.com
SKY Index	www.sky-software.com
SKY Index Users mailing list	groups.yahoo.com/group/skyindexusers
SKY Index wiki	skyindex.pbwiki.com
Society of Indexers (UK)	www.indexers.org.uk
Society of Indexers (UK) website index	www.indexers.org.uk/site/index.htm
Society of Technical Communicators (STC) – Indexing SIG	www.stcsig.org/idx/articles/judge.pdf
Society of Technical Communicators (STC) – India	www.stc-india.org
Sonar Bookends (Virginia Systems)	www.virginiasystems.com
SongTapper	www.songtapper.com
Spell checker for botanical names	www.webindexing.biz/IndexingResources
State Records NSW 'About keyword classification'	www.records.nsw.gov.au/recordkeeping/ about_keyword_classification_431.asp
State Records NSW indexing projects	www.records.nsw.gov.au/archives/ indexing_projects_4566.asp
Statement of knowledge for recordkeeping professionals	www.rmaa.com.au/docs/profdev/ StatementKnowledge.cfm
StepTwo designs	www.steptwo.com.au/papers/
Suite 101 indexing beginner articles	suite101.com/articles.cfm/indexing/more
Surname information	digiserve.com/heraldry/surnames.htm
Sydney morning herald	www.sl.nsw.gov.au/infoquick/about.cfm
Tagcloud.com	www.tagcloud.com
Tasmania Online	www.tas.gov.au/tasmaniaonline
Tate Gallery, London	www.tate.org.uk

TaxoCoP mailing list	groups.yahoo.com/group/TaxoCoP
Technology in Australia 1788–1988	www.austehc.unimelb.edu.au/tia/bookindex.html
TechRepublic's Builder.com	builder.com
TermTree thesaurus construction software	www.termtree.com.au
Text Encoding Initiative	www.tei-c.org
TExtract software	www.texyz.com/textract
The argus	www.nla.gov.au/argus
The history and heritage of scientific and technological information systems	www.chemheritage.org/pubs/pub-nav3.htm
The indexer: the international journal of indexing	www.theindexer.org
The mathematica book index	documents.wolfram.com/v4/MainBook/Index
Therapeutic guidelines indexes	www.emispdp.com
Thesaurus construction (Tim Craven)	instruct.uwo.ca/gplis/677/thesaur/main00.htm
Thesaurus for graphic materials I: subject terms	www.loc.gov/rr/print/tgm1
Thesaurus for graphic materials II: genre and physical characteristic terms	www.loc.gov/rr/print/tgm2
Thorpe weekly newsletter	www.thorpe.com.au/products/products_wbn.htm
Timekeep for Windows	www.the-indexer.com/timekeep.htm
Tom Murphy's site	www.brtom.org/ind.html
Tower Records faceted music metadata	www.towerrecords.com
TREC text retrieval conferences	trec.nist.gov
UKOLN (UK Office for Library and Information Networking)	www.ukoln.ac.uk/metadata/interoperability
UMLS (Unified Medical Language System)	www.nlm.nih.gov/research/umls
University at Albany list of search engines	www.internettutorials.net/choose.html
University of Bristol KWIC index	www.bris.ac.uk/index/full
University of Texas SMIL samples	www.gslis.utexas.edu/~l384k9/smil/smilindex.html
UNIX manual	unixhelp.ed.ac.uk/index/index.html
Usability guidelines	www.usability.gov/guidelines
USC Shoah Foundation Institute	www.usc.edu/schools/college/vhi
Useit.com (Jakob Nielsen)	www.useit.com/papers/heuristic/heuristic_list.html
Vivisimo	vivisimo.com

W3C (Worldwide Web Consortium) – RDF	www.w3.org/RDF/FAQ
W3C (Worldwide Web Consortium) – SKOS core guide	www.w3.org/TR/2005/WD-swbp-skos-core-guide-20051102
W3C (Worldwide Web Consortium) – SMIL	www.w3.org/TR/2005/PR-SMIL2-20050927
WebBrain search interface	www.webbrain.com
Webchoir thesaurus construction software	www.webchoir.com
Webindexing.biz (Glenda Browne and Jon Jermey)	www.webindexing.biz
Wikipedia (in English)	en.wikipedia.org
Willpower (thesaurus information)	www.willpower.demon.co.uk
Wine Diva	www.winediva.com.au
Winwriters (now WritersUA) articles	www.winwriters.com/articles
Wondir	www.wondir.com
WordEmbed	wordembed.jalamb.com
Wordmap	www.wordmap.com
XMetal	www.xmetal.com/index.x
XML schemas	xml.silmaril.ie/authors/schemas
XRefHT32 ('shreft')	publish.uwo.ca/~craven/freeware.htm
Yahoo! directory	au.dir.yahoo.com
Yale Undergraduate Regulations Index	www.yale.edu/ycpo/undregs/pages/indexpage.html
YouTube video gallery	youtube.com
ZING – Z39.50 International: Next Generation	www.loc.gov/z3950/agency/zing

Index

This is an index to subjects. The only cited works that have been indexed are standards and style guides. Figures are indicated by the letter 'f'. Word-by-word filing has been used, with entries filed 'as is' rather than 'as if'. The metatopic – indexing – is treated as a significant entry point. Nonetheless, as the whole subject of the book is indexing, not everything can be indexed under that term, and specific headings have been used as necessary. The word 'indexing' has been removed from headings where possible (e.g., using 'encyclopedias' not 'encyclopedia indexing'). Individual website names have not been indexed, but are listed in the appendix. The index was created by Glenda Browne, a registered member of the Australian and New Zealand Society of Indexers.